"The true impact of *Being the Boss* is its ability to capture the critical lessons of leadership growth that come only from making mistakes and living to tell the tale. This book should be part of every training program for developing managers in today's dynamic and global business environment."

—Praveen Akkiraju
Senior Vice President and General Manager, Cisco Systems Inc.

"It is often said that physicians make lousy managers—and in fairness, most physicians would freely admit that they did not go to medical school to become a manager or even a leader. Nonetheless, leadership and management have clearly become the purview of the modern-day physician. This book provides an easy-to-read road map for developing one's own leadership and management style. The liberal use of stories brings to life many of the important concepts put forth by the authors. The practical leadership constructs offered by *Being the Boss* will prove informative and enlightening to those who bridge the gaps between healer, leader, and manager.

—William D. Chey
Professor of medicine, and Director, GI Physiology Laboratory,
University of Michigan Health System

"*Being the Boss* realistically characterizes the complexities of the manager role in the twenty-first century. Linda Hill and Kent Lineback provide a logical framework for organizing this complexity and emphasize the importance of regular self-examination in diagnosing and addressing personal managerial challenges. Today's managers will find this work compelling and a practical addition to their toolkit."

—Tanya Clemons
Chief Talent Officer, Pfizer Inc.

"*Being the Boss* is a refreshing read, superbly organized, that covers very intelligently almost every one of the management problems and issues I have encountered in my long years as a CEO. It is packed with insightful ideas and advice."

—Ibrahim S. Dabdoub
Group CEO, National Bank of Kuwait

"This is an indispensable guide to evaluating yourself as a boss and understanding what you can do to improve your performance. This book covers all the relevant areas in a helpful and pragmatic way that will enable both novice and experienced bosses to achieve more. A wonderful book for self-renewal."

—Geraldine Haley
Head of Leadership Effectiveness and Succession,
Standard Chartered Bank

"*Being the Boss* delivers a remarkably comprehensive, delightfully readable guide for developing the capabilities critical for highly effective leadership. Most distinctively, *Being the Boss* challenges and enables you—at a personal level—to assess yourself honestly, offers practical approaches for improvement, and inspires you to live up to your full potential as a leader."

—Ted Hoff
Vice President,
Center for Learning and Development, IBM

"*Being the Boss* is an easy and fun read. Each chapter opens with an all-too-familiar story—a remarkably effective means to help readers reflect where they stand on the journey and what it will take to master the art of leadership. If you have your mind and heart set on becoming a world-class leader, this book will prove an ideal companion—part compass, part toolkit—as you work your way through the everyday struggles of management."

—Steven Moran
Senior Vice President, Corporate Human Resources
Strategy and Controlling, Bertelsmann AG

"A very engaging and impactful hands-on guide to truly becoming the boss. The conversational writing style is a very powerful tool for delivering the book's essential concepts. Should be required reading for all new people managers."

—Wendy Murdock
Chief Payment System Integrity Officer,
MasterCard Worldwide

"Leadership is not a science; it calls for constant learning and growth. Self-awareness and a clear understanding of our impacts as leaders are essential elements of success, and perhaps the most difficult to attain. This book adds clarity and sense to this bewildering journey, with logical, well-illustrated, practical steps to success. It should sit permanently on the desk of anyone with ambition."

—Nicholas Mutton
Executive Vice President, Four Seasons Hotels and Resorts

"*Being the Boss* is a refreshing, human look at what it means to be a good manager in the fullest sense of the word. Hill and Lineback, both steeped in the knowledge and practice of leadership, write in a compelling, honest voice and provide important tools and questions for reflection. It is a must-read for managers who take seriously their own journeys of personal development and growth. I strongly recommend it."

Jacqueline Novogratz
CEO, Acumen Fund; author, *The Blue Sweater*

"Most books on leading others read like platitude-filled works of fiction. Hill and Lineback describe the dilemmas that bosses confront and offer intelligent and practical advice on how to deal with the real—and messy—world of organizational life."

—Jeffrey Pfeffer
Professor, Stanford Business School; author,
Power: Why Some People Have It and Others Don't

"*Being the Boss* highlights the extraordinary self-awareness and perseverance required to become a successful manager. Using a creative narrative device punctuated with helpful checklists, the authors have crystallized the essential insights necessary to aid the reader on this difficult journey. It is a great resource for both government and private-sector managers making the transition from individual performer to 'being the boss.' I wish I had read it years ago."

—Daniel M. Price
Partner, Sidley Austin LLP; former senior White House
adviser on international economic affairs

"After leading global teams for twenty-plus years, I strongly believe that developing high-performance teams and retaining talented people drives organizational excellence. This book provides practical perspectives augmented with focused examples of how leaders enhance their people development capabilities to build competitive advantage."

—Nick van Dam
Global Director, Human Capital Practice,
Deloitte Consulting LLP; founder and Chairman,
e-Learning for Kids Foundation

"No high-potential or top individual performer can effectively manage in today's business environment without continuously transforming him- or herself and positively inspiring others. Linda Hill and Kent Lineback present the three imperatives for becoming a great leader through an extremely smart sequence of powerful and engaging situations and self-assessments. This book will help guide you through the long and challenging—and exciting!—journey of becoming a better boss."

—Philippe Vivien
Senior Executive Vice President
of Human Resources, AREVA

"Being a successful manager can be challenging, and many find themselves failing to live up to their potential. But with *Being the Boss*, that can change. Accessible and clear, this book provides you with tools and advice that can be put into action immediately. There are no easy answers, but there are always possible solutions. Linda Hill and Kent Lineback provide many practical ways to reflect and move forward effectively."

—Jaime Augusto Zobel de Ayala
Chairman and CEO, Ayala Corporation

BEING
THE BOSS

BEING
THE BOSS

THE 3 IMPERATIVES

for BECOMING

a GREAT LEADER

LINDA A. HILL

KENT LINEBACK

HARVARD BUSINESS REVIEW PRESS

Boston, Massachusetts

Library of Congress Cataloging-in-Publication Data

Hill, Linda A. (Linda Annette), 1956-
    Being the boss: the 3 imperatives for becoming a great leader / Linda A. Hill, Kent Lineback.
        p. cm.
    Includes bibliographical references.
    ISBN 978-1-4221-6389-4 (hbk. : alk. paper)

    1. Supervision of employees.   2. Executive ability.   3. Management.
4. Leadership.   I. Lineback, L. Kent, 1943—II. Title.

    HF5549.12.H554 2011

    658.4′092—dc22

                                                        2010024951

The paper used in this publication meets the requirements of the American National Standard for Permanence of Paper for Publications and Documents in Libraries and Archives Z39.48-1992.

CONTENTS

PART THREE
Manage Your Team

ACKNOWLEDGMENTS

Many hands write a book, and this one is no exception. We're grateful for all the help and advice we received along the way. Whatever merits *Being the Boss* possesses are due in large part to the time, effort, and advice generously given by others.

We deeply appreciate those who read the manuscript—no small task—and offered their thoughtful comments: Greg Brandeau, Joline Godfrey, Benjamin Esty, Boris Groysberg, Rakesh Khurana, Anthony Mayo, Tom DeLong, Henry Mintzberg, Sandra Glitten, Peter Naegeli, Susan Anastasi, Christopher Galbraith, Kwan-Kit Lui, and the anonymous readers the Press enlisted. Three reviewers focused on the story that opens each chapter: Bonnie Binkert, Robin Heyden, and Cinny Little. Their comments, details, and corrections made it far better than it would have been without their assistance.

Others who helped in essential ways include our always thoughtful editor, Jeff Kehoe, whose calm patience and good advice never failed us; Carol Franco, agent and wife, who read every chapter in its multiple forms and always managed to combine encouragement with high standards; Emily A. Stecker, Linda's research associate, who supported Linda from the beginning and whose careful and insightful readings of the manuscript along the way were invaluable; Barbara Devine, whose steady hand throughout helped us in many ways, not least in bridging the distance between

Boston and Santa Fe; Jennifer McNamara, who helped us in preparing the manuscript; and Carla Fantini, who helped us think about cultural diversity. Linda also extends a special note of thanks to the Harvard Business School Division of Research for providing her with the time and resources to complete this work.

Our families deserve special recognition. Their love and support provided the emotional sustenance and time needed for the arduous effort every book requires. For Linda, that includes Roger Breitbart, Jonathan Hill Breitbart, and Dana Hewett, and for Kent, his wife, Carol Franco. They all endured not only our absence but our anxiety and preoccupation as well as we struggled to get something complex right. A special note of gratitude from Linda goes to her father, Clifford Hill Sr., who taught her that integrity and caring are at the heart of great management.

WHY WE WROTE THIS BOOK

Linda Hill

This book is intended for managers who want to make a difference—those who want to be great at working with and leading others. For almost thirty years, I have been doing research on what effective managers do and how they have learned to do it. One thing is crystal clear: management is hard and is getting harder.

As faculty chair of the Leadership Initiative at Harvard Business School, I spend much of my time working with high potentials—MBAs and executives from around the globe who want to contribute to their organizations and build fulfilling careers. These are well-intentioned, smart, accomplished individuals. There is nothing that gives me more pleasure than watching those managers who progress and fulfill their ambitions. But too many derail and fail to live up to their potential. Why? Because they stop working on themselves. Leadership is about using yourself as an instrument to get things done. It can be learned, but only if you are willing and able to engage in serious self-development.

In the first edition of *Becoming a Manager*, I simply provided a forum for new managers to speak for themselves and share the trials and tribulations of their first year on the job. My hope was that others could learn vicariously from them. It is gratifying to see that the stories still resonate. Notes and e-mails continue to arrive from managers writing to share how relieved they are that others find the promotion to manager "painful" at times too. In the second edition of *Becoming a Manager*, I addressed the three concerns most often raised by new managers as they cope with their new role and its associated challenges: How can I be more effective dealing with organizational politics and in influencing my peers and bosses? How can I develop and lead a diverse team in times of change? How can I build a successful managerial career? In this expanded edition, I offered frameworks and prescriptions tested and refined during my experience as the faculty course head for our required MBA Leadership course.

Much to my surprise, many senior managers have contacted me over the years to thank me for *Becoming a Manager*. Perhaps one said it best when she observed, you never know whether you have learned the right lessons from the "sink or swim school of management." And indeed it is very hard to get honest feedback not only about what you are doing, but also about how you are doing it. The latter is the key to becoming a world-class manager.

Like *Becoming a Manager*, *Being the Boss* is about the fundamentals of management. But *Being the Boss* is not simply for the novice; it is meant for the more experienced. If you have been at it for a while, how do you know whether you are good enough? Anyway, don't you want to be great?

Kent Lineback, an experienced executive and most generous colleague, approached me about writing a book that addressed the essence of what it takes to play a leadership role in organizations these days. We wanted to provide a rich yet parsimonious and workable model of management, one that would provide guidance on how you should focus your attention and energy as you carry out your responsibilities. We wanted to address common misconceptions and missteps. We wanted to provide insight into those matters that we know keep managers up at night. How do we know what we write is true? We know from research and our collective and complementary experiences of managing, teaching, and consulting with literally thousands of managers in diverse organizations and in varied roles from all around the world.

We have written this book to mirror the personal transformational process we know is associated with learning to manage and lead. One of the managers I interviewed early on compared learning to manage to becoming a parent; opportunities and challenges continue to evolve and become more complex. He observed, somewhat wistfully I might add, that he could only hope he would grow wiser over time and be prepared to provide his children with what they would need to flourish over their life stages.

Being the Boss is written to encourage self-reflection and insight about how to continue to your desired destination. It is designed to help you translate your learning into productive action. The good news is that we are all human and even the greatest manager is imperfect. But I am willing to bet that those managers you admire most are people who understand that the mastery of their craft requires discipline, persistence, and commitment. We hope that you will come to treat this book as one of the tools in the tool kit you keep close at hand to do necessary repairs and build your dream.

Kent Lineback

For nearly thirty years, I was a boss in a variety of settings and organizations. I managed projects for a consulting firm. I ran the business side of a national not-for-profit television network and moved to the same function in a quasi-governmental agency in Washington, where I dealt with the Office of Management and Budget and congressional appropriations committees. That was followed by a stint in charge of marketing for a closely held professional publisher. Then I built a successful internal start-up selling products for PCs, after which I became general manager with a mandate to reenergize virtually the entire company.

I worked at all levels, from project management to the C-suite, and I focused on a variety of concerns, from completing projects for clients to turning out daily work on time and on budget, to rethinking basic corporate purpose, design, and strategy.

In all those positions, I never considered myself more than a competent boss. I had strengths and weaknesses and a too-human tendency to overrate the strengths and recognize the weaknesses mostly after the fact.

But if anything set me apart from other managers I knew, it was that I always paid close attention to the nature of the work I was doing and what it required. I did that in part because it was my nature to pay attention—I've always combined the paradoxical roles of player and observer—but there were other reasons too.

I never set out to be a boss. If anything, my earliest and most basic ambition was to teach. Parts of management fit nicely with this inclination, but much of it cut against the grain of my impulses. I started out, for example, trying to motivate people through friendship, until I realized that didn't work. Whatever I achieved came from constantly stepping back and reflecting on what I needed to do to succeed. I was a student of my craft because I had to be.

Most of all, though, I paid attention as a boss because of the happenstance of how my managerial career began and ended.

In my first job out of graduate school, I was fortunate to work for someone who had spent his professional life thinking about management. J. Sterling Livingston was a professor at Harvard Business School and is still remembered as the author of two classic *Harvard Business Review* articles: "Pygmalion in Management," which focused on the power of managerial expectations, and "The Myth of the Well-Educated Manager," which focused on the lack of correlation between success in business school and subsequent success in work and life.

I knew Sterling not as a professor but in his other life as a serial entrepreneur. I worked for his latest creation at the time, Sterling Institute, whose humble purpose was to remake management education. I became his assistant and that meant I spent much time with him, which provided opportunities to listen as he expounded on his key ideas.

Some of those ideas you will find in subsequent pages here: first, the notion that becoming a manager is a difficult life transition, on a par with leaving home, marriage, retirement, and the like. This was Sterling's intuitive conclusion that Linda's subsequent research confirmed empirically and with much greater depth. Second, that management was a practice, a discipline, and, above all, a process, and that good managers were therefore systematic. They uncovered what worked and made sure those things got done over and over. Third, at a time when management wisdom said to "match authority and responsibility," he derided the notion. Responsibility will always exceed authority, he said, and good managers are those who find ways to fulfill their responsibilities nonetheless. It was the basic rationale for what we now call networking. Finally, he talked about how good managers use the daily work to do their managerial work. Most of all, he spoke of this in regard to developing people, which he considered the heart of management: good managers structure the work that must be done in ways that develop the people doing the work.

Sterling's final lesson for me came from his actions rather than his words. In spite of all his insight, he was a terrible manager, a conclusion reached by virtually all of us around him, and he knew he was. For instance, he constantly had me, a kid, carry messages to his senior people that he should have carried himself. Once, when I more or less suggested he should do himself what he wanted me to do, he said in exasperation, "Look, I know what it takes to manage. I just don't want to do that." Until then, I'd never thought of management as a matter of will, discipline, and courage that could make demands of us we may not like, demands we could ignore but only at our peril. I believe it's fair to say that for all Sterling accomplished, he did not fully reach his ultimate goals, at least as I understood them decades ago.

Working for Sterling early in my career sensitized me to all these ideas—most of all the idea that management is an activity that can be studied and learned, a more or less discrete set of activities with related skills, knowledge, values, and competencies. It was something I could and should pay attention to. That fit neatly with my natural tendencies, and so I did pay attention through the rest of my career. For all that, I'm deeply in his debt. He was a seminal figure in my life and his hand is on this book. I was saddened, as were all who knew him, by his recent death.

Twenty-five years later, after all the positions I noted at the beginning, I worked at Harvard Business School Publishing.

There I collaborated with management experts, many on the Harvard faculty, to produce programs about how to manage. If Sterling was the prelude to my management career, this was the coda. It was an opportunity to reflect on my experience in relation to the content of the programs I was producing and finally make sense of what had worked, and where and why I had fallen short. What I learned is the heart of my contribution to *Being the Boss*.

While at Harvard, I came across Linda's work with new managers and read it with deep and personal interest. It played a large role in helping me understand my own experience.

I'm grateful for the opportunity to collaborate with her on *Being the Boss*. I wish I had been able to read it forty years ago. Assuming I had the maturity then to practice what it says, it would have made me a better manager and saved me and the people around me some turmoil. I hope it will serve that purpose for others. In many ways, it represents a return to my original aspirations of explaining, teaching, and helping others succeed.

INTRODUCTION

Where Are You on Your Journey?

Are you as good a manager as you need to be? Have you truly mastered the fundamentals of being a boss? Do you know how to get the best possible performance from the people who work for you? Are you ready for increased leadership responsibility? Are you good enough to achieve your career aspirations? Or have you stopped making progress?

Being the Boss will help you answer these questions. It's not just about good management, it's about *you*—about how *you* can assess your current capabilities as a manager and how *you* can become the great boss you want and need to be.

Are you up to the challenge? Do you know *how* to get better?

To help you think about these important questions, consider Jason Pedersen, who's just taken a new position that's going to test his managerial skills to the limit. We'll open every chapter with another episode from the Friday of his first week on the job as he struggles to understand the responsibilities he's taken on. Imagine yourself in his position and think about how you might deal with the challenges in front of him.

6:10 a.m.   Unable to sleep, Jason Pedersen arrives at work before dawn at the London office of Reynolds Educational, a $630 million publisher of educational materials for preschool through college.

From his backpack, he pulls out a laptop, along with all the materials he read last night at the company flat, his temporary home for at least the next six months.

Today, Friday, is his fifth day as publisher of Project Emerge, a six-month-old start-up within Reynolds Ed. It's aimed at offering a college-level technical curriculum that's presented entirely online but sponsored and administered by local schools in emerging economies.

Reynolds Ed is a Boston-based division of Reynolds Company, a $12.3 billion international media company headquartered in New York that publishes (besides educational materials) business news, trade publications, fiction and nonfiction books for the general public, and scientific and technical journals.

Jason joined the company six years ago in IT, where he spent his time integrating the IT systems of publishers acquired by Reynolds Ed. Wanting to have more impact in the company, he transferred to editorial, where heading two complex and successful product development projects has made him something of a rising star.

Only three weeks ago, he was offered the job of publisher by Fred Whitelaw, Reynolds Ed CEO, and Ray Sanchez, executive vice president of editorial. They said a pilot course in computers, Introduction to Programming, was almost ready to launch. They expected it to validate the new business model—online courses with local sponsors—and lay the foundation for a rapidly growing business. The next day, when Jason accepted the position of publisher, Sanchez, his new boss, seemed relieved. "This is very important," he said. "The world is changing and Reynolds has to change with it. Project Emerge is a big part of that evolution. We're counting on you. You showed us you can develop great new products. Now show us you can build and lead something."

Jason has spent the past week getting to know the business and the people involved. He's talked to the six individuals who report to him, a diverse group that includes individuals from India, Korea, China, the United States, Argentina, and Nigeria who range in age from twenty-seven to fifty-seven. As of yet, he has only spent time with his direct reports and not with the other nine people in his group. He's also talked in person or by video-conferencing to the five Reynolds Ed senior managers he'll work with regularly, including, besides Whitelaw and Sanchez, the heads of international sales, educational technology, information technology, human resources, and finance. He's also on three corporate task forces but doesn't yet know how much effort they'll require. Right now, they feel like distractions to him.

As he lay in the dark last night, trying to sleep, his mind kept spinning through the litany of expectations, problems, and complaints he'd been hearing all week. Project Emerge is the most visible new venture in the division, and everybody seems to have their own views of what it will accomplish, how it will affect them, and what's wrong with it. Now, full of anxiety, he's come in early to sort through the voluminous notes he made over the past four days.

7:40 a.m.   After more than an hour and two mugs of coffee, he finishes typing out the last item in his summary of the issues he faces. Last Tuesday he tried to call his predecessor Frank Rigby, who'd gone to another division. Rigby hasn't called back and now Jason is beginning to fear the worst, that Rigby jumped ship just before the hole in the hull became obvious.

Jason studies his list of problems. The big issues fall into three key categories: First, Project Emerge's critical relationship with a nongovernment organization, the International Fund for Technical Education (IFTE), seems troubled and perhaps even at risk. Second, the program to sign up schools for the initial course is just under way, but critical initial steps are behind schedule. The international sales group and the IFTE haven't yet done what they committed to do. Finally, the schedule for production of online materials for the all-important inaugural course seems in doubt. He's still trying to find out where it stands.

Solving these problems—indeed, the ultimate success of Project Emerge—depends significantly on people and groups outside Jason's Project Emerge team. One reason he left IT was to avoid the constant haggling associated with merging different computer systems. In developing new products, he had to coordinate different groups, but the organizational issues were manageable. Now he realizes he's back in the organizational stew and will be spending much time dealing with people and groups he doesn't control. It's a disconcerting, almost helpless feeling he thought he'd left behind.

Yesterday on the phone, Sanchez seemed reluctant to hear any details of what Jason had found. When Jason alluded to problems and what other groups hadn't done, Sanchez only said, "That's exactly why we put you there. There's nothing wrong some good leadership can't fix." Jason suspected that was supposed to encourage him, but it had the opposite effect.

A disturbing thought begins to nag at Jason: How will I ever get everyone to do what they have to do? This is like herding cats.

Quite a change since Monday, he thinks. He walked in that first morning full of confidence, sure he could take on this exciting project, produce a great win, and build something important. It would be his breakthrough opportunity. If results met expectations, he would grow his group to forty people within a year and far beyond that over time.

Now he wonders whether he's up to the challenge. Does he know enough? he worries. Is he ready to pull this off? He remembers the arrangement Whitelaw and Sanchez offered him: six months to convince them he can lead a rapidly growing business, not just develop great product. In six months he can move his family to London—if he succeeds. If he doesn't, he'll return to Boston, and then who knows what will happen? For the first time, the possibility of failure seems real, and he realizes he's never failed at anything before.

Does this sound familiar? Sooner or later, most managers face a situation like this when they realize that becoming an effective manager is an enormous challenge and taking a management course or getting an MBA isn't sufficient preparation.

Obviously, the details of your work differ from those Jason faces in Project Emerge. But can you imagine yourself in his situation? Have you encountered a moment of reckoning, when you realize how much is really required of you and how much further you must grow in your role as boss?

This is a common experience for new managers—when they often wonder, Does anyone know I'm faking it? But it can come later too, after years on the job. One day you realize you're stuck, going nowhere, no longer growing or advancing. Or your people aren't performing as they should, and you have a nagging suspicion that you're probably part of the problem. Or you may have thought you were doing fine, but you've recently been given a daunting new assignment, or perhaps you've received some negative feedback about your leadership. All these suggest that you have more to learn, more distance to cover before you're fully effective.

If this moment hasn't happened for you yet, it surely will if you aspire to greater responsibility and impact.

Why Is Becoming a Manager So Difficult?

Why, for most who enter it, does management present so many surprising hurdles and frustrate so many preconceptions and expectations? Progress will come more quickly and easily to those who understand the challenges they face. The answer has two parts, based on research we and others have done, our own observations, and our personal experience.

Management Is Different

First, management is different from anything you've done before. Becoming an effective manager is difficult because of the great gulf that separates the work of management from the work of individual performers.

Many managers think at first that managing others will be an extension of managing themselves. They assume they will be doing what they did previously, except they will exercise more control over their work and the work of others. Instead, they find they must make a great leap into a new and strange universe unlike anything they've encountered before.

This is especially true if you're a producing manager who must combine the roles of individual contributor and manager. At first, you naturally tend to think the managerial role is simply a broader version of managing yourself. Only with time and painful experience will you discover it's totally different.

Becoming a Manager Requires Personal Learning and Change

Second, becoming an effective manager requires that you not only acquire new skills and knowledge but also undergo difficult personal change.

Those who become managers must learn to see themselves and their work differently. They must develop new values, deeper self-awareness, increased emotional maturity, and the ability to exercise wise judgment. Many managers, for example, are accused of being control freaks because they don't delegate. But a desire for control often isn't the problem. Instead, it's an issue of identity. They haven't yet changed how they think about themselves and their contribution, the value they add as managers. They resist giving up the role of doer because they believe, if only unconsciously, that's who they are. They have not learned to see themselves as the boss.

In fact, becoming a manager requires so much personal learning and change that it is truly a transformation, akin to the transformations required by such life events as leaving home, finishing school and beginning a career, getting married, or having a child. Like these profound inflection points, becoming an effective manager will call on you to act, think, and feel in new ways; discover new sources of satisfaction; and relinquish old, comfortable, but now outmoded roles and self-perceptions. It requires you to consider anew the questions, Who am I? What do I want? What value do I add?

Becoming a Manager Is a Journey—A Journey Most Managers Fail to Complete

Such a transformation cannot occur overnight. It takes so much time and effort that it's helpful to think of it as a journey. The changes are so deep and personal that they require time to take root, usually years. And they cannot be taught. You and every other manager must make them yourself, based on your own experience as a boss. You make progress on your journey as you learn and change, step-by-step.

Where are you on your journey? How far must you go to become a fully effective manager?

Unfortunately, most managers begin to make progress, but many—perhaps most—fail to complete their journeys. They stop short of acquiring the necessary skills, knowledge, values, outlook, self-knowledge, judgment, and emotional competence.

Most new managers start out receptive to change and learning because of their initial discomfort in their new position. But as they begin to learn the ropes and no longer fear imminent failure, too often they grow complacent. Every organization has its ways of doing things—rules of thumb, policies, standard practices, unspoken rules and guidelines—such as "no overtime," "promote by seniority," "smooth over conflict," and a host of others. Once learned, they are ways of getting along, and new managers use them to get by. Instead of confronting a performance problem, they fill out the compulsory annual appraisal form and simply negotiate the wording with the person involved. They do enough to meet budget because that's all that's required of them. Indeed, they stop thinking of what's possible and focus on what's expected. They hire people who are good enough and will blend in.

They progress to the point that management no longer feels new and strange. When they no longer fear imminent failure, they grow comfortable. They "manage," in the worst sense of the word. That's why years of experience are not necessarily an indication of managerial effectiveness.

This surely accounts for the wide range of mastery among managers, even those with considerable experience. Based on what we have seen, most organizations have a few great managers, some good managers, a horde of mediocre managers, some poor managers, and some awful managers. Like most of us, you've probably had, at one time or another, a boss whose ineptitude made you wonder how someone like that could become or remain a manager.

That so many stop short of completing their journeys is hardly surprising given the difficulty and discomfort involved, the time and commitment required, and the limited or elusive sources of help available. Full mastery comes slowly, as with any serious craft, and requires steady progress in a world that keeps throwing up ever more complex challenges and opportunities. We know highly competent managers who consider themselves still learning even after years of experience. It hardly helps that most organizations both fail to provide enough initial help for inexperienced managers and seldom confront the shortcomings of those with experience.

Were You a Star as an Individual Performer?

If you were a high performer in your work before becoming a manager, you may find the journey into management particularly difficult. Because of their previous success, stars are understandably reluctant to give up the attitudes and practices they think produced their success thus far, and they're unwilling to change themselves. They don't know how to develop or coach people because they never needed much coaching themselves, or so they believe. They don't know how to deal with people who lack their motivation. Because they've never failed, they've had little practice reflecting on and learning from experience. No wonder many former stars turn into mediocre bosses. If you were a star, be aware that the very success that produced your promotion can now work against you.

Former stars or not, most managers stop developing, we suspect, not as a matter of personal and conscious choice. They simply don't know better. Ignorant of what's required to be fully effective, comfortable in their roles, and understandably reluctant to undergo sometimes painful personal change, they simply believe they've journeyed far enough.

How else can you explain the fact that, in study after study, a majority of managers rate themselves "above average"—how can everyone be above average?—and that many bosses in 360-reviews rate themselves more highly as managers than they're rated by the people they manage.[1]

It's hardly necessary to point out the corporate and personal cost of all this. Poor management directly affects the ability of a company to perform, meet customer needs, compete successfully, and innovate in a changing world. And it limits the ability of managers to have the impact they want, advance in their careers, and satisfy their aspirations.

Being the Boss Can Help You Complete Your Journey

Where are you on your journey? Have you made sufficient progress to be comfortable? Have you learned the ropes enough to get by? Or are you as effective as you could be? Are you a great boss? How far must you still go to master your crucial role?

We wrote *Being the Boss* for individuals in their early and mid-careers who realize they need to become more effective managers. If you're willing to challenge yourself and keep making progress, it will help you improve. *Being the Boss* can provide the insights you need to become a great boss, regardless of your level in the organization. For higher level managers responsible for business units, it lacks coverage of only two key aspects of their responsibilities: organizational design and competitive strategy.

It will help you understand the nature of your journey into management and what to expect along the way. Making progress requires an understanding of management and why it's difficult. If you don't know what to expect, you're much more likely to give up because you think you're alone and your problems are unique.

It will help you understand the purpose of your journey. What is a fully effective manager? What does such a person do, and how does she do it? What does it mean to reach mastery and become a great boss? Many managers stop their journeys because they don't realize how much further they must go.

It will help you understand where you are on your journey and how much further you have to go. This is truly important. You cannot make progress without assessing yourself periodically and identifying both your strengths and where you need further development.

If you haven't completed your journey, that should spur you to action, not discourage you. Indeed, what we've said should give you hope. Since it's a journey, you can *become* what you need to be. Good managers are made, not born.

But why should you keep striving to improve? You should continue your journey for two good reasons:

First, the people for whom you're responsible need you to keep going. In the long run, they cannot perform better than the quality of management you provide. You are ultimately the primary limit on their performance as a group. Management actually does make the difference between poor and superior performance.

Second, you cannot achieve your own aspirations if you don't keep making progress. Think of how many people you know who were high potential at one time but now are stuck or their careers derailed. Organizations may not be good at confronting inept managers, but—usually—they don't keep promoting them either. What we cover in *Being the Boss* can guide your work as a boss through middle management. Senior managers and executives face additional challenges, but even their work is built on the foundation we present here.

As you make progress, you will feel a growing sense of mastery. You will discover the exciting challenges and deep pleasure to be found in making others more productive in doing worthwhile work. As one manager said, "It's fascinating to see you have impact. It really feels good."[2] And you'll uncover new sides of yourself, new talents, new sources of satisfaction, a richer work life.

Where are you on your journey? Are you as good as you want and need to be? How much further must you go to master the fundamentals of being a great boss?

There's no limit to the size of organization you can lead or the accomplishments possible if you have the will and courage to keep going.

1

YOUR 3 IMPERATIVES
AS A MANAGER

Making Sense of Your Journey

7:52 a.m. Jason picks up his phone messages. The first came at 9:25 p.m. yesterday from Dr. Schmidt, a computer scientist at a major U.S. university who's on the Project Emerge editorial advisory board. Speaking rapidly, Schmidt presents a litany of problems with the outline of the initial course, Introduction to Programming. The second message is from Barry Hultgrund, a call Jason didn't take when it came earlier. Barry is the finance analyst assigned full-time to Project Emerge—he more or less works for Jason—and he's reminding Jason that preliminary budget numbers are due today for the next fiscal year, which begins in less than four months.

Jason feels another twinge of anxiety. He knows the budget is looming but he forgot the numbers are due today. He adds it to his list.

7:58 a.m. Jason sends an e-mail to Sumantra Tata, his senior editor, telling him to get back right away to Dr. Schmidt, the adviser who called, and reminding him it's the second message from Schmidt in two days.

8:00 a.m.   Jason receives a call from Jacques Levanger, his contact and a senior official at the IFTE. Levanger has been out all week until today; he and Jason are scheduled to meet on Monday when Jason will take the train to Paris, where the IFTE is head-quartered. Levanger is calling to ask whether there's a problem, because, like Jason, he arrived at the office early and found a message from Dr. Schmidt. Jason tells Levanger he'll be in touch with Schmidt today. "Yes, please do," says Levanger. "We don't need more problems with Project Emerge now. In any case, I look forward to our meeting."

Jason adds a note about Schmidt and the IFTE to his list. The International Fund for Technical Education is a strategic partner crucial to Project Emerge. Funded by the aid organizations of the world's largest economies, philanthropic foundations, and international companies desperate for skilled local talent, its strategy is to jump-start commercial interest in markets that might not yet seem attractive. For Jason, the IFTE's specific role and critical contribution is to help create partnerships between Project Emerge and the over two thousand local educational institutions in its network.

8:05 a.m.   Jason's mobile vibrates. A text message from Laraba Sule, Project Emerge marketing manager. A Nigerian who attended the London School of Economics, she's worked in media and marketing at Reynolds for eight years and is a recent mother who works flextime. Her message reads, "We want to conduct an orientation session at International Sales Conference for the sales team assigned to help sell our programming course. But people in sales claim no time is available on the agenda. Please approach Mr. Jack Cavit about this important matter. It is very important for our plans."

Jason sighs. This is not good news. Cavit is vice president of international sales, and his people pitch instructors at schools outside North America to adopt Reynolds' materials for their courses. Every publisher's sales live or die on the attention received from these people. Sales Conference, where they all gather to learn about coming new products, is a critical forum for convincing them yours is worth their interest. Publishers vie to get on the agenda. Other publishing groups have apparently convinced Cavit they're more important than Project Emerge.

8:09 a.m.   Jason looks at Cavit's online calendar and sees that .he's not free today and will be traveling next week. With apprehension, Jason calls Cavit's assistant, gets no answer, and leaves a phone message asking for a callback ASAP.

8:12 a.m.   Jason leaves a note on the desk of his assistant, Kim Young, asking Kim to bring in the analyses Jason assigned to various people earlier in the week.

8:16 a.m.   Glancing at his laptop, Jason sees a new e-mail from Sumantra, who's forwarding an e-mail exchange with Kathy Wu, an assistant editor in New York assigned half-time to Project Emerge. Wu's role, as Jason understands it, is to identify and take a first look at possible additional courses for the Project Emerge portfolio. Sumantra insists that she works for him. She insists that she works for the project publisher. Sumantra ends his e-mail to Jason with "We must have a VERY serious talk about this VERY soon. Please let me know your pleasure."

8:19 a.m.   Jason adds this to his list in the section for miscellaneous problems that includes a potpourri of other issues about salaries, performance reviews, promotions, sour work relationships, family problems, and who should get an empty cubicle with windows. He's put off dealing with any of these until he gets to know people better. He's still figuring out whom he can trust, who's good and who's not.

8:23 a.m.   Jason tries Cavit's assistant again. She's just in and Jason explains why it's important that he talk to Cavit.

"Project Emerge," he says, "is supposed to have four sales people assigned to it full-time for three months. They'll work with the IFTE in placing the new Project Emerge programming course with schools in the IFTE network. And we're supposed to run an orientation session for them at Sales Conference. But no salespeople have been assigned so far, and now I'm hearing there's no time available at Sales Conference."

Cavit's assistant promises to check with her boss and get back.

As he hangs up the phone, Jason realizes that if nothing happens at the conference and the salespeople can't get started on schedule, it will throw into doubt all the projections for the coming academic year. And if Project Emerge is in trouble, he thinks, then his position, his career at Reynolds Ed, is in trouble too.

In the introduction, we said becoming a manager is a difficult journey of personal transformation that requires you to learn from experience over a long period, typically years, a journey most managers stop short of completing.

But why is management so difficult?

What Is Management and Why Is It Difficult?

What makes management difficult isn't the *idea* of management. That couldn't be more straightforward.

Management is responsibility for the performance of a group of people. It's a simple idea. The people you manage do the work and you're responsible. Yet, if the idea isn't difficult, putting it into practice is. Why? Because . . .

To carry out this responsibility, you must influence others, which means you must make a difference not only in what they do but in the thoughts and feelings that drive their actions. Management is defined by responsibility but it's done by exerting influence. That, in a nutshell, is what you do as a boss—influence others in ways that make them more productive as individuals and, especially, as a group. Thus, the central question we address in *Being the Boss* is this: *How* do you exert influence? *What* do managers actually do to shape and even change the behavior, thoughts, and feelings of others?

Watching real managers in action provides clues but no clear answers to these questions. We know from systematic observation that managers spend their time in an unending parade of mostly small events consisting mainly of person-to-person interactions, the majority of them unplanned encounters, with a wide variety of people, and covering a seemingly random mix of topics.

Half the managers' activities took mere minutes to complete. Only a small percentage received more than an hour.[1]

Even at higher levels of an organization, general managers who run significant business units spend 70 to 90 percent of their working time with others, face-to-face, on the phone, conferencing on the Web, or interacting online through e-mail or more sophisticated social networking tools. Whatever form they take, most of their interactions are reactive, not proactive; many are interruptions. Most interchanges are quick; a single topic seldom gets more than ten minutes. Even brief exchanges typically cover a wide range of topics, both business and nonbusiness. The business issues discussed are a mix of the trivial, mundane, and important. Rarely is any subject explored in great depth. Time working alone occurs mostly at home, while commuting, or when traveling for work.

In all their interactions, managers rarely make definitive major decisions. They do spend much time trying to influence people, but mostly by asking, requesting, kidding, cajoling, nudging, persuading, and coercing—almost anything but issuing direct orders, which they do rarely.

Because much of what they do is fragmented and unpredictable, what they actually do is often different from what they planned to do. As one manager said, "Each day I go into the office with some preplanned action and at the end of the day, I have to regret that all the various things I [did] are very different."[2]

Many managers think the problem is their lack of knowledge, experience, or skill, especially their inability to manage time. In fact, the problem in large part is the fundamental nature of management itself, which at virtually all levels is unavoidably pressured, time-constrained, fragmented, and hectic.

So forget the notion that managerial work is organized, reflective, and carefully planned, or that a good manager moves thoughtfully and systematically from planning, to organizing, to coordinating, to controlling, to the other activities on the traditional list of what managers do. As one researcher concluded, "Managers do one darn thing after another!"

Management Is Difficult Because of Its Inherent Paradoxes

The work of managers seems so fragmented, improvisational, and superficial because it embodies a panoply of paradoxes.[3]

A paradox is a statement that contains contradictory elements but is true or useful nonetheless. For example: "To focus on the work people do, focus on the people doing the work." To make sense of this, you must find either the right balance point between the contradictions (focus on work versus focus on people) or the right way to combine them (deal with the work *through* the people doing it).

We describe here some of the more fundamental and difficult paradoxes that reside at the heart of management. This list is hardly exhaustive, and we'll point out others as they apply in subsequent chapters.

Paradox: You Are Responsible for What Others Do

Performance is the point of it all—the work done by your group. That's what you're responsible for. When your boss wants to know why an initiative is in trouble, he won't call in your whole group. He'll call you in, and you alone will sit in the hot seat. You're responsible and no one else. Yet you don't, or shouldn't, do the work.

How can anyone be truly responsible for what someone else does? Good question. We say it easily—*responsible for the work of others*—without appreciating its obvious and inherent difficulty. It makes complete sense only if you assume that in every situation you know what should be done and that people will do exactly what you say. Obviously, those assumptions are flawed, and only when you relinquish them can you understand what a difficult undertaking it is to answer for the work of others. To be successful at it requires that you work *through* others—that you include and work with them, rather than simply issue directives they must follow—a difficult task for anyone who prefers direct action and personal results.

Paradox: To Focus on the Work, You Must Focus on People Doing the Work

Many managers think they manage the *work*. They don't. They're *responsible* for the work, but they get work done by influencing the people who do the work. What makes this complicated is what Peter Drucker pointed out: when you hire a hand, it comes with a head and heart attached.[4] So you must pay attention, lots of attention, to the whole person—head *and* heart—because you need more than your people's time and attention. Most work now requires knowledge, judgment, thinking, and decision making, and so it matters if people care about what they do. You cannot simply give them orders and criticism. That rarely produces the kind of engagement you need. Other, less direct but more effective forms of influence—such as support, development, and encouragement—are needed that engage the whole person.

Paradox: You Must Both Develop Your People and Evaluate Them

It is a boss's dual responsibility both to foster the development of her people and to determine if and when those same people must be removed because they cannot do the work. Logically, assessment is necessary for development, but the conflict of the paradox arises when the boss must abandon the goal of development and act solely in the interest of the group by releasing a person who cannot perform the work needed by the group. How do you, as manager, determine when it is time to make that tough choice? How do you work to develop someone and invest yourself in that person's progress—and then abandon him? How do you find the right balance between someone's need to learn and their need to perform? It's as much a psychological as a logical paradox, which makes it all the more difficult. Dealing with the opposing roles of coach and judge will present some of the most difficult emotional and managerial challenges you will face as a boss. You will be sorely tempted to abdicate one of the roles.

Paradox: You Must Make Your Group a Cohesive Team Without Losing Sight of the Individuals on It

Many managers think the word *team* is simply another name for the group of people they manage. Some eventually realize that success depends on converting the group into a true team— *a group of people who do collective work in committed pursuit of a common goal.* Every team is a group, but not every group is a team. In every team, there's a strong sense of "we" and a shared belief that "we" succeed or fail together. Yet a team needs to be diverse as well—members must bring different competencies, experiences, mind-sets, and individual interests—if the team is to be innovative. You will struggle constantly to balance the dual needs for diversity and cohesiveness.

Paradox: To Manage Your Group, You Must Manage the Larger Context Beyond Your Group

You may prefer to think you can focus only on your own group. But every group operates in a larger organization or context composed of many groups that depend on each other.[5] Goals, priorities, needs, and interests all differ from group to group because the job of each group differs and resources are scarce. Because you cannot impose what you want on others, or they on you, then to succeed you must constantly manage your group in the context of others' needs and interests.

To achieve your group's goals also means there will be times you must influence and even challenge the organization beyond your own area—including your boss, other superiors, colleagues, and outside stakeholders. Too many managers see themselves as subjects of the larger organization who simply follow orders from above. Such thinking is too narrow. To deliver expected results may mean that you sometimes act as change agent both within *and outside* your group. You are responsible for creating the conditions needed for your own success.

Paradox: You Must Focus on Today and Tomorrow

You need results today, but if you don't prepare today for the future, you won't get results tomorrow when *tomorrow* becomes *today*. Focusing on today and tomorrow requires trade-offs because limited resources will prevent you from focusing on both at once. But when does one take precedence?

Paradox: You Must Execute and Innovate

To survive and succeed, all groups must simultaneously change in some ways and remain the same in others. They must execute *and* innovate, stay the course *and* foster change. Yet the group skills and mind-sets required for serious change and innovation differ from those for continuity and steady execution. To do both demands an accomplished manager who can act as both change agent and steward of continuity. Your task is to discern when one versus the other is required.

Much business thinking tends to distinguish management and leadership.[6] It says management focuses on doing work on time, on budget, and on target—*steady execution*—while leadership focuses on *change and innovation*. A few years ago, management was the broader term and *included* leadership. In *Being the Boss* we return to that approach. We believe leading and managing are equally essential and actually work together. In any case, the same person—you, the boss—must do both, and so we employ the term *manage* to mean *all* effort necessary to influence others in ways that make them more productive, including *both* execution *and* innovation, continuity *and* change, management *and* leadership.

Paradox: You Must Sometimes Do Harm in Order to Do a Greater Good

With managerial influence and authority comes the ability, often the necessity, to make choices for the greater good that harm some of the individuals or groups involved—for example, when you must cut costs, lay people off, or promote only one of three candidates. Such harms are not the goal but the consequence of actions you must take, yet they are real and painful to those who suffer them.[7]

As a manager, you cannot avoid decisions that affect the work and lives of others in profound ways. They appear all the time, a burden of being the boss. What makes them truly difficult is that you must weigh competing considerations that render your choices anything but clear and obvious. "Nothing is black and white," one new manager observed. "It's all gray. My job is to manage trade-offs."

If you don't see such ethical dilemmas as part of the job, you're likely to treat them as exceptions, distractions that don't deserve real attention. But they're not exceptions. They're built into your everyday work as boss.

Since you cannot avoid ethical dilemmas, you must be prepared for the personal anguish they can create. You probably don't see yourself as someone who consciously harms others, and so confronting the necessity of inflicting harm, however inadvertently, will force you to examine your identity and think hard about what you're willing and not willing to do. To these dilemmas you must bring both emotional competence and a set of personal values developed over time through experience—another reason becoming a boss is a long and difficult journey.

The Paradoxes Define the Fundamental Nature of Management

Remember the paradoxes. You will encounter them every day in almost everything you do as the boss.

They are never fully and truly resolved. That's why a certain amount of fragmentation, conflict, tension, instability, and general messiness is built into the basic nature of managerial work. Only those who ignore the paradoxes think "good" management will produce a workplace of constant calm cooperation, a perpetually smooth-running machine.

Because of them, the "right" management action will always be a matter of judgment. Be bold or patient, directive or accommodating, developmental or judgmental? These and a thousand other choices will depend on a full consideration of the context and the goals being sought. And it's not just knowing *what* to do but *how* to do it as well. Mastery requires judgment.

The paradoxes explain why management is so stressful. Even successful managers report feelings of overload, conflict, ambiguity, and isolation.[8] The paradoxes are a key reason. They come at you relentlessly—day after day after day. You must find the proper weight for each and keep them all in balance simultaneously as conditions change around you.

The paradoxes explain why the world needs management. Without it, they will eventually undermine the ability of groups to do productive work. They are the primary reason organizations fail and groups fall apart.

The paradoxes explain why becoming a manager requires a lengthy, difficult, personal journey. You will need time and experience to learn how to cope effectively with all of these conflicting interests, forces, and needs at the heart of management.

The paradoxes explain why management requires self-knowledge. Every time you encounter a paradox, you will bring to it a predisposition to favor one side or the other. For example, you tend to focus on the individual over the team—or vice versa. Or you focus on the work and not the people—or vice versa. To each paradox, you apply a default response. Taken together, these predispositions or default responses make up your style, the way you tend to lead as a boss.

What are your default responses? If you're not aware of them, you will follow them without thinking rather than make choices best suited to the circumstances.

What's Your Leadership Style?

Mark where you fall on each of the following scales to identify your style profile:

Do you tend to include others in the way you manage, or do you tend to give directions and tell others what to do?

1	2	3	4	5
Give directions				Include others

Do you tend to focus on the work or on the people doing the work? In other words, do you tend to confront and criticize, or do you support people and give them what they need to do good work?

```
1            2            3            4            5
├────────────┬────────────┬────────────┬────────────┤
Focus on                                     Focus on
work and                                   people and
confrontation                                 support
                                        them with what
                                           they need
```

Do you tend to focus more on evaluating your people or on developing them—on their performance or on helping them learn?

```
1            2            3            4            5
├────────────┬────────────┬────────────┬────────────┤
I tend to                                   I tend to
judge and                              develop people
evaluate
people
```

Do you tend to focus on your team as a whole or on the individual members who work for you?

```
1            2            3            4            5
├────────────┬────────────┬────────────┬────────────┤
Mostly on                              Mostly on team
members                                   as a whole
```

Do you tend to focus on your team or on the broader organization in which it operates?

```
1            2            3            4            5
├────────────┬────────────┬────────────┬────────────┤
Focus on                                     Focus on
team                                     organization
                                         outside team
```

Do you tend to focus on today's challenges, or do you prefer to deal with the future and what's coming?

```
1            2            3            4            5
├────────────┬────────────┬────────────┬────────────┤
I stick pretty                               I prefer
much to                                 planning and
"now"                                 thinking about
                                          the future
```

Do you prefer execution—getting steady work done—or innovating new things and ways of working?

1	2	3	4	5

I prefer
execution

I prefer
innovation

Are you reluctant to do anything that might harm someone or some group? Or are you able to cause some pain to some people to accomplish a greater good?

1	2	3	4	5

I avoid any
kind of harm
or pain to
anyone

I can pursue a
greater good
even if it causes
some harm to
someone

There are no "right" answers that always and everywhere apply. The right choice will in every case depend on the situation and the people involved. But you need to know what you *prefer* to do, what response you will make automatically unless you stop and think about what you're doing. These preferences arise from your personality, your values, and your work experiences. And so, as you'll discover, they're not easy to change. The goal is to manage them by being aware of them and sensitive to when they come into play.

Keep your preferences and your style in mind through the rest of *Being the Boss*. They are your preferred ways of managing, and you'll find they shape everything you do and every choice you make.

Add to the Paradoxes a Dynamic Workplace and a Changing Workforce

As if the paradoxes aren't enough, the workplace and the workforce are constantly changing and making your job as manager increasingly difficult. You're being called upon to assume rising levels of responsibility, manage increasing numbers of people, respond to more change, and cope with mounting diversity.[9]

Globalization and technological change, and the heightened competition they bring, are forcing organizations to become ever more agile and responsive. As a consequence, organizations have become flatter, more far-flung, and hence more multicultural, as well as more complex and fluid in their structure.

Many companies have stopped using organization charts. Reporting relationships change frequently, and many organizations now depend on ad hoc work groups—teams, task forces, boards, and councils—that cross functional, geographical, and hierarchical lines. Such changing complexity has led many companies to give up trying to describe their structure with simple lines and boxes.

While organizations are changing the way they function, the work force itself is shifting too. Employees of *different generations*— there are now four in the workplace—bring to work diverse aspirations, motivations, values, and feelings about authority and organizations. Imagine the challenges of managing a collection of workers ranging from twenty to sixty-five years old. That's not an unusual work group today.

In addition, as organizations spread around the globe, their workforces embrace *multiple cultures.* As a result, there's growing similarity among cultures in the way people dress, talk, and interact socially. Yet these superficial similarities often mask fundamental differences in attitudes about such key work matters as time, deadlines, hierarchy and authority, how to manage conflict, and even how to communicate.

To complicate matters, such diverse group members are often located around the globe, and so relationships among them must be created and maintained through technology rather than face-to-face.

The management implications of more fluid organizations and more diverse employees are both obvious and subtle. What's obvious is that managers must learn to produce results in spite of constant change, ever-growing complexity, as well as basic and often unspoken differences within their groups driven by culture and generation and mediated by new technology-driven ways of interacting. Running a multifunctional, multicultural, multi-generational team of thirty people with different training and experience, and spread over three continents, can be someone's first job as a boss.

At a more subtle level, managers must now work with a changing *psychological contract*.[10] This is the unspoken agreement that employee and employer bring to their relationship. It's what each party expects from the other in such areas as rewards, recognition, amount and quality of work, and loyalty.

Today's contract is increasingly temporary and transactional. Work relationships now tend to focus not on building long-term relationships but on pay-for-work, and both sides recognize work ties will last only as long as they make short-term sense for all involved. We see this in the proliferation of different work arrangements. Besides permanent full-time employees—once the vast majority—the proportion of part-time, job-sharing, free-lance, and independent consultant/contractor "employees" is growing dramatically.

Here's the challenge presented by this shifting psychological contract. How do you manage a multifaceted and transient work-force that feels little personal investment in the long-term success of your organization? How do you create in your people a sense of real commitment to the work? Why should they care? What will cause them to invest the extraordinary effort that good results usually require? This burden now falls largely on your shoulders; you represent the company for those reporting to you. The old saying that "People go to work for a company but quit a boss" is probably more true today than ever.

This is an urgent problem for you and your organization. Low birthrates, an aging workforce, and other factors are shrinking the labor force in developed economies. And with growing educational and economic opportunities in emerging economies, the aspirations and expectations of the labor force there are on the rise.[11] As a result, only good bosses, supported by well-run organizations, will be able to hold good people.

How Do You Manage in Such a World?

As all those changes make management even more fluid, hectic, fragmented, and discontinuous, how can you, as a boss, do anything but react to what comes at you day by day? How can you get beyond merely coping with the chaos? Unfortunately, many managers don't. We know that too many have no sense of where they're going and simply react to events as best they can.[12]

But effective managers do more than cope. They *use* the apparent chaos to do their work as managers.[13] They resolve problems by referring to some sense of the future they're trying to create, rather than arranging endless ad hoc solutions. If they need information, they use a chance encounter to ask a key question. Indeed, a ten-minute meeting on one subject may end up covering four or five topics because the manager deliberately uses the opportunity to raise them. In short, effective managers bend each interruption and problem to achieve a managerial end. They find in every activity thrust on them a seed of progress.

The Manager's 3 Imperatives

To apply this approach, you need a clear underlying sense of what's important, where you and your group want to be in the future, the priorities that spring from that foresight, and how you will achieve your goals. You need a mental framework that you can lay over the chaos and into which you can fit all the messy pieces as they come at you. For that, you need a way of thinking about your work and, in particular, a way of thinking about what you must do to influence your people to make them productive and achieve the results you need.

We offer a way based on studies of management practice—what effective managers actually *do*—and on our knowledge of where managers tend to go wrong.

We call this approach *the effective manager's 3 Imperatives: manage yourself, manage your network, manage your team.* We believe it can be used to guide every aspect of your work. Each imperative is critical to your success, and, taken together,

The effective manager's 3 imperatives

1. Manage yourself
2. Manage your network
3. Manage your team

they encompass the crucial activities all effective managers must do to influence others. Mastering them is the purpose of your journey.

Manage yourself. Many managers, new and experienced, think the third imperative, manage your team, covers the whole of their work. It's not obvious to them that effective management begins with them as individuals. Thus, *manage yourself* deals with changes required in how you think about yourself and your role, how you relate to others as a boss, and especially how you try to influence others.

Manage your network. Many managers disdain and actively avoid the political side of organizations. Others relish the internal competition and focus on it so much that winning organizational battles becomes their primary goal, the source of satisfaction for them. Both kinds of manager fail to appreciate the need to work effectively in political environments without becoming enmeshed in or controlled by them. Instead of the fly caught in the web, you must become the spider that creates the web—your own network—and dances lightly over it.

Manage your team. This is about managing all those in your group for whom you're responsible. In managing their own people, however, many managers never grasp the critical difference between simply managing a collection of individuals and managing a real team. *Manage your team* is about building a high-performance team that's more than the sum of the individuals involved.

The 3 Imperatives summarize the essence of what you must do to fulfill your responsibility as a manager. They are the fundamental levers of influence you can use with both the people who work for you and those who don't. They provide the tools for managing the paradoxes, and they're flexible enough to accommodate the changes now occurring in the workplace and the workforce.

Above all, the 3 Imperatives make sense of your journey by making clear its purpose: to become an effective manager by mastering them. Mastery means not perfection but the ability to perform the 3 Imperatives with a consistently high level of proficiency. Each imperative reveals not only how to manage well but also how you must change if you want to act, think, and feel like a manager. Each is a key piece of the transformation management requires.

The remainder of *Being the Boss* is organized around the 3 Imperatives, with three or four chapters devoted to each.

Part I, Manage Yourself, focuses on the person-to-person relationships you form with others, especially those who work for you—which are the basis for how you influence others. Chapter 2 deals with the limited role of formal authority as an enduring and effective source of influence. Chapter 3 looks at the pitfalls of using friendship to influence others. And chapter 4 examines the real foundation of influence: trust.

Part II, Manage Your Network, is about exercising influence with integrity and for constructive purposes, given the political realities of organizational life. Chapter 5 stresses the critical need for you to create and sustain, with careful deliberation, a network of groups and people you must work with and whose help you need. Chapter 6 describes in detail how to build such a network. And chapter 7 examines your critical relationship with your boss.

Part III, Manage Your Team, focuses on what's required to create a real team of those who work for you. Chapter 8 deals with the need for you to make both written and unwritten plans to guide your team and give it a sense of purpose. Chapter 9 describes team culture and how to foster the right norms, values, and standards for productive teamwork. Chapter 10 explains how to work with and manage the performance of *individual* team members. And chapter 11 reveals the fundamental action model—*prep-do-review*—at the heart of all you do as a boss and how it can help you use every management activity, including problems and unexpected events, to pursue your managerial agenda.

Finally, chapter 12 will help you assess yourself against the 3 Imperatives and determine your strengths and where you need to make more progress in your journey. It also provides helpful advice for learning from your day-to-day experience.

As you read through *Being the Boss*, you'll discover a consistent theme: the critical role of self-assessment. What's covered in these chapters is based on management research and our extensive experience both managing others and helping others learn how to be effective bosses. Instead of theory, we provide how-to prescriptions through a process of self-discovery. The bottom line—becoming an effective boss—is about knowing how to use yourself as an instrument to get work done and contribute to your organization. Throughout, you will be encouraged to examine yourself in light of each imperative and, through a series of headings and subheadings that are actually probing questions, assess yourself against its requirements.

If you're an experienced manager who's already made much progress on your journey, you'll be familiar already with some of the questions and material in *Being the Boss*. Nonetheless, it will be useful as a reminder and summary, a way to identify where you still need to make progress, because there's often a gap between what we know to do and what we actually do. Also, as work and circumstances change, your job can temporarily call on some aspects of the 3 Imperatives more than others, and so it's good practice periodically to take a comprehensive look at yourself and where you stand.

Whether you are experienced or new to management, assess yourself with care and thought. Your success will depend on your ability to make progress, and progress depends on a clear sense of your current strengths and weaknesses. Over and over, we find managers at all levels who underperform, and whose careers are stalled or derailed, because they have not mastered the imperatives.

We hope you emerge from *Being the Boss* with a richer sense of yourself as a manager and a commitment to moving ahead on your journey. If you aspire to greater responsibility and impact, continuing progress on your journey will provide them. With commitment, there's no limit to where your journey can take you.

Part One

MANAGE YOURSELF

MANAGEMENT BEGINS WITH YOU—who you are as a person.

It begins with you because what you think and feel, the beliefs and values that drive your actions, matter to the people you must influence.

Each day people examine your every word and action to uncover your intentions and motives. They want to know whether they can trust you. How hard they work, their level of personal commitment, their willingness to accept your influence will hang largely on the competence and character they see in you. And their perceptions will determine the answer to this fundamental question every manager must ask: am I someone who can influence others to produce the results we need?

The chapters in part I will help you find the answer. They focus on the very core of management: the relationship between you and the people you manage. What is that relationship? What does it require of you? What about it creates the influence you must exercise?

Chapter 2, I'm the Boss! looks at formal authority, a manager's ability to exercise influence on behalf of the organization. It's an ability many managers misunderstand and misuse. They focus on the rights, privileges, and status—rather than the duties and responsibilities—that come with their title. We conclude that formal authority is a useful but very limited means of influence.

Chapter 3, I'm Your Friend! looks at a different source of influence: the personal relationship between boss and subordinate. In an authority-based relationship the manager says, "Do it because

I'm the boss." But in a personal relationship, the boss says, "Do it for me because we're friends." Though sometimes created consciously, such relationships usually develop because the manager simply wants to be liked and believes that a close, personal relationship is the best way to influence others. Unfortunately, it is not, and such relationships can create obstacles that limit the manager's effectiveness.

Chapter 4, Can People Trust You? answers this question: if influence doesn't arise from fear ("I'm the boss!") or from being liked ("I'm your friend!"), where does it come from? It comes from people's trust in you as a manager. Trust is the foundation for all forms of influence other than coercion. In this chapter we examine the sources of trust—people's belief in your competence and character—and encourage you to examine how well you do those things that foster trust.

As you read these chapters, we hope you'll consider carefully the many questions they pose. Use them to reflect on your own practices and your ability to influence your people, peers, and superiors.

This is where management—and your management journey—begins.

I'M THE BOSS!

Don't Depend on Your Formal Authority

8:31 a.m.   Kim Young, Project Emerge assistant, enters Jason's office waving the note Jason left on his desk.

"What's this?" Kim asks.

"Last Tuesday," Jason says. "I asked Jay, Sumantra, Kathy, and Barry for progress reports by end of day yesterday. I copied you and asked you to combine them into one file for me."

"Now I remember," he says. "Nobody sent anything."

"Did anybody say they'd be late?"

"No." Seeing the look on Jason's face, he adds, "Frank was pretty relaxed." Frank Rigby was Jason's predecessor. "He didn't believe in lots of reports or meetings or bureaucracy."

"Apparently not." Jason takes a deep breath and fights back the anger he can feel building inside himself. "Please go check with them," he says firmly but calmly to Kim. "Remind them I said this is important. Let me know when they expect to have their reports. And ask them about the other things I wanted. Sumantra's going back and taking a close look at our agreement with the IFTE—I want to know how they can bow out of Project Emerge, if that's what they're thinking of doing. Laraba is supposed to be comparing the IFTE's network of schools against the schools where Reynolds' materials are already being used. I'll call Barry myself. And make sure Jay covers what's going on with eMedia." Jay Bradshaw is manager of online production in charge of producing the actual online materials for all Project Emerge courses, based on a syllabus developed by Sumantra Tata, Project Emerge senior editor. eMedia is the outside production house Jay is using. Jason has heard eMedia is having problems staying on schedule.

8:35 a.m. Jason finds Barry's report in an e-mail that just arrived and spends a few minutes scrolling through it. With a sinking heart, he realizes it's not all he asked for. He wanted a sensitivity analysis of Project Emerge's numbers next year if development of the first offering, Introduction to Programming, is delayed or interest in it is less than expected. Barry only considered lower demand and ignored the possibility of production delays. Jason checks the e-mail he sent Barry. It clearly said to consider both demand and a delay.

8:43 a.m. Jason calls Barry. "I need to know what happens if Introduction to Programming is delayed."

"If it is, heaven help us."

"When can you redo the report?" Jason asks. "I can't submit any preliminary budget numbers until I see it."

"End of today."

"Then we won't have numbers until Monday."

"They won't like that," Barry says. "Why not just put in the original pro forma numbers?"

"We know more now, and I'm not signing up for funny numbers," Jason says. "I like reality."

"Be careful. Reality can bite you around here." Barry laughs.

8:46 a.m. Kim returns. "Those reports you wanted—Sumantra's half done. Jay says he's been too busy. Besides, he's meeting with eMedia at lunch today. He'll know more then. I can't reach Laraba. She must be on her way in."

In a fit of frustration, Jason shoots out a curt e-mail to all of them saying he needs their reports and other information by 4:00 p.m. *without fail*. "Let's see if they ignore *that*," he thinks.

8:51 a.m. Jason looks around to see Julia Morgan standing in front of his desk. She's an editorial assistant who works for

Sumantra. She asks for a minute and makes an impassioned plea for the empty cubicle by the windows. She has seasonal affective disorder (SAD), and unless she gets as much light as possible in the winter months, she gets depressed. "I've been diagnosed," she says. "I'm not making it up." Jason tells her he hasn't decided yet but will consider her request very seriously.

8:59 a.m. Still no word from Jack Cavit's assistant. Jason takes the elevator up to the seventh floor, hoping to catch Cavit in his office there. No luck. He asks Cavit's assistant to double-check his schedule. Nothing. No free time at all, not even a few minutes.

9:08 a.m. Jason takes the stairs down, instead of the elevator, to work off some nervous energy. "This is turning into a big problem," he thinks. "I can't believe Project Emerge and my future at Reynolds Ed depend on getting ten minutes with this one guy just to make sure he keeps his promise to assign people and give us time at Sales Conference."

Many managers take an authoritarian "do this, do that" approach with their people. It's not that they necessarily enjoy controlling others but that they believe exercising authority is the most efficient way to influence others and get results.

For many of them, this approach reflects the reason they became managers. They want to have an impact on their organizations, to be the ones who "drive the business," the ones "who make things happen." As one said, "I . . . always wondered what it would be like to be in charge and get people to do things the right way." When they issue a directive, they're essentially saying, "Do it because I'm the one who's been given responsibility and put in charge. I'm the boss."

What approach do you take? Do you rely on the authority that comes with being a boss to get the results you need? Do you try to influence people by telling them what to do? Do you think that's what you're supposed to do?

If you do, you may be among the many managers we see who misconceive the nature and purpose of their formal authority.

Many think it's the center of their work, the key means of influencing others. They think it is literally what makes them managers. And some even think it changes who they are and their place in the world.

Misconception: Do You Think Authority Is Your Key Means of Influencing Others?

"I'm the boss!" It's a common mistake to think management is defined by formal authority—the ability that comes with a title to impose your will on others. In fact, formal authority is a useful but limited tool.

People Want More Than a Formal, Authority-Based Relationship with the Boss

Many managers—especially those who were achievement-driven stars as individual performers—don't even think about relationships. They're so task oriented that they put the work to be done and their authority as boss at the heart of what they do and assume they can ignore the human aspects of working with others.[1]

The problem is that most people don't want your authority to be the be-all and end-all of the relationship. They want a personal, human connection, an emotional link. They want you to care about them as individuals. They want you to encourage their growth and development. Research tells us this kind of human relationship with the boss is a key factor determining an employee's level of engagement with the work.[2]

We know of a small-company owner, a warm, decent woman, so pressed for time she consciously decided to avoid small talk at the office. She never opened up to people about herself or asked about their lives and interests. She didn't, that is, until her people rose up and expressed, through an intermediary, that they hated how she treated them. They wanted a real, human connection with her, even if she was "the boss."

The Limits of Formal Authority

Most managers soon discover, often to their dismay, that authority isn't very effective for influencing people and getting results.

Your Formal Authority Often Fails to Produce Compliance

You may think people are perverse or stubborn, but there are many reasons they don't always follow your instructions.

They disagree with you. They think there's a better way and feel free to exercise their own judgment.

They think something else is more important. It's up to you to set deadlines and make your priories clear.

They don't understand what you want. Making directions more and more explicit can only go so far. Most work today requires some judgment and thought, and so it's almost impossible to give instructions specific enough to eliminate all misunderstanding or cover every contingency.

They find circumstances have changed, invalidating your directions and forcing them to improvise.

They dislike being bossed around. Peremptory orders given in a tone of voice or choice of words that's belittling only invite minimal compliance or subtle disobedience. As someone told us, "I fixed my boss. I did *exactly* what he said to do." Be aware that some people are especially sensitive to "being bossed around." They bring to work a history of troubled dealings with authority figures. By the time you meet them, they've accumulated a set of ambivalent and even negative feelings about authority, which they apply to you and any instructions you give. At the extreme, these are the people from whom a simple directive can produce angry resistance.

People may have a view of authority that differs from yours. They may bring to work generational or cultural attitudes that lead them to distrust and question authority. That will make them less likely to comply. This is not personal. It's simply a different point of view that you and they will need to work through. As companies and work groups become more diverse, these differences will appear more often.

Finally, people may not comply because they're confused. The growing complexity of the workplace and more fluid organizational structures with multiple bosses and temporary teams can complicate and blur lines of authority. Many employees may be confused by what seem to them conflicting demands and expectations. Also, in virtual teams with members spread far apart, distance diminishes the ability of formal authority to create compliance. It's easy to forget about a boss 3,000 miles away, especially when there's another just down the hall.

All of these reasons create a workplace in which authority is at best an uncertain means of influence.

Your Formal Authority by Itself Cannot Generate Commitment

You need more than people's simple compliance. You need them to be engaged with their work and want to do it well. You can command how your people spend their time, even where they direct their attention, but you cannot decree what's essential for good work—you must win their commitment by winning over their heads and hearts. When you rely primarily on your formal authority, you're fundamentally managing through fear—fear of the consequences of disobedience. Fear is a limited, ultimately corrosive and demeaning way to get what you want from others. It certainly will not generate personal commitment or real engagement with the work and the team.

Your Formal Authority Cannot Create Genuine Change

Change often brings uncertainty, loss, and pain for those it touches. Yet those are usually the very people who must embrace the change and make it work. Real solutions can only come from those involved, and real change requires that they alter not only their behavior but their thinking, assumptions, and values as well. Authority cannot compel such change.

Your Formal Authority Is Less Likely to Elicit People's Knowledge and Insight

Every individual in an organization possesses knowledge, skills, and new ideas of potential value. (If they don't, it's your responsibility to replace them with people who do.) Managing people primarily by exercising your formal authority—by telling them what to do without truly seeking their input—is far less likely than a more open approach to capture that full value.

Insisting on "I'm the boss!" places a huge burden on you. The head of a large high-tech company told us of a discussion she once had with her head of HR. Her company had installed a program to encourage broader participation in decision making, and she was frustrated that product development seemed to be moving too slowly. "Maybe we have to go back to the old command-and-control system," she said. "If that's what you want," said the HR person, "I'll help you. But there's one problem. You have to be right all the time." Laughing, the CEO said, "I'll never forget what he said. I told him, 'That's never going to work.'"

No one person can possibly possess the knowledge, experience, and wisdom needed to make every decision. Organizational success today requires the involvement of everyone at all levels. Less authority-driven organizations are more likely to elicit and take full advantage of the talent and experience of their people. We see firms in all cultures moving in this direction, even those that are traditionally hierarchical.

For example, a leading Indian IT firm introduced several practices to encourage employee engagement and foster innovation.[3] Those practices include 360-degree feedback for all managers, including the CEO, who posts his reviews on the company intranet and encourages others to do the same. In Indian culture, which has historically valued hierarchy and the status it provides, that's a shocking move, but it models the openness the company is trying to achieve.

Misconception: Do You Think Your Authority Defines You Personally?

You're at a social gathering chatting with a stranger who asks, "What do you do?"

Do you answer, "I'm in charge of..." or "I run..."?

Or do you say, "I'm responsible for..."?

It's a small distinction but a telling one.

Here's another question: visualize yourself and your group. Do you see yourself *above* your people, directing them from a higher level? Or do you see yourself in the center, the hub connecting all the pieces?[4] Organization charts, which literally place managers over those they manage, certainly encourage the "I'm above you" point of view.

Both these questions begin to reveal the dark side of formal authority—that those who have it begin to believe it's about them, that it changes who they are.

Do you think it's about you? Do you believe it sets you apart personally? As one senior manager once told us, "Sometimes I forget what it was like before I was a boss."

Ask yourself this: "Do I take pleasure in being able to tell others what to do?" We don't mean pleasure from the accomplishment of work. We mean gratification from seeing others obey you. Do you *enjoy* the simple act of exercising your authority?

You needn't be an egomaniac to admit you do. Virtually everyone does. Society, the media, and popular fiction all encourage it. Indeed, we all care about status and influence. We scan our environment to figure out who has it and to assess how much we have in comparison. Such concerns are wrapped up with the human instinct for survival. So for us to view our job as boss in personal terms is a natural impulse.

The issue is one of degree. Is your sense of the personal privilege conferred by your authority overblown? Do you make too much of it? Is the personal status that comes with formal authority the central feature for you of being a boss?

Research confirms the old saying that "power corrupts." The frequent exercise of formal authority can lead you to inflate your own sense of self-worth and denigrate the value of those on whom you exercise it. [5] As a manager who had recently taken over a group described his experience: "Then review time came around . . . it was quite an exercise . . . You hold their job, their career, in your hands, so to speak. They have an inbred fear."

As people defer to your authority, as you sense that fear, you may be tempted to believe they defer to you personally—it's *you* they fear. Once that belief takes root, you'll be tempted to exercise your authority even more. Its seductive effects on your ego and self-esteem tend to grow the more you use it. No wonder you hear almost every day of powerful people whose inflated sense of personal importance led them to perform stupid, inconsiderate, and even illegal or unethical acts. You think such things only happen to other people, but they can happen to anyone, including you.

It can happen insidiously, a tiny step at a time. We know managers who at first took pains to explain the reasons for what they wanted. But they became so accustomed to compliance that they stopped explaining and simply issued orders. They didn't even realize what they were doing.

What this means in practical terms is simple: *don't let being the boss go to your head*. The use of authority without respect for others or to satisfy personal needs rarely sits well with others. Such use can take several forms: issuing orders without explanation, demanding personal loyalty and praise, foisting your opinions on others, stifling disagreement, focusing on the perks that come with your title, or any number of other actions that advance you personally at the expense of others who are "below" you.

If you see yourself primarily as "the boss," the one in charge, the one above those you manage, it will limit the willingness of others to accept your influence.

Are You Abdicating Any of Your Management Responsibilities?

We know managers at the other end of the spectrum—bosses who shrink from exercising their authority.

They're uncomfortable with providing guidance and direction. They hesitate to issue orders even in situations like a crisis that demands immediate action, when orders are needed and appropriate. In failing to use their authority, they're abdicating responsibility.

So don't draw the wrong conclusions from what we're saying. You cannot ignore your authority and never use it. It's not the use but the *misuse* of authority that creates problems.

Be aware that abdication doesn't just mean doing nothing. It can also mean doing only part of the job, as seen in the following types of bosses.

The boss of some but not others. You may be comfortable managing some people in your group but not others. Perhaps you tend to ignore those older than you, or more experienced than you, or more expert or knowledgeable than you. You may ignore people you don't like.

The bureaucrat. Perhaps you see yourself as the implementer of orders, rules, policies, and strategies from above. You hesitate to make any decisions without direction or, lacking that, full consensus of all involved. If so, you're abdicating your responsibility to ensure real direction yourself.

The technocrat. Perhaps you see your organization as a rational, even mechanical "system." Problems are technical challenges with a "right" solution, and the messy human element is something you can and should ignore.

The social director. Perhaps you see yourself as one who coordinates, facilitates, referees, and counsels those doing the work. Your primary task is to promote harmony and keep things running smoothly. You rarely take a stand or make a difficult choice. You seldom criticize anyone and never allow conflict, on the assumption that all discord or controversy will hinder good work.

Do you see yourself in any of these descriptions? Does exercising authority make you uncomfortable? We've cautioned against too much reliance on it, but failure to use it when necessary and appropriate is a management failure too.

Do You Want to Influence Others?

Effective managers do. If you don't, you'll struggle to be an effective manager because having an impact on others is the essence of management.

But if you seek influence because you enjoy dominating others and seeing them do what you say, that will create problems. The most effective managers are driven by a strong need to have an impact on others—not for their own satisfaction or self-aggrandizement but to achieve the goals of the group.[6]

That's a critical distinction. Effective managers don't view authority as a source of personal superiority or primarily as a means of satisfying personal needs. Instead, they consider it a tool for helping others accomplish something worthwhile. In short, they use authority to do useful work, not to serve their own ends.

Some managers find it valuable to think of their authority, being the boss, as a role they play, a means of helping others become more productive. They distinguish this role from themselves as individuals. Thinking this way can help you maintain some perspective when people display deference or negativity because of your authority. If you think, "They're reacting to the role I've been given to play, not to me personally," you won't take the disagreement or negativity to heart, and the deference won't go to your head.

Effective Managers Know When and How to Use Their Formal Authority

Effective managers understand the benefits and pitfalls of authority. As they try to influence others, they understand what authority can and cannot do well. They know when and how to use it. Here are some questions that will help you compare your use of it with their experience.

Do You Understand That Formal Authority Works Best as a Two-Way Relationship?

Authority will be most useful if you treat it as a two-way relationship ideally an equitable series of exchanges, give-and-take, over time. For you to use your formal authority most effectively, your people must say, in effect, "We accept you. We will let you influence us." In short, you must earn the right to exercise authority, for it comes with obligations to those you manage. They expect you to solve problems, make decisions, develop them, protect them, obtain necessary resources, give out rewards and recognition, advocate and negotiate for them, care about them, and more. Subordinates who feel you're letting them down can find a thousand ways to comply formally with your directions without achieving what you want.

Do You Apply Ethical Judgment in Using Your Authority?

Your formal authority and the responsibility to your organization that comes with it don't free you to ignore the side effects of your decisions and actions. Your people, and any other stakeholders, expect you to recognize and try to deal with the harms you do while seeking a greater good.[7] This is a key way you earn the right to exercise authority.

Do You Use Your Authority Sparingly?

Authority works best when it's exercised rarely and only when truly necessary. Keep it handy, but the less you pick it up and use it, the more powerful it will seem. Most of the time, people will simply do what you ask. Consider it a last resort. As one manager told us, "You have the ability to hire and fire, but the moment you rely on that authority or imply it, I think the battle is lost."

Do You Involve Others in Your Use of Authority?

We know a manager who discovered that his people accepted and implemented his decisions more willingly when he explained the reasons for them. Another realized his direct reports were much more willing to cooperate if they were first allowed to offer ideas and reactions.

Wise managers solicit opinions, get information, and ask advice. They involve those who will be affected by a decision or plan. They act transparently by making clear both what they do and why. They manage with the door open, so to speak. They know there's no better way to win support and commitment.

In fact, effective managers go beyond involving others. They share or delegate their authority by giving others freedom to act within their own areas of responsibility. The secret of successful sharing is in knowing the capabilities of those to whom you're delegating and then setting constraints, as in the guideline below.

Do You Understand When It's Appropriate to Exercise Your Authority?

Don't misunderstand. We are not saying that you should never or rarely exercise your formal authority directly and explicitly. There are situations when it's both appropriate and necessary.

In an Emergency, When Fast, Decisive Action Is Required

When you face a big problem and there's little time for consensus building, people will look to you for clear and decisive direction.[8] This is not the time for lengthy discussion and a full airing of all points of view. You'll want to gather information, identify alternatives, and then take decisive action.

When Members of Your Group Cannot Reach Agreement

It sometimes happens that your group, after full discussion of alternatives, cannot reach consensus. Here you'll need to make a choice in order for the group to move forward. You'll have to explain the reasons for your decision, especially to those who preferred some other course of action, but most people in such situations will prefer progress to impasse.

To Maintain Group Standards and Norms

You may need to step in when your group is about to violate or ignore some important element of group culture—group values, standards, and norms, such as quality, meeting a deadline, fairness, openness to all points of view, and recognizing the rights and requirements of other groups. This can happen when pressures mount to take shortcuts or skip steps or simply choose a more expedient course.

To Set Useful Boundaries or Outer Limits

Effective managers use their authority less to give directives than to set outer limits within which people are free to act. Much of the 3 Imperatives is exactly that. Goals and strategies say, "Go in this direction, not some other." Plans prescribe certain actions and not others. Group standards and practices suggest preferred ways of behaving and proscribe others. Budgets set limits. Policies, laws, regulations, and ethics create borders. Specific guidelines for specific tasks—"Don't go further than this" or "Don't spend more than X dollars"—shape the constraints to the specific circumstances and the individuals involved. Think of authority as the way you create the arena within which your people can act with initiative and creativity.

To Focus People's Time and Attention on What's Truly Important

There is a powerful prerogative of authority that few dispute but is often overlooked: the simple ability to command people's time and attention. Suppose you fear customer service is being ignored. But instead of imposing new procedures, you have your people join you in talking about service to ten customers each. Such assignments, along with asking for reports or calling meetings, can bring attention to an issue or problem and let people discover it for themselves. That's usually better than dictating a solution.

In the end, effective managers realize that formal authority is neither the heart of management—it's not what makes them a boss—nor the only or best way to influence others. It's simply one useful source of influence, a limited source that, by itself, cannot produce what they ultimately need: the engagement of their people and the cooperation of those they don't control.

All this has been captured in a timeless way by Mary Parker Follett, who studied workers and the workplace nearly a century ago: "The test of a [manager] is not how good he is at bossing," she wrote, "but how little bossing he has to do."[9]

To move forward on your journey, give up the myth of authority—the belief that it's the key way you have impact. Accept your dependence on others, including those who work for you, and learn to use more effective tools of influence.

What are those tools? That is the subject of the rest of the book.

3

I'M YOUR FRIEND!

Beware the Pitfalls When You Create Relationships That Are Too Personal

9:13 a.m. Jason hears his name called as he walks down the corridor. He turns to see Jay Bradshaw, his online production manager, coming up behind him. Jay's in charge of producing the materials for all Project Emerge courses.

Of all the people in the group, Jay is the only one Jason already knew when he arrived Monday. He'd known Jay since both joined the Reynolds Ed IT department around the same time. They shared some common interests, notably the use of technology in education, and found themselves having lunch now and then. Jason enjoyed Jay's outspoken opinions about everything. They'd stayed in touch ever since. Eventually Jay, like Jason, moved into editorial. The two of them never actually worked together, though they always stayed in touch.

"I'll get you that information this afternoon," Jay said. "But I have a great idea, a way to save you time. Let me sit on the educational technology task force so you don't have to bother with that corporate baloney."

Jason found out only two days ago that he was a member of this corporate task force when he received several long documents to review before a meeting today. He's barely had time to skim them.

"My first meeting is today," Jason says.

"Great! Let me go. You can start saving time right away."

The idea has appeal for Jason. The material he received looked only moderately interesting, and he certainly has more pressing concerns. He's also on two other task forces on emerging markets and custom publishing. Each entails more meetings and more to read.

On the other hand, Jason is hesitant about unleashing Jay on the rest of Reynolds. Until now, he's only known Jay as a work friend, but in the past week a decidedly mixed picture of him has begun to emerge: he's talented but also someone who delights in goading anyone who disagrees with him. Jason isn't sure he wants someone like Jay representing Project Emerge on a company task force. He's generally considered a talented loose cannon. Besides, Jason thinks, there are people on the task force I rarely see otherwise, and as we roll out Project Emerge, a couple of them could be key.

"Let me think about it," Jason says. "I should go to the first meeting."

"Come on. There's nothing to think about, and I *really* want to do this. Really. Humor me."

"Jay, I said I'd think about it. I'll think about it."

Jay stops and lets Jason walk ahead. Jason glances back in time to see the unmistakable look of disappointment on Jay's face.

"I applied for your job, you know," Jay says. "It wasn't your job then. I didn't know you were being considered. When Frank told me he was leaving, I talked to Sanchez. I thought I'd be a good choice. Why bring in somebody midstream? He barely gave me the time of day. I almost quit."

"I didn't know," Jason says.

"And I didn't know you were coming until Monday," Jay says, "the day you showed up. You didn't even call me."

Jason is taken aback. Things were so hectic. "I'm sorry," he says. "It happened so fast. Things just . . . I should have. I apologize."

Oh, just let him do it, Jason thinks. Is it worth upsetting him? It's one task force. Why disappoint him? He's been a work friend for years. He's very smart and probably knows more about educational technology than anyone else. It seems important to him.

In the last chapter, we explored the deficiencies of formal authority as a means of influencing those who work for you.

But what's the alternative? Is it the opposite, a relationship focused on building close, personal ties between you and subordinates? That's an approach many managers, and perhaps you too, have chosen to take. Or, perhaps, it's a way of working together you've simply fallen into without much thought.

Should It Be a Close, Personal Relationship?

Do you consider your direct reports your friends? Perhaps you're driven by a deep need to be liked. Your first instinct in any interaction is to build close, personal relationships, and you will do almost anything to protect them. One new manager said he had to "fight the burning desire to be accommodating . . . so that [my people] would like me." To confuse being liked with being trusted or respected is a classic trap for all managers.

Perhaps you hate conflict. You avoid doing or saying anything that might cause tension or upset others. When strife of any kind arises, you leap to remove it or tamp it down. As another manager discovered about himself: "I don't react well in conflict situations. I back off. It really hurts me to have people get mad at me."

Perhaps you're simply uncomfortable with the idea of disrupting others' lives. This aspect of being a boss unsettles many managers. As one explained, "What really makes it tough is that you get to know the person fairly well and you know he has a wife and two children and owns a home and has debt like the rest of us.

You're saying, 'Look, you aren't cutting it.' And you're assaulting their self-image and threatening their whole lifestyle."

Perhaps you've made a rational choice: you think close personal relationships are the best way to influence people. When you ask people to do something, you're saying, in effect, "Do it for me because we're friends." What could be more compelling?

If you create or allow close personal ties with your subordinates for any of these reasons, you will struggle as a manager. You won't be able to make tough but necessary people decisions or evaluate people accurately and give critical but helpful feedback. If you try to stay on good terms with everyone, you'll make exceptions for individuals that others consider undeserved or unfair. Relationships that are primarily personal can only produce disappointment for your people in the long run and make you much less effective.

Do you tend to create such relationships? Think of your people one by one and ask, If his performance slipped and didn't improve, would I be able to terminate him? If she made repeated serious mistakes in spite of careful coaching, could I cut back her responsibilities or tell her she won't get a raise?

If you're reluctant to discipline or terminate someone because of the harm it might do to your relationship, then your ties to that person will prevent you from doing your job as the boss.

Why Being a Boss and Being a Friend Are Often Incompatible

Consider the differences between being a boss and being a friend.

Friendship Exists for Itself

Friendship is not a means to some other end. As social beings, we need close, supportive connections with others. That's not, however, what drives the boss–subordinate relationship. That tie exists to accomplish work. If something prevents a direct report from doing his or her job, then the relationship must end.

Friends Are Equals

Bosses and direct reports are not equals inside the organization. Even if the boss keeps her stick of authority hidden most of the time, she will still need to use it on occasion in ways that may not please her subordinates. Not many friendships can survive such status inequality when that happens.

Friends Accept Each Other as They Are

Friends don't actively evaluate and try to change each other. They certainly don't make their friendship contingent on such change. Yet an effective manager must constantly assess his people's performance and abilities and press them to develop and change. Such benevolent but real pressure is an important, unavoidable part of managing.

Friends Don't Check Up on Each Other All the Time

Managers continually press their people to report on progress, evaluate themselves, and commit to future results. Friends do have expectations of each other, but they're mutual, not one sided, and less demanding.

As a Practical Matter, You Cannot Be Friends with All Your People Equally

If you choose to make friends of your people, human chemistry will come into play, and you'll develop closer ties with some than others. You can imagine the havoc that will wreak with your efforts to manage a smooth-working team, especially a virtual team with far-flung members.

If you create friendships with your people, if you try to motivate them through the personal ties you've created or allowed, you're likely to find yourself having to choose between maintaining the ties or obtaining the best results possible. If you maintain the ties, you will compromise results or make unethical choices that harm others not for a greater good but for the good of a friend. If you choose work and the work group over the wishes of a friend, as eventually and inevitably you must, the friend will feel betrayed.

Sooner or later you must decide against, disappoint, criticize, discipline, demote, or even fire someone who works for you. To someone who thought you were friends, those actions will feel like a personal betrayal and will damage or destroy that person's commitment to the work.

Another Paradox: Caring, Even Close, but Focused on the Work

Your relationship with your people should be driven by neither control nor friendship, defined by neither affection nor authority, though affection and authority should certainly be pieces of the puzzle.

In a word, the boss–subordinate relationship is another paradox, one of the most profound you will encounter as a boss. It's a paradox because it must be genuinely human and caring—even close, since you and your people strive toward a common, worthwhile purpose.[1] But it must remain a relationship that never loses sight of one fact: it exists to accomplish work. It is a means to an end. You and your people need to connect as humans but always, in the end, to focus on the work. You and they need to be friendly— no one will work hard for a cold, distant, uncaring jerk—but ultimately not friends in the true sense of the word.

We've heard some say, "Then it's just manipulative. You only care in order to get work from people. You use them. You don't truly, genuinely care about them." We understand how someone might reach that conclusion. We're sure many managers feign concern only to get what they want.

Still, we maintain, it is possible to care deeply while focusing on the work. Consider other relationships. Do you expect or want your lawyer, doctor, accountant, or therapist to be your close friend? You want them to care deeply and genuinely for you. But you want their insights and expertise, and you don't want those clouded by affection for you. Think of a great teacher you had. You wanted her on your side, caring for you, but you understood that if you didn't know the exam answers, she would grade you accordingly. Think of a coach. Again, you wanted him to care for you and help you develop, but you both accepted that his ultimate goal was to field the best team. Whether you made the team, whether you played or sat on the bench, depended not on his feelings for you but on your performance.

Management is no different. It works best as a cordial, genuinely caring relationship, but it's not about the relationship. It should be an open, positive relationship, but one in which there is ultimately some distance, a line never crossed. If you create relationships in which the primary goal is to sustain the relationship rather than do work, you will be creating a trap that sooner or later will snare you.

Why It's Hard to Get the Relationship Right and Keep It Right

Given its paradoxical nature, the boss–subordinate relationship is easy to get wrong. Instinct, gut feel, and natural chemistry are poor guides. They'll push you away from people you instinctively don't like and pull you toward those to whom you feel naturally attracted.

Yet, it falls on you, as a boss, to work with and create the right relationships with both. All your relationships should be bounded and defined. They're not about liking, chemistry, or personality. While those factors don't disappear, and you will have to deal with them, they do not and should not define your fundamental relationship with your people.

You must take responsibility for defining the relationship, for setting limits or boundaries that keep all your relationships focused on the work and its successful accomplishment. It's a good idea to be explicit about this. As you make decisions, especially those that involve people and their personal aspirations, be clear from the beginning how you will make them.

At the same time, you must create and maintain good working relationships with those you don't naturally like. The first step is to recognize your feelings. You needn't change them, but you do need to deal with such people in spite of them. Periodically review your contacts. If necessary, create a contact schedule—say, a weekly meeting or phone call—to build and maintain good working relationships with them. It may help to remind yourself that friendship is *not* the goal.

Preexisting relationships present inherent challenges.[2] Family firms in which family members work with and for each other, business ventures begun and run by friends, a friend hired by a boss, or a close-knit team now headed by a member who was promoted will all require special care. The clash between authority and blood, or authority and other preexisting personal ties, can either diminish your effectiveness or destroy the preexisting relationship, or both. There's no easy solution for the potential problems except frank and ongoing discussions of roles, expectations, and consequences. Those involved must often separate their personal ties from their work relationships and mutually decide how they will operate in each sphere. It's no surprise that many family firms, as well as partnerships begun by friends, eventually disband—often with a big bang—because the relationships are so complex and the tensions so extreme. It can be helpful to enlist outside assistance from an executive coach who specializes in these matters. Such assistance can help you anticipate and prevent or work through the inevitable dilemmas that arise from the mix of family, friendship, business, and wealth.

Seeking the right balance in the ties between you and your people means you'll always have a certain level of tension in the relationships—a constant but, we hope, easy give-and-take as you and each of them constantly negotiate boundaries and appropriate mutual expectations. Relationships often tend toward one of the extremes—toward distance or toward friendship. Only steady care *by you* will keep each relationship on track: caring, human, but always with a little distance, and always focused on the group and its work. Friendly but not friends. The penalties of failing this requirement will be painful to you, both as a boss and a person. It's easier to get these things right from the beginning than to repair them after they've gone wrong.

CAN PEOPLE TRUST YOU?

Influence Begins with Trust

9:33 a.m. Jason's phone rings. It's an irate Brenda Baldwin, director of online support, widely considered number two in the educational technology department. She's in charge of Reynolds Ed's company Web site.

"You guys are letting us down," she says in a voice heavy with accusation.

"What's the problem?" Jason manages to ask in spite of his surprise. Another problem. More anxiety. Jason has met Baldwin but he's never worked with her. She has a reputation for being tough to deal with, someone who always tries to keep others on the defensive.

"All the marketing and promotion material you're supposed to have ready for the Web site, right? We're doing a major revision, including the addition of Project Emerge, and the deadline was yesterday close of business. You better have a good talk with your marketing wizard. This is the third deadline she's missed. Get your stuff in if you expect to have some room on the site. From what I hear, you guys expect everyone else to accommodate your schedule."

"I'll find out what's going on, Brenda," Jason promises, as Baldwin hangs up without saying anything more.

Great, Jason thinks. Baldwin comes across as a jerk, but the Web site is critical. It's a key way interested schools will be able to get information about all aspects of Project Emerge and its courses.

Jason's thoughts turn to Laraba Sule, his marketing manager, and the problem she's created. Why couldn't she meet the deadline? I'm still trying to understand why the program to sign up schools seems in trouble, and I don't know yet how good she really is. She's never mentioned something is due and she wouldn't have it on time. Is she part of the problem? Can she be trusted?

9:39 a.m.   Jason picks up the phone and tells Laraba a problem has come up and she needs to come see him right away.

9:41 a.m.   Ray Sanchez, Jason's boss, calls with a question, and while they're talking, Laraba appears in the office door, looking nervous. Jason waves her to a chair. She sits and waits anxiously while Jason finishes answering Sanchez's question.

Suppose you were the one sitting in that chair across the desk. What's it like to work for you? How do people experience you, especially in a tense situation like this? How do you make people feel about themselves when they deal with you? Do they know they'll be treated fairly, supportively, and with respect? Or do they know you never check your emotions and blurt out whatever you happen to be feeling? If you do, beware. It matters to those you manage. The quality of work they do, the care and commitment they devote, their willingness to expend extra effort, all depend in significant part on the kind of person you are. It's the question we first raised at the beginning of part I: are you the kind of person who can influence others to produce good results even in the face of adversity?

In the last two chapters, we discovered that neither formal authority nor friendship is sufficient. You need other means of influence, all of which begin with trust.

Trust is the basis for all forms of influence other than coercion. It's a necessary element in effective relationships in all cultures.

It's critical to the effective functioning of today's more fluid, fast-moving organizations with their emphasis on collaboration. So the "kind of person" question can be boiled down to the essence of who you are as a manager:

Can people trust you?

Whether it's called trust, respect, reputation, or credibility, it all comes down to whether people believe they can *count on you to do the right thing*.[1]

Almost certainly, you consider yourself trustworthy, but has it ever occurred to you that people may not trust you *as a manager*? Are your people confident you'll do the right thing as their boss? The answer will determine whether they accept your authority and leadership and give the work their utmost care and commitment. Nothing will be more fundamental to your success and your progress than your ability to generate trust. Trust in you as a boss is the foundation of your influence as a manager.

Be clear about what trust is and is not. It's not about being liked. It's not about being "nice." In fact, it's based on two beliefs:

People's belief in your *competence* as a manager

People's belief in your *character* as a person

In the remainder of this chapter, we'll explore these two elements.

Competence: The First Element of Trust

Do your people believe you're competent as a manager?

Competence means you know *what* to do and *how* to get it done. It means you have some expertise as a boss. Confidence in your competence will grow as you demonstrate that you know the "what" and "how" of managing, especially as you develop a track record of managerial accomplishment.

Few managers doubt the importance of competence, but too many view it too narrowly. They focus on technical know-how, knowledge of the nuts and bolts of the business, when they should take a broader view. We think of managerial competence as having three elements: *technical* competence, *operational* competence, and *political* competence.

Technical Competence

Technical competence is about knowing what to do. For a boss, it means both knowing the business and understanding what managers do, the 3 Imperatives.

Technical expertise doesn't mean you must be the expert, the ultimate authority, in everything your group does. You cannot be that, and too many managers waste their time striving to fill that role. But you must know enough about the work and how it's done to guide others and, most of all, to make intelligent decisions and judgment calls. Accepting that you cannot be the technical expert is especially difficult for producing managers, who often consider that a key part of their role.[2]

If you don't know how your business works and you're not sure what managers do, how can anyone trust you to do the right thing as their boss?

Operational Competence

Technical competence is about *what* you know. Operational competence is about knowing *how to apply it.* Knowing and doing are different. You need to know how and when to apply technical knowledge in your business. It's the same with managing: Knowing you need a plan doesn't mean you know how to produce an effective one. Knowing one of your people is struggling and that it's your job to provide support doesn't mean you know how to help. Operational competence is knowing how to put your knowledge into practice effectively.

Political Competence

The group you manage is part of a larger organization, and you need to know how to function effectively in that context. That means you must know how organizations, yours in particular, work and how to get productive work done in them. Political competence is about knowing who does what and how to influence them. As one direct report said of his manager, there's "nothing worse than working for a powerless boss"—that is, a boss who couldn't get anything done in the organization.

Do you possess the technical, operational, and political competence you need?

Character: The Second Element of Trust

Do your people consider you a manager with character?

Character is about believing in and following a set of values. It's about possessing an internal compass. While competence is about *knowing* the right thing to do and how to get it done, character is about your *intention* to do the right thing. People want to know what you *will* do, and the only way they can predict that is by knowing your values and motives.

That's why people analyze the statements you make and the actions you take for clues about your intentions. They want to understand how you think and feel, what's important to you. That shouldn't surprise you. Almost certainly, you did it with every boss you ever had and do it even now. Still, it can be unsettling. As one manager told us shortly after taking a new managerial position: "I knew I was a good guy, and I kind of expected people to accept me immediately for what I was. But folks were wary, and you really had to earn it."

We define *trust* as people's belief that you will do the right thing. But *the right thing* isn't always obvious, and people will vary in their definition of it. Indeed, to a large extent, defining *the right thing* and coping with the associated trade-offs will be the subject of constant negotiation between you and everyone you work with. However, some "right things" are so universal that they apply to all managers in virtually all situations. We include here the ones that seem most important.

As we identify them, we'll ask you a series of questions to help you assess people's perceptions of your character. The questions will encourage you to think long and hard about yourself and your actions.

We pose the questions in terms of what *others* think of you. What matters most is not what you think but what *others* think of you. They're the ones you must influence.

Character: People Believe You Value the Work

How much would you trust a boss who thought the work you all did was just a way to earn a living and had little value otherwise? What if this boss didn't care about quality or about those who used what you made? Would you trust him to make good decisions? What if he valued himself and his own success more than the work, if he considered the work only a means to his personal ends?

Where do you stand against this aspect of character?

Would people say you think the work of the group matters? If your group and its work disappeared today, would the world be different in some substantial way tomorrow? Without a fundamental belief in the value of what you do, you will struggle to gain people's trust. Why would anyone believe in the intentions of a boss who belittles the value of the work she and her people do?

Would people say you work hard? People respect a good work ethic and tend to trust a manager who invests great personal effort—does homework, comes prepared, and takes the work seriously. If you work hard as a manager, it means you value the group and its work and want it to succeed.

Do people think you walk the talk? In your own actions, do you practice the work values and standards you espouse and expect of others? Are you consistent in what you believe, say, and do? This is integrity. Do you demonstrate in your own work the commitment you want from others? Are you willing yourself to make the sacrifices you expect of your people? Being a manager doesn't give you the right to make exceptions for yourself.

Would people say you worry more about your people and the work than you worry about yourself? The people who work for you can tell whether you truly care about what they do. They know whether you're focused on your personal success and value them only as they contribute to it. What you think and feel about "I" versus "we" will be crystal clear over time. If it's "I," don't expect them to devote any more time and effort than necessary to keep their jobs or ensure their individual success.

As you go home at the end of the day, do your thoughts dwell on what *you* achieved or on what your *group* accomplished? What gives you the most satisfaction: your own performance or the performance of your people as a group? As one manager we know said of her people after she finally began to let go of her need for personal recognition: "When they made a good cold call or closed a deal, I was as excited as if I had done it myself."

Most managers understand the need to make this shift, but they can't give up focusing on their own achievement. Their prior success as individual stars blocks them from making a fundamental change in where and how they derive a sense of accomplishment.

Must you give up your own desire for personal success? Not at all. You would have to be a saint to do that. But it does mean you must grow beyond your own ambition to focus more on the success of your group and organization. The paradox here is that your personal success now requires that you find satisfaction in the success of those who work for you.

Character: People Believe You Value Them as People

We once interviewed a manager in a large steel company who had posted a sign in his office that read, "It's hard to soar like an eagle when you're surrounded by turkeys." When we asked about it, he said, "It's a joke." How would you feel if your boss put up that sign and then said it was a joke?

Do people believe you genuinely care about them? All relationships have some emotional component, including, not least, the boss–subordinate relationship. Do you truly want your people, as a group and as individuals, to succeed? Do you believe in the inherent value of others, beyond their role at work? Are you concerned for them as people and not just as workers? If one of your people suffered a personal calamity, would you genuinely care? Do your actions and words reflect your concern? You cannot hide these kinds of feelings. If you don't care, how can you expect anyone to care about you or the work you manage?

Would people say you consider their interests when making difficult decisions? Exercising ethical judgment becomes critical here because you cannot always satisfy people's personal desires and needs. When you must disappoint some individuals to accomplish a greater good, it can seem to signal a lack of caring—unless you clearly recognize their interests, weigh them seriously in your decision making, and provide empathy and emotional support for their disappointment.

Do people believe you strive to preserve every person's dignity and self-respect, no matter the circumstances? Are you generous? Do you praise in public and criticize in private? Are your day-to-day interactions considerate and respectful? When you terminate someone for poor performance, do you let him go in a way that allows him to depart with dignity and self-respect?[3] It may seem irrelevant, but it's a useful indicator: do you say "please" and "thank you" to the receptionist and the mailroom clerk? We know an executive recruiter who nixed a candidate because he was rude and disdainful to a waitress.

Would people say you try to see the world from their point of view? This is empathy, the ability to understand how someone else sees a situation and why she reacts as she does.[4] It doesn't mean you must agree with or accept her point of view, but you should be able to understand it. A critical distinction: empathy isn't about putting *yourself* in someone else's position. It means seeing through *their* eyes based on *their* experience, needs, and values.

Do people believe you accept their personal differences without judgment? This is increasingly important as the workforce becomes more diverse. How do you react when someone differs drastically from you in background, experience, dress, speech, attitude, and style? Many managers realize only slowly that their people can't be managed like copies of themselves. Only when they recognize and respect each individual's uniqueness can they begin to manage effectively.

Do people consider you fair in the way you treat them? Fairness doesn't mean you treat everyone exactly alike. Individuals differ. "To treat people fairly is to treat them differently," said one manager when she discovered the tough, challenging approach that inspired one of her people only discouraged others. The key question is this: would all your people say they receive from you what they want and need for their work? Above all, do they *perceive* your treatment of them individually to be fair and without favorites?

Do people think you listen well? You may think you do, but here's what it means to truly listen. When you're talking to someone, *are you willing to change your mind?*[5] If not, you're telling and selling, not listening. Don't think of listening as a passive activity. Active listening means you engage with someone, ask questions, and proactively explore what they're saying. It means not only that you say the words that express interest but that you communicate active interest in nonverbal ways too: body language, tone of voice, demeanor, and manner. (Indeed, such nonverbal cues need to be present in all these areas.)

Would people say you trust them enough to delegate? Trust works both ways. To get it, you must give it, as it's earned and deserved. Delegation, the granting of some authority and decision-making power to direct reports, is both a fundamental act of management and a mark of genuine trust.

Character: People Believe You're Emotionally Steady and Dependable at Work

Call it emotional maturity, intelligence, or dependability, it's the ability to deal effectively with your own and others' feelings at work.

You may prefer to think of work as rational and unemotional. But, in fact, the workplace is an arena where feelings of all kinds are felt, expressed, and acted out. A moment's reflection about your own experience will surely confirm this, both in the emotions you've seen on display and in your own feelings at work.

Handling emotion can be a challenge. Under the right circumstances, anyone can be hijacked by their own or others' emotions at work—irritation, anger, frustration, fear, pride, jealousy, unreasonable competitiveness, and even positive feelings taken to an extreme, like excessive gratitude. All of them can lead you to say or do things that you regret and that reduce your effectiveness.

The solution is not to ignore or suppress feelings. What's required is the ability to recognize your own and other's emotions but not be controlled by them. This is what's called emotional maturity or emotional competence, and management will reveal how much you have.

Would people say you handle your own feelings well at work? Your reactions must always be constructive, forward looking, and in the best interests of the group. Your people are constantly watching for cues about how to feel and act. One manager told us he'd discovered that "you can't be pessimistic on the job. The amount of your enthusiasm translates directly into how your people feel and how much effort they put into the job." Or as another concluded, "Be like a duck—on the surface calm and serene and underneath paddle like hell."

Do people consider you discreet? As a manager, you often receive sensitive and personal information from your people. Can they count on you to keep it private and use it with tact and prudence? Do you hold yourself above gossip within your group?

Do people think you handle their mistakes constructively? Direct reports are particularly sensitive to the way the boss handles errors. No one expects to be excused for catastrophic or repeated blunders. But on occasion everyone falls on his face. People want to know whether the boss will berate and punish them or help them stand up, correct the error, and learn how to avoid missteps in the future.

Would people say you seek out what they think and are open to fair criticism? Do you encourage and allow people to be candid with you? Are you able to hear what others say without becoming upset, angry, or defensive even when their words seem critical, painful, or even unfair?

Would people say you're able to acknowledge your own errors, ignorance, or shortcomings? Some managers compound their problems by not seeking help or not revealing what they don't know. They're trapped by their fear that people will consider them weak or ignorant. Do you ever say these words at work to your people?

"I'm sorry."

"I made a mistake."

"I was wrong."

"I don't know."

"Would you help me?"

"Could you explain this to me. I'm not sure I get it."

"What do you think?"

"What would you do?"

These are important words. They can produce learning, better options and solutions, and they can help repair a strained relationship or restore damaged trust. There's nothing about being a boss that should prevent you from using them when they apply. People know when you are wrong or have made a mistake or need help. They're reassured when you know it too, and they respect your willingness to say so.

We know a new manager who took over a trading desk in a global investment bank where he oversaw a group of experienced traders. Like many other new managers, he first used a directive approach, giving detailed instructions for adopting or closing specific positions or trying different trading strategies. The traders resented his commands and demanded to know his rationale, even though many acknowledged privately his talent for timing trades. Tension grew between them. He did recognize his lack of knowledge about foreign markets, however, and one day he asked a trader a simple question about pricing. The trader spent several minutes explaining and even suggested they talk again at the end of the day. It provided an important insight for the manager, who said he learned to stop talking all the time and begin listening. Once he made that change, he said, he began to learn about the work, and people questioned his calls less. In short, people began to trust him.

We recognize that there's a fine line here. On one side of it, people respect your honesty and willingness to be candid about your own shortcomings. On the other side, however, too much expression of weakness, error, and uncertainty will diminish rather than foster people's trust in you. In every situation, you must find that line and stay on the positive side—yet another example of the judgment management requires.

Would people say you're able and willing to recognize and deal with their emotions? Managing the feelings of others doesn't mean you must simply put up with others' feelings. What's required is more than that: you must actively recognize their emotions and take them seriously, even if you disagree or consider them misplaced, and even when they're directed at you and feel personal. Sometimes simple acknowledgement of a person's feelings and allowing him to talk are enough. Of course, you need not condone behavior that exceeds the bounds of respect, civility, and decency.

Recognizing others feelings doesn't mean you should take them personally. Do you internalize every expression of anger and frustration aimed at you? Do you take personally the deference you receive as boss and let it go to your head? Without doubt, much of it—both the negative and the positive—is aimed at you as boss, at the role you play, and not at you personally.

Would people say you're able to step back and keep control of emotional situations? You need the ability to step back figuratively or even literally and look at a situation objectively. Taking a deep breath, getting a cup of coffee, counting to ten, or some other simple device can help. Loss of self-control may lead to a sudden, ill-considered response or tilt a decision in the wrong direction and do harm that cannot be easily undone.

As we said in chapter 2, a particularly good way to do this is by distinguishing between self and role. This is not easy, especially for smart managers accustomed to relying on first impressions and quick interpretations. But it can help you step back, slow down your thinking, do some diagnosis, avoid defensive interpretations, respond thoughtfully, and prevent yourself from being hijacked by someone else's emotions. What makes this difficult is that emotional attacks often *feel* personal. Sometimes they'll even be phrased in personal terms.

Character: You Possess a Strong, Resilient Sense of Yourself

Everyone suffers frustrations, setbacks, and failure at times. Your journey will be full of them. The question is, How do you respond?[6] Do you keep going? Do you find a way to keep making progress? We once heard a senior manager at a successful company describe it this way: "To succeed as a manager here, you have to have a strong ego. Not a big ego, not someone who's 'me, me, me' all the time. We don't like that. That person won't last one day here. But you have to have toughness, a strong sense of who you are and what you're about. When you get whacked, you keep coming back. You can do that because you're focused on the work and what you and your team have to do."

Think of it as a good kind of self-confidence. A healthy sense of self—a strong but not big ego—is the foundation for virtually all other elements of character: for valuing others and treating them with respect; for empathy; for the ability to hear criticism, learn, and change; and for emotional maturity. Most of all, it's the basis for dealing with the world as it is, including others' opinions of you as a manager. Often, a big ego puffs itself up because it feels weak and uncertain. In contrast, a strong ego is resilient because it's focused on something outside itself, such as the work and its ultimate purpose. A big ego seldom cares about anything but itself.

You need a strong ego to maintain people's trust. As we said, there's more to trust than the values and behaviors we've described. Indeed, every vital relationship in a changing world requires constant negotiation of *the right thing*—what people expect of you. Your people and you will engage in constant give-and-take about expectations and how they apply in specific situations. A strong ego will let you undertake these ongoing negotiations in an open and honest way and help you hear the negative feelings they sometimes reveal about you and what you do.

With all the questions in this chapter, we've pushed you hard to look at yourself and the kind of person you are as a manager—especially from the viewpoint of your people. How do they experience you?

To be trusted, you must reveal yourself in order to demonstrate your competence and character. To create trust requires that you take pains to be explicit about what you value as a manager, how you work, what you want from others, and, not least, who you are.

We hope you've given some thought to the many questions and from them gained some appreciation of where you stand against the standards of trust—competence and character—required by management. The evidence is clear: these things matter.

We admit there were many questions—more, perhaps, than you wanted or could deal with all at once. Yet they weren't simply a hodgepodge of unrelated traits. All of them taken together can be boiled down to something fairly simple: they describe the characteristics of a decent person, someone who connects with others in a steady, clear, forthright, and honest way. It comes down to little more, or less, than that.

Did you fall short? Almost certainly you did, if you were fully honest. We all do. We're all human, not saints. We're all flawed. We all have strengths and weaknesses as people.

The best we can do is strive constantly to close the gap between who we are and who we need to be if we're to be effective bosses. None of us will ever be without fault, and so we need ways to compensate for our shortcomings, always seeing them clearly, understanding which are important enough to derail us, and always seeking to become the kind of person who can influence others to produce good work.

Getting the right relationship with your people is the foundation of all else on your journey. It alone will not produce success, but without it, success will be elusive. Management begins with who you are and how people perceive you. Don't focus your relationships around either authority or friendship. Build them on trust in your competence and character.

Where Are You on Your Journey?

Imperative 1: Manage Yourself

Did you pay attention to the questions asked throughout the last three chapters? They focused on the kind of person you are and how you think about yourself as a boss. These are important considerations because, as we noted at the start of part I, management begins with you.

Here are some questions that will help you summarize not just the key ideas in part I but your strengths and weaknesses around the first of the 3 Imperatives.

Do You Use Your Formal Authority Effectively?

Do you consider your formal authority a useful tool but not the primary way you influence others or the key driver of relationships with your people?

1	2	3	4	5
No, I depend on it heavily				Yes, I use it rarely

Do you exercise your authority transparently—making clear what, how, and why you do what you do—and even share it with others when possible and appropriate?

1	2	3	4	5
No, I need to be more transparent				Yes, I use it transparently

Do you focus more on the duties and responsibilities that come with authority than on the personal rights and privileges it provides?

1	2	3	4	5

No, the rights
and privileges
are
key to me

Yes, I focus
more on the
duties and
responsibilities

Do you avoid creating relationships focused on authority in which you think of people merely as instruments to carry out your instructions?

1	2	3	4	5

"I'm the
boss!"

People are
more than
extensions of
my authority

Do You Create Human, Caring, but Not Personal Relationships with Your People?

Are you able to create and maintain relationships that are supportive and rich in human connections but always focused on the purpose and goals of the team and the organization?

1	2	3	4	5

I struggle with
this

I can find the
right balance

Do you avoid trying to influence people by making friends of them—creating relationships that are close and personal in which the relationship itself is ultimately more important than the work it's meant to accomplish?

I really need
to be liked

I care but
always keep
work foremost

Do Others, Especially Your Own People, Trust You as a Manager?

Do others believe they can count on you overall to do the right thing? Is your belief based on more than your personal opinion—do you have data or have you talked directly to others about this?

1	2	3	4	5
No (or I don't know)				Yes (I have real data)

Do others believe in your technical, operational, and political competence?

1	2	3	4	5
No (or I don't know)				Yes (I have real data)

Do others believe in your character—your intentions, values, and standards, as well as your emotional resilience and maturity?

1	2	3	4	5
No (or I don't know)				Yes (I have real data)

Do You Exercise Your Authority and Influence Ethically?

Do you consistently and systematically, before taking any important action, identify stakeholders and their interests, weigh those interests, and then, when acting, try to mitigate whatever harm may come to some because of what you do?

1	2	3	4	5
I need to work on this				I always weigh all relevant interests

Part Two

MANAGE YOUR NETWORK

A S A MANAGER, you face a critical choice.
You may have made it already because it's often made unconsciously. It arose when you discovered two fundamental features of organizations that may have surprised you.

The first surprise is the level of help and cooperation you need from others, and they from you. No group can succeed by itself. As a result, *instead of the freedom and independence you probably expected as a boss, you found dependence—or, more accurately,* inter*dependence*. Expecting to have more opportunity to "drive the business" yourself, you discovered that everything you do requires the cooperation of others, some of whom you formally control but most of whom you don't. As the boss, you're both dependent *and* accountable. Instead of the autonomy you expected—and that you may have enjoyed previously as an individual star—you find yourself constrained, enmeshed in a great web of your own and everyone else's needs and expectations.

The second surprise is related to the first: you find political conflict everywhere because the diverse groups in your organization, though they depend on each other, also differ in their immediate wants and needs. And these differences can be huge—in goals, priorities, points of view, values, interests, and practices. Thus, you must negotiate and compete constantly for scarce resources, including the attention of your management.

Dependence *and* disagreement. It is here, entangled—trapped, many would say—in this problematic combination, that you face your choice.

You can turn inward, focus on your own group, and deal with others only as some specific need arises. Stay above the fray, you think.

Or you can turn outward and proactively engage the broader organization by building a network of ongoing, mutually supportive relationships with others.

What choice have you made?

Perhaps you're not sure because you've never thought about the issue so explicitly. If so, consider these questions: Have you consciously identified and built a broad network of those you depend on and who depend on your group? Do you nurture this network daily? Or do you deal mostly with those you work with every day and with others only when some problem or issue arises? Implicitly or explicitly, every manager makes a choice. What is yours?

Now consider a second question.

How much influence do you have in your organization?

Are you consistently able to change the actions and thoughts of your colleagues? Is your group able to pursue new ideas and initiatives? Does it get the cooperation, support, money, people, and other resources it needs to do its work well? Are you able to protect your group from outside distractions or interference? Do others pay attention to you?

Would you like to have more influence? If you had more, could you and your group be more productive?

Influence is how conflict in organizations gets resolved. Groups whose managers have influence tend to get what they need. Those whose bosses lack it don't. If your group is to perform at its best and produce the results you want, you need organizational influence.

How do you influence people you don't formally control? By making the second choice—reaching out and interacting with the broader organization. If you choose consciously or unconsciously not to do this, you're severely limiting the potential of the people you manage and your own ability to succeed.

Unfortunately, it's the choice we see too many managers make, and it's a major reason so many fall short of their full potential.

Why, then, do so many—including you, perhaps—make that choice?

It's not hard to understand. Building and maintaining relationships takes time, effort, and, for many, some social discomfort. Doing it can certainly feel less urgent than daily problems.

If pressed, many managers would probably add another reason. They're uncomfortable engaging in the constant give-and-take of organizations. They want to avoid what they consider organizational "politics." They became managers vowing to devote little or no time to such activities, which they consider a waste of time.

In fact, by holding themselves apart from—many would say "above"—the constant struggle for organizational influence, they trap themselves in a cycle of failure. Their instinctive distaste for political conflict keeps them from understanding and accepting how organizations really work. This ignorance limits their ability to create and exercise the influence they need to create the conditions for success—for example, they cannot obtain the resources and support their group needs.

These are the issues we address in part II, Manage Your Network. It's a natural sequel to part I, where we explored your one-on-one relationships with those you formally control. Here we focus on your equally important relationships with all the others you need but *don't* control.

Chapter 5, Understand the Reality of Your Organization, explains what organizations are and why they work as they do, particularly why conflict is so pervasive and why it's not necessarily dysfunctional. For those who share many managers' low view of organizations and the "politics" they spawn, we offer here a more productive (and accurate) point of view. All organizations may be inherently political environments, but you *can* succeed in them without feeling trapped in unhealthy interactions or surrendering your integrity.

Chapter 6, Weave Your Own Web of Influence, explores the most effective way to build organizational influence: by proactively creating and nurturing a broad network of relationships with those you need, and who need you, but over whom you have no formal authority. Included are the steps for building your own web and a description of what network building requires of you.

Chapter 7, Don't Forget Your Boss, discusses this crucial relationship with one of the most important members of your network, someone managers often struggle to understand and use productively. Your boss can be a key source of influence on your behalf.

As organizations turn to more complex and fluid forms—temporary teams, multiple bosses, matrixed responsibilities, self-organized groups, collective problem solving—they become more political, not less, which makes the insights and skills covered here even more essential for your success and progress.

As you read the following chapters, examine yourself and your attitudes about these matters. Are you able *and willing* to develop the organizational influence you and your people need?

5

UNDERSTAND THE REALITY OF YOUR ORGANIZATION

You Need Influence to Make Your Team Effective

10:27 a.m. Jason arrives for the meeting of the educational technology task force. Another member, a publisher of a line of materials for K 8 (kindergarten through middle school), is already there. On a large video screen can be seen three others sitting at a table in Boston, including two publishers of college-level materials and the head of IT for Reynolds Education. In a moment, Eric Wingate arrives. The head of educational technology for Reynolds Ed, he chairs the group. The remaining member, a manager from finance, shows up at precisely 10:30.

Wingate starts by addressing Jason. "Welcome. We're glad you're here. Your predecessor rarely came. We hope we'll see more of you."

"I'm glad to be here," Jason says. He looks at the video screen. "Nice to see some compatriots from Boston."

"Let's start," says Wingate, "with the last-minute agenda item I e-mailed around this morning. It's the question of royalties when one imprint repurposes content developed by another imprint."

Jason saw and read the e-mail. It said some publishers in the division had raised the question of whether an imprint, a line of business, should pay fees to another imprint when it used content belonging to that other imprint. Since Project Emerge was being built on a business model of recycling or repurposing existing materials from traditional imprints, any fees would have a direct effect on the project's operating costs—one not assumed in the original projections.

"Question," Jason says. "Would this represent a change in the current policy that no charge will be made for using another imprint's content so long as it's not used in a way that cannibalizes sales for that imprint, the one that developed it?"

"That's right," says Wingate.

"That's a well-established policy," Jason says. "If we change it, it will play havoc with most of the imprints. There's always been a willingness to share if there were no opportunity costs."

"It will touch most of the imprints," says one of the Boston publishers, "but . . . play havoc? Only with those that make their living by sponging off what others paid to create."

"Like Project Emerge," Jason says. "'Sponging' seems a little strong, Gena. You know Project Emerge is built on that policy in its current form. That was the whole idea."

The Boston publisher is Gena Rowland. Her imprint, Edison Books, specializes in college-level engineering texts and related materials, including software development. Project Emerge is planning to repurpose much of her content in its Introduction to Programming course. The other Boston publisher in the meeting heads Commonwealth Books, which also publishes college-level texts.

"If you say so," Gena says. "But we think it's time to change the policy. It's only fair."

"I'd like to get a sense of the group on this," says Wingate, "so I can pass it on. Comments?"

As Jason listens to others talk, he's struck by the fact that the three publishers and the person from finance are speaking in perfect accord, as though they have the same script. Then he realizes they do. Obviously, they held their own meeting before this one and worked out a common position, and there are enough of them to carry the task force. Wingate will pass on their point of view as the opinion of the group.

When Gena said "we think," Jason wondered who the "we" included. Other publishers, obviously, but not him or Project Emerge. I'm a publisher, too, he thinks. He knows what they said wasn't personal, but it felt that way. He understands the publishers want to pursue emerging markets themselves. Company leadership decided to do it through a dedicated new group. The other publishers disagreed with that decision, and so now they resent Project Emerge for stealing an opportunity they feel should be theirs too.

How do you react when something like this happens? Do you feel sabotaged by office politics? A subgroup meets beforehand—you imagine them huddled in a back room hatching plots—and decides what is supposed to be decided by a larger group. Do you feel superior? "Office politics! I can't stand them! I'll never play those juvenile games!" Do you feel excluded? "Why didn't they include me? I'm a publisher!" Do you become defensive? "Those guys are only out for themselves, not the good of the whole organization."

Or do you feel disappointed in yourself? "Maybe I should have set up that premeeting myself and made the case for Project Emerge and what we're trying to pioneer. Reynolds Ed has to find new ways of doing business."

Perhaps you're not likely to find yourself in this situation because you're savvy about organizations. You're naturally inclined to seek out partners and create a coalition. If so, you're fortunate because an inability to understand and work effectively in organizations can derail both your journey and your career as a manager.

What Do You Think About Organizations and How They Work?

Is the meeting just described the kind of political situation you, like many managers, anticipate with anxiety and distaste? You know such things happen all the time. You feel blindsided, or it seems that others have ganged up on you. You lose an argument in spite of the merits of your position. Or your group finds itself with unrealistic or unfair quotas, goals, assignments, or budgets.

Many managers understand that dealing with the political dynamics of organizations is part of their jobs, but they're reluctant to "play the games," as they call it. They dislike conflict and competition and consider the political give-and-take mostly an ego-driven waste of time. To them, it's all about coercing or manipulating others, a world where "who you know" is more important than "what you know," where winners win because they're better connected, not because their business case is stronger (in their opinion, at least).

So they deal with others in the firm as needed, which means they typically deal with others only when there's a problem or specific need. Otherwise, they focus on their group and its work. "Judge me by results," they think, "not by how many people I know or backs I slap."[1]

That's the extreme view. Do you share it to some degree? If you do, you're not alone. We see many managers become disillusioned and even cynical about the way organizations work. And so they step back. That's an understandable but wrongheaded response. The fact is, they cannot do their jobs as managers without vigorously engaging the organization.

Do You Realize the Political Roles You Already Play?

As a manager, you have no choice but to deal with the rest of the organization all the time. Consider the many organizational roles you play as manager of your group.[2]

You Troubleshoot for Your Group

Two employees who must coordinate their work disagree because their different groups have different priorities. When problems arise between your group and others, you're the one who must deal with them to keep the work flowing smoothly. If you don't confront them quickly, they have a way of suddenly blowing up in your face. We know of a manager whose customer service group carried on a running dispute with the sales department over promises made by salespeople to important customers. As this dispute festered, frustrated customers began shifting to a competitor.

You Act as Information Conduit Between Your Group and the Outside

You're the central clearing house of information passing into and out of your group. Your people deal with others in the organization for day-to-day work, but most nonroutine information passes through you. The new product in another division is failing. Not your problem? It will be when there are budget cuts for everyone as a result. The IT department is thinking about a major infrastructure upgrade next spring, with inevitable system downtime, just when you plan to install new design software. In order to get such critical information, you must be actively plugged into the broader organization.

You Negotiate for Your Group

Do you think your bosses know what you and your group need or that they'll provide it if you merely ask? Resources like money, space, and administrative support, as well as less tangible needs like time and information, are always scarce. You must negotiate with your bosses and colleagues for them. You also negotiate arrangements and expectations with others—what will be done, how, and when. If there's important giving and taking to be done, you're the only one who can ultimately decide what to ask for and what to give up. You're the only one in your group who can create and join coalitions of like-minded colleagues in support of common interests.

You Speak for Your Group

You are your group's official spokesperson and its champion, ambassador, lobbyist, advocate, and public relations flack. Both your people and the organization expect you to play this role. How your group is perceived by outsiders will depend largely on your efforts. Did it successfully complete a big project and come in under budget? It's your job to spread the good news. We know a group that failed to hit an important deadline, and its manager saved the day not only by leading the group to find a solution but also by personally going around to all other groups involved and explaining the cause of the delay and the solution. Only you, the boss, can do this.

You Protect Your Group

You serve as a buffer between your group and outsiders, whether that's senior management, other groups like yours, or outsiders. Your people expect you to challenge inappropriate or unrealistic directives from "upstairs" and protect them from excessive bureaucracy. You act as a gatekeeper for pressures and demands up, down, and across your organization as you manage the paradox of serving the sometimes conflicting needs of your team and the organization. A weak manager—one without influence—can only pass on others' demands.

In short, it's your job as manager to *integrate* your group in the organization and keep all parties working together. You stand with one foot inside your group and the other outside. This is a role that comes with your formal authority, for that authority not only puts you in charge but makes you the contact point for your group with outsiders. Knowing how to play this role is a key component of the operational competence you must demonstrate to win the trust of others.

Note that all of the roles we just described require you to exercise influence. How well are you performing them? How much influence do you have?

You Cannot Manage Without Actively Engaging the Organization

What's clear from the list of roles above is that you cannot avoid the political side of your organization and still do your job. If you don't engage the organization and exercise influence effectively, if you hold yourself above the political push-and-pull, you will limit your effectiveness as a manager. Consider the consequences of *not* performing all the roles noted above:

- Problems go unresolved between your group and others.

- Disagreements consistently get resolved against your wishes.

- Your group and others operate on incomplete or inaccurate information.

- Others constantly misperceive and misunderstand your group.

- Others constantly distract your people because no one negotiates, filters, or mediates outside pressures.

- Your people lack the resources they need.

- Your people think you're letting them down—as a manager, you're both incompetent and lacking in character because you don't care enough about them and their work to provide what they need.

In all organizations, there are unprincipled game players who derive satisfaction not from the work they do or the purpose they serve but from plotting, scheming, and winning internal battles. And, sadly, there are organizations with poisonous political climates that encourage such behavior. If you find yourself in such a place, our advice is to look for work somewhere else. Fortunately, most organizations in our experience are not like that.

Most organizations are, however, political environments where decisions are made and conflicts resolved through influence. To succeed in them, you need influence. And that may create a dilemma for you: to build and exercise influence, you have no choice but to manage the inevitable political dynamics in your organization. You cannot hunker down and focus on your group and its work alone, because no group can succeed in isolation.

Imagine you have no influence. That means you and your group are at the mercy of what others demand of you. Yes, power can corrupt, as Lord Acton said, but power*less*ness corrupts too. Witness all those throughout history who have explained the harm they did by claiming, "I had no choice. I had to do what I was told."

If you want to be a force for ethical judgment and fairness when important decisions are made, you need influence.[3] What's at stake with influence is not just getting what you want. It's also a matter of being able to stand up for what's right and just when expedience pushes others in a different direction. If you have influence, you can resist pressure to go against your standards. If you have none, you can only give in or get out.

If you've ever worked for a boss without influence, recall how frustrating that was, even if you liked him personally. You couldn't get the resources or attention you needed. No one took you or your group seriously.

In addition, there are bullies in organizations, those who aggressively pick organizational fights and get their way through intimidation. These people and situations can be difficult, but the answer is not to withdraw. You can resist them only with influence of your own, which you use to find allies and build coalitions in support of your position.

The simple fact is this: you must influence others—people and groups over whom you have no formal control—to get what your group needs and to work for what's best and right. Your own people count on you to do this because they cannot do their work well otherwise. The organization depends on voices like yours to keep it on the right track.

The right approach, then, is not to avoid the political aspects of your organization but to take part in positive ways for good ends. The struggle for influence can be dysfunctional and personal, but it need not be. In fact, influence is inherently neutral. It can be used for good or ill, depending on how it's wielded. There's no reason in organizations, as within the group you manage, that you cannot engage others and participate in politics effectively while conducting yourself by standards of openness, honesty, fairness, and respect. "Playing politics" and wielding influence in a political environment aren't the same.

Start by Understanding How Organizations Work

Start developing influence by understanding the beast. Managers often dislike and avoid the political side of organizations because they misunderstand organizations and how they work.

Do you see organizations as rational hierarchies in which information flows up the chain of command and directions come down? Do you believe influence in organizations should come from position or title, perhaps augmented by track record and expertise? Do you consider any effort to gain influence in other ways to be little more than an egotistical drive for status or control, an effort to manipulate others or build empires? Do you believe that organizational differences should be settled by a rational search for the "best" or "right" solution, which will be obvious to all intelligent, right-thinking people, all of whom share the desire to work together? Do you consider conflict a failure of management or organizational design?

Unfortunately, real organizations are much more complicated than this because they're composed of humans and because management is largely about negotiating the paradoxes and trade-offs of organizational life. Because of that, there are certain realities that all managers must recognize in order to deal with organizations as they are, not as they should be.

Today's Organizations Actually Work Fairly Well

In spite of their political natures, organizations are probably the best way society has found so far for large groups to do complex collective work productively over time.[4] Hierarchy has been with us for millennia. No alternative has yet been shown to work better, and so hierarchies composed of specialized groups working interdependently are unlikely to go away soon. They certainly are changing form and at the moment becoming less structured. And the relationships between enterprises and people are changing too. But these changes will tend to heighten, not lessen, the political nature of organizations because they will increase the need for informal communication, coordination, and cooperation. Organizations will always be imperfect, but you must deal with them nonetheless.

Organizations Are Both Rational and Social Institutions

You may wish organizations were entirely rational, but since they're composed of people, they're also social, emotional communities in which diverse groups with often conflicting needs must depend on each other. They function through dispassionate, analytical decision making *combined with* messy, murky processes of developing and applying influence.

That's why good ideas, the right strategy, or the best course of action will not be obvious to all. Hence, even plans or ideas that seem obvious to you will need to be sold to others. This has been true of organizations throughout history—business firms, churches, government agencies, charities, not-for-profits, nongovernment organizations—*all* organizations *all* the time. The effective manager finds a way to integrate and work within both the rational and the emotional realms inside them.

Organizations Generate Conflict—and That's Not Bad

Conflict is a characteristic feature of every organization, the primary source of politics, and the reason you need influence. Some firms allow it to show; differences within them are discussed and worked out openly. Others actively discourage it, though they succeed mostly in suppressing not its existence but its overt expression.

Conflict arises unavoidably from three fundamental features of all organizations:

Diversity. Specialization and division of labor, which are key to organizational effectiveness, create different groups, each seeking its own goals, struggling to work within its own limited resources, and necessarily pursuing its own set of priorities. In the long run, the work of all must combine to produce the work of the whole. At any given moment, however, it's unlikely that every group's goals, resources, and priorities will match perfectly.

Interdependence. In spite of their conflicting goals and needs, these diverse groups depend on each other, and that means their differences cannot be ignored.

Scarce resources. There's never enough time, money, or other resources for every group to do everything it wants to do. So they all compete for a larger share of a finite pie.

To eliminate the political nature of organizations, you would have to eliminate organizational conflict. To eliminate conflict, you would have to eliminate diversity, interdependence, and resource scarcity. This is unlikely to happen and unrealistic to hope for. It would also be undesirable because conflict among diverse groups can be healthy and productive. Indeed, diversity and conflict are essential drivers of creativity and innovation.[5]

Organizations operate on the tacit assumption that contention, working through conflict, is the most effective way to find the best course of action. Indeed, most organizations count on a degree of conflict for this purpose, no matter what they say publicly about the virtues of harmony. That's why effective managers must be willing and able to engage in constructive conflict.

Much organizational conflict is misinterpreted. It's construed as a merely personal, parochial struggle between warring egos, quests for personal power. In fact, most conflict involves much more. People and groups struggle over *real and legitimate* differences in interests and points of view.[6] That such disputes often contain interpersonal elements doesn't diminish their essentially reasonable nature. People in organizations aren't merely competitive personalities vying for personal power and control. They represent instead a tangle of legitimate, genuinely different, and often incompatible points of view that need to be worked through for the good of the whole.

What can be confusing or even confounding is that people often do engage in power struggles based only or mostly on ego needs.

Legitimate conflict over real issues and differences often does degenerate into battles for personal power, especially if those involved are less mature and self-secure than they should be. Conflict can be mismanaged and become destructive and personal. Groups can regress to tribal behavior, view other groups as "us versus them," and engage in destructive internal competition.

As a result, conflict must be managed. Every effective organization must find ways to keep it constructive and work related, not destructive, dysfunctional, or personal. The challenge is not to eliminate it but to direct it to constructive ends and even, at times, to foster it for the right purpose.

Organizations by Definition Are Instrumental

Organizations are instruments that serve a purpose or achieve some end. So everything about them, including the relationships among people and groups, is instrumental as well. That means everybody wants or needs something and is constantly pushing and pulling on each other to get what they desire. That's the nature of the beast. It explains why most relationships in them are reciprocal—that is, exchanges in which each party provides something of value to the other. There's nothing inherently wrong with such ways of relating; virtually all relationships contain some element of reciprocity. The real question is not whether relationships in organizations should be altruistic—"I do for you because it's right"—rather than reciprocal—"I do for you because you do for me." The real question is whether the ultimate organizational purposes being served, the goals, are worthwhile.

Organizational Skills Are Important

It's easy to underestimate the soft and hard-to-define skills that foster collaboration and success in organizations. We know young managers who disparagingly ascribe some senior managers' success to their political skills. "They only tell customers what they want to hear." Or, "They really don't know much, but they're great schmoozers."[7]

But those young managers who saw the same senior people up close and actually worked with them came away with a different story. They recognized, instead of political skills, an important ability to communicate with clients in a way that didn't threaten or irritate them but made them feel important. They saw an ability to bring together people from feuding groups. They saw an ability to synthesize points of view in ways that moved people forward. They recognized the skill required to run a meeting well—what questions to pose, for example, or the sequence in which people are called on. Organizational skills matter.

Do You Know How to Engage Your Organization Positively and Constructively?

The political environment within organizations can lead to destructive *or* constructive outcomes, depending on how people conduct themselves. That environment can produce pathological behaviors, such as narrow-minded infighting and personal power struggles. Or it can lead to useful creativity and innovation.

We're not suggesting that every aspect of a political environment is constructive or always works for the good of everyone. People do use influence for petty, personal, or parochial purposes. Organizations can indeed be high school for grown-ups. Destructive infighting, personal politics, and egomania can block progress, discourage initiative, reduce morale, and stifle innovation. Not to recognize this would be naive. But it need not be that way.

In the end, the question isn't whether you should seek to exercise influence in a political environment but *how* you should do it. Here are some suggestions.

Keep your efforts clearly focused on the good of the enterprise, and don't be surprised when well-meaning people disagree about how to achieve that good. The best you can hope for is that you win some and lose some. Resilience is critical. When you lose, do your best to support the decision made and help it succeed. Expect others to do the same.

Avoid the extremes of cynicism and naïveté. Organizations aren't evil incarnate; nor are they or should they be utopias. They're messy human enterprises. None is ever perfect or ideal. The way to deal with what ails them is to engage your colleagues more, not turn away.

Don't make disagreements personal or let them become personal. Here's where a strong but not big ego is critical. Stay engaged with those who disagree with you. Don't demonize others or let your group fall into the "us versus them" trap.

Remember, building organizational influence, just like influence with your own people, is based ultimately on trust and is fostered in the same way.

Conduct yourself according to a set of standards important to you: honesty, forthrightness, openness, dependability, integrity. Even if others don't follow the same standards, stay true to yours.

Find people in your organization who possess organizational skills and use them well. Study what they do and how they operate. If you can, talk to them about these issues, express your respect, and seek their counsel.

We're not saying this is easy. As you try to acquire and use organizational influence, there will be times you feel pressured or even compelled to act in ways that violate your personal beliefs. You will sometimes feel wronged. You will need to make trade-offs, to do a smaller harm—such as refusing some colleague's legitimate request—to accomplish a greater good. But even in taking such difficult steps, you can do them with respect and integrity.

As a manager, you cannot make progress or succeed by holding yourself above the conflict and negotiations found in all organizations. So resolve to engage the organization around you fully and proactively, with honor, integrity, and the best intentions, for worthwhile ends.

WEAVE YOUR OWN
WEB OF INFLUENCE

Exercise Influence by Building a Network of Key Relationships

11:03 a.m. As Jason returns to the Project Emerge area, his senior editor, Sumantra Tata, rushes up to him.

"I knew this would happen," Sumantra says.

"What happened?"

"Copies of some course materials Jay is producing have been obtained by people at Edison and Commonwealth, and they're up in arms. Oh, they're very upset." Edison and Commonwealth are two Reynolds Ed imprints whose publishers were in the educational technology meeting Jason just attended. Jay Bradshaw is in charge of producing all Project Emerge online course materials.

"I knew something like this would happen," Sumantra says.

"Is it a problem?" Jason asks.

"Yes, naturally. They didn't give permission."

"He didn't ask them?"

"He did," Sumantra says, "but they refused."

"How could they refuse?"

"Because they own the material."

"Then how could he get it without permission?" Jason asks.

"I don't know. He has technical friends who have access, I assume. That's possible, isn't it?"

"The publishers wouldn't let him use their content," Jason says, "so he got it some other way."

"Yes, I believe so," says Sumantra. "What shall we do?"

After a moment's thought, Jason says, "Nothing—for the moment. Nothing's left the company. It's still an internal matter. I'll talk to Jay. Did you specify the content in your syllabus?"

"Yes," Sumantra says, "but I told him we had to obtain permission. If we could not, I said we would have to develop it ourselves."

"But we can't. The whole idea is to repurpose existing content. Have you talked to Edison and Commonwealth?"

"Oh, no. I should not insert myself between Jay and the publishers."

"You can't specify something and not be involved, Sumantra. Isn't that what you're supposed to do? Didn't you review the syllabus with people at Edison and Commonwealth?"

"Oh, no. After they complained to Frank [Rigby, Jason's predecessor], he said not to involve them. It would only complicate matters. I agreed."

Jason sighs, not sure at the moment where to take this. "By the way," he says, "did you talk to Professor Schmidt?" Schmidt is the adviser who called Jason and Project Emerge's strategic partner, the International Fund for Technical Education, to complain.

"No," says Sumantra. "I must talk to you about that.

"Isn't he on your editorial advisory board?"

"Yes, but he's also on the board of the IFTE and—"

"Wait," Jason says. "You mean he's on the board of directors at the IFTE? Why didn't you tell me?"

"It's in the material I gave you."

"I'm sure it is," Jason says, "on one of the three hundred pages you gave me. All right, give me his contact information. I'll call." More politicking, Jason thinks. Just what I need now.

Sumantra looks at his watch. "He's in California," he says. "It's three o'clock in the morning there. I'm sorry. I should have pointed it out."

Organizations by their natures are political environments. To succeed in them, you must acquire influence. You do this by pro-actively creating a network of personal contacts—your own web of interdependence—and then using it to exchange the support, resources, and information you and your network partners need.

The wisdom of a network may seem obvious, but creating one is something many managers dread, and so few do it actively or well. Do you? Learning to do it—indeed, being *willing* to do it and then actually creating a network—will be a significant milestone on your journey.

Have You Created a Real Network of Your Own?

Everyone builds relationships in the course of doing their work. So you already have a set of contacts. What's needed, though, is not merely contacts but a network: a set of ongoing, enduring relationships with those you depend on and who depend on you, based on a real understanding of each other's needs and mutual dependencies.

How is this network different from the haphazard contacts that you and all managers create in the course of doing your work?

- It's likely to be *bigger and more complete* since it should include everyone you need and everyone who needs you.

- It's composed of *ongoing partnerships* with network members rather than one-off contacts made only when needed.

- It is *both present- and future-oriented* since it includes those you need to accomplish the daily work *and* those whose support will be critical in the future.

- It's essential to create such relationships *before* you need them. If you connect only when you must resolve a problem, you'll be interacting only at times of pressure and even conflict—not the best way to begin or sustain a fruitful relationship.

Even in a network of ongoing relationships built around long-term mutual benefit, there can still be differences, even tension and conflict. But they will occur in a context of underlying trust, understanding, and partnership that has already been established.

Effective managers use their networks to pursue plans and goals in four key ways.

Do You Use Your Network to Obtain and Provide Information?

An irony of management is that as you step back from direct involvement in the work, your need for information goes up. Consequently, you must develop new ways of finding out what you need to know.[1]

The role of your network in filling this requirement couldn't be more important. From network members, you will gain (and provide to them) the information that helps your and their groups succeed. Through members, you can scan the environment—ask questions, listen, observe—for not only what's happening but what might happen as well. Much of it will be tidbits, gossip, details, and assumptions you assemble into a coherent picture, impossible to create any other way, that becomes your foundation for better-informed decisions and plans.

Information isn't available for the asking. Because it truly is power, people often hoard it, releasing it only to those they know and trust. And even if you do hear something useful, but you don't know the people providing it, you cannot evaluate what they say or interpret its implications.

Do You Use Your Network to Link the Work of Your Group and the Rest of the Organization?

This is the role we discussed in the previous chapter of *integrating* your group and the wider firm. Here you troubleshoot problems; speak for, protect, and promote your group; and obtain the resources it needs. A rich network is key to performing this role well.

Do You Use Your Network to Form Coalitions of Those Who Seek the Same Goals?

A *coalition* is a collection of people who align themselves in pursuit of a common goal—a new strategy, a new product, a different way of doing business. It's a case of strength in numbers, a way of mobilizing support and negotiating from a position of greater influence. The meeting of the educational technology group at Reynolds Ed that opened the previous chapter was a good example. Few organizations decide issues by vote, but every senior leader understands the risks of acting in opposition to many voices speaking in unison.

Do You Use Your Network to Exercise Ethical Judgment?

A network will help you identify and assess the consequences of a planned action or decision. It will help you negotiate trade-offs among stakeholders. And it will help you deal with the dark side of political environments, such as pressure to compromise your standards of quality and integrity or to oppose organizational bullies who seek only their own interests.

Build Three Networks

Ultimately, you need to create three related but different networks.

Your *operational network* comprises those involved in your group's daily work.

Your *strategic network* will consist of those who help you prepare for the future by answering the questions, "What should we be doing? Where are we going and how will we get there?"

Your *developmental network* includes those who help you grow and provide personal, emotional support when you need it.[2] It can overlap with the others to some extent, but it's also likely to have several unique members, given its personal nature and purpose.

How to Build a Network

You may be thinking, "That's all great—for someone else. I know it's important, but it's not me! I like people, but I'm not good at meeting and greeting. It's like going to a party where I don't know anybody, and I hate that!"

We understand. Building a network certainly takes effort, but we don't agree that you must be an extrovert to do it. Why? Because you already have a preexisting reason—your mutual dependence—to approach all who will be in the networks you build. Everyone in them is already connected to you and you to them through your present or future work. You depend on them, and they on you. Create your relationships by identifying and building on those preexisting ties.

Given this mutual dependence, networking doesn't require a particularly outgoing personality. It's a skill, something anyone can learn through practice. Once you start doing it, you may even enjoy it.

In fact, if you're naturally gregarious, you will face your own trap: creating a network that takes on a life of its own. Like organizations, your network is instrumental and exists to serve a purpose. What you do must be driven primarily by the demands of the work, not by the personal relationships created along the way. Balancing the personal obligations a network can create with the needs of your work can present challenges you must resolve.

There are five major steps in building a productive organizational network.

1. Know your business and organization.

2. Know where your group is going.

3. Map your web.

4. Create your network.

5. Sustain your network.

We don't mean for these steps to be performed mechanically. We present them this way because we know from experience that if managers don't approach this important task systematically, they probably won't do it or do it to the extent necessary. Think of the steps as a regimen, like an exercise program, that you follow with discipline.

Step 1: Know Your Business and Organization

Start by creating a solid foundation of knowledge about the business you're in. This is the context for everything that follows. Nothing will make sense until you understand what the organization does, how it works, the challenges it faces, where it's trying to go, how it's planning to get there, and who does what.

Organizational conflict usually reflects competing *legitimate* interests—that is, points of view and issues driven by the business's challenges, goals, and strategies and the way those affect each group differently. Understand the business to understand those differences.

Understand Your Business

Start at the level of the business (or business unit) as a whole. Look at internal sources of information and what's available online from analysts, business publications, government or regulatory sources, and blogs. Attend trade and professional meetings. You want to know the company's longer-term goals, strategies, business model, and plans. You also need to understand its history, especially the recent past, and the issues, challenges, and threats it currently faces.

Understand, too, how the market it's in operates. See it through the eyes of its stakeholders: customers, investors, and suppliers. Learn what market forces shape its industry. Get to know the competition.

Understand How Your Organization Actually Works

Now look at the various divisions, departments, and other groups inside the organization—what they do and how they work together. In particular, make sure you understand the role of your division or department and how your group fits into it.

Figure Out Who Has Influence in Your Organization

Determine how influence is actually distributed throughout your organization.[3] What is the *informal* organization chart? The opinions of people and groups with influence carry greater weight when important decisions are made. These are the folks you want on your side. Pay attention to certain clues:

Who has formal authority? Start with a person's or group's status in the hierarchy. Formal authority is far from the only source of influence, but it is a factor.

Who is listened to and why? In meetings and other settings, identify the individuals and groups whose voices command more attention. Whom do people in the organization talk about more? Whose opinions seem to carry more weight?

Whose work is important to organizational objectives? Some people or units play larger roles in relation to the organization's goals. If the company expects most of its growth to come from Asian markets, those connected to that effort will be more influential than those linked to the West European market where sales and profits are flat.

Who's "plugged in"? Personal ties are important. A CFO may be only one of several senior managers, but his personal working relationship with the CEO may give him more influence than his peers. In the same way, being part of a key network imparts influence. The head of the West European division wields influence, in spite of flat sales in her market, because she sits on the company's management committee and has daily contact with other senior managers. This is one reason serving on task forces can be useful.

Who has critical expertise? The vice president of information technology may be especially important to a CEO who considers himself weak in technical matters.

Step 2: Know Your Current Work and Where You're Going

Perhaps it's obvious, but to map your web you must begin with a good understanding of your group and its work. What does it do and how does it do its work? What are its critical success factors? Its key metrics—measures that define progress and success? Whom does it depend on? Who depends on it?

Equally important, you must know where your group is going. What are your plans? Where do you expect to be in a year? In three or more years? How will the future be different from today? How do you plan to get there? What will change along the way? What resources and whose help and support will you need to create the future you want?

Step 3: Map Your Web

Now you're ready to name the people and groups who should be part of your networks (see the figure below).

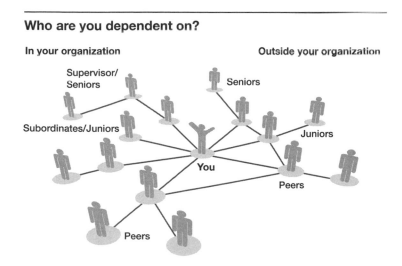

Who are you dependent on?

In your organization   Outside your organization

Supervisor/Seniors   Seniors

Subordinates/Juniors   Juniors

You

Peers   Peers

Peers

Identify Who Should Be in Your Networks

Given today's *and* tomorrow's needs, identify all the people and groups you and your people need or that need you. Ask yourself:

Whom do I and my group depend on now, and who depends on us? (Your operational network)

Whom will we depend on, and who will depend on us in the future? (Your strategic network)

Write down these names! Make two lists, one operational and the other strategic.

Beside each name, note the nature of the relationship: how are you dependent on that person or group, and how is that person or group dependent on you?

Watch out for common traps or mistakes as you make your list:

Don't focus just on people you see and work with daily. If your networks don't extend beyond the location where you work or the people you see often, if they don't anticipate future needs, you almost certainly aren't reaching far enough.

Seek diversity over sheer size. You want bridges to parts of your work world you don't normally inhabit. This will give you access to a broader range of talent, ideas, and resources.

Include adversaries or competitors. Don't exclude people or groups because they may have opposed or failed to support you in the past. If you need them, or they you, add them to your list.

Don't forget outside dependencies. Have you included everyone you need outside the organization? Key vendors, customers, consultants, freelancers, government or trade groups, other services?

Assess Those on Your List

First, for each person on your list, ask, *How important* is this contact to my group? Rank each on a simple scale of 1–3, where 1 means "important," 2 means "more important," and 3 means "very important."

Second, assess the *current quality of the relationship*. Are there mutual trust, expectations, and a willingness to work together, even on difficult problems? Again, use a simple number scale, where 1 means "could be stronger or more positive," 2 means "not necessarily perfect but a generally good current relationship," and 3 means "very strong and positive." Note that a 1 has two possible meanings: no relationship currently exists, or it exists but is very weak or problematic. Perhaps a recent dispute left a bitter memory and there's some mending to be done. In assessing relationships, look at them not just through your eyes but through the eyes of the other side as well.

Third, compare the two rankings. Are there relationships rated 2 or 3 in importance but only 1 in current quality? Those are important disparities to address. In the long run, you want every relationship to be 2 or 3 in quality, with all important relationships a 3.

This simple analysis can be very revealing. How many relationships did you mark 1 because you really have no relationship yet? If many fall into this category, it's an indication of the new networks you need to establish.

Look, too, at the relationships you marked 1 that already exist but are strained. If you have several, ask yourself whether there are common reasons for the problems. This may shed light on how you're perceived or the way you deal with colleagues.

Step 4: Create Your Network

Here is where you begin to create the actual relationships that make up your network.

Make Contact with Network Members

To begin, systematically work through the list of people you identified. Contact each, note how you're dependent on one another, explain that you want to discuss ways of working together better and helping each other, and, if possible, arrange a face-to-face meeting or a video call.

For many managers, this is the hard part: initiating contact in the absence of an immediate problem or some other compelling reason. Be opportunistic. Attend functions or meetings where you're likely to find people on your list. Consider joining task forces because they're good ways to make connections. Invite contacts to join your network via social networking tools; ask to receive their blogs or RSS feeds, if they offer them. (RSS, or "really simple syndication," refers to software that makes it easy to keep track of blogs that interest you.) Or offer yours to them.

Establish both a professional and a human connection. You want an ongoing relationship based on mutual dependence and trust, but nothing will really happen between the two of you until you connect as humans. If you observe effective managers, you're likely to see that their interactions include humor and such nonwork matters as family, sports, personal interests, and background. (But be careful of humor; it often falls flat and can even be inadvertently offensive when used across cultural lines.)

As you make these contacts, learn something of the person's culture and what that culture expects of a work relationship.[4] In many cultures, there are certain proprieties to observe, such as the need for socializing before discussing anything to do with work, or not asking personal questions early in a relationship—for example, questions about family or children. Other cultures are so task driven—people get together to perform a task, and the relationship ends when the job is done—that people you contact may want some specific work reason to get together. So be prepared with a shared goal, work process, or some other common issue to explore. Then use that discussion to begin a broader conversation.

In the beginning, you may find some individuals slow to reply to e-mails or phone messages. Keep at it in a professional way. Get on their calendars, even if the earliest available time is two months away. Above all, don't wait for a problem to arise. Remember, as you make these contacts, you're dealing with busy people. Provide as compelling a rationale for meeting as you can. Recognize that if you're not the solution to an immediate problem, *you must provide the energy that gets the relationship started.*

Connect, too, with people who've opposed or competed with you in the past. Instead of ascribing their previous positions to unpleasant personality flaws ("They're jerks, stupid, ignorant, self-interested . . ."), try to understand what underlying business issues or interests motivated them. Approach them by saying you want to understand your differences and find ways to work together more productively. Be prepared to take some heat before moving on to create a better relationship.

All the while, be yourself and use your own style of interaction. If you tend to be naturally shy or socially reactive, you do need to be proactive, but otherwise you needn't become a different person. Put together a plan for contacting the people on your network list, and then work the plan systematically. It may help to observe others who do relationship building well. Don't just mimic their style mechanically. That seldom works, because you're not them. But you can pick up insights and approaches for your own use.

All this will become easier as your network and knowledge grow. The more contacts you have, the more you can make through referrals. Your ability to link people and ideas, along with your organizational insights, will make you an increasingly valuable person to know.

Use Current Members to Extend Your Network

As you build your network, ask members whether they know others you should add. You're particularly looking for connections or ties that will extend your world and provide access to useful information and insights not available through those in your workaday world.

Don't Put Off Your Strategic Network

Once you and your group have a plan, you can begin creating a network to achieve your longer-term goals. Building this network will require even more discipline because its real benefits may only come in the future. Start with those in your operational network who are also important to you strategically. Branch out from there to include those who are less important now but will become important in the future. Be proactive and opportunistic—use everyday activities, such as a meeting or presentation or an encounter in the cafeteria, to approach or reconnect with others. However you approach them, be clear about your plans and how you may be working together in the future.

Your Attitude Is Important

Take care to approach network building with the right mind-set because the underlying spirit you bring to it will shape everything you do. If you are driven entirely by your own needs—How can *I* get what *I* want?—it will be obvious to others, no matter how well you think you're camouflaging your fundamental self-interest. It's the nature of networking that to get what you want, you must give others what they need. So understanding others and their needs is important. Ask questions: "What's your goal and how are you planning to get there? What are your top three priorities? What's the biggest obstacle you face? How can we help?"

Step 5: Sustain Your Network

Your network will wither and die unless you sustain it by using it as often as you can.

Share—don't hoard—information, point out threats and opportunities, send a heads-up about something of interest, volunteer to help with a problem, actively support others' causes when you can, contribute ideas, give honest and constructive feedback. If you know someone is interested in a subject and you find a good article or podcast that applies, forward it to them.

Be a bridge yourself. Act as a link between two members of your network who share some work interest but wouldn't normally connect with each other in the normal course of events.

Build coalitions of network members who seek a similar goal. Work through your common interests, and find ways to express your single voice where it can influence the actions and decisions of others.

Take opportunities to make a human connection. Send e-mails saying, "Thanks," "Congratulations," "I'm sorry for you," or whatever is appropriate and genuine. The test here isn't whether you normally do that sort of thing; instead, ask yourself, "What would I say if the person were standing in front of me?" Say it in a quick call or e-mail. Small, human touches are important.

Periodically step back and assess your relationships with your network partners, as you did in the beginning. Are important relationships being ignored or underserved? Do any need to be repaired or revived?

Use all interactions to maintain and strengthen your long-term relationships with network members, not just to resolve an immediate problem. Conduct negotiations, no matter how tough, on the assumption that both of you want to maintain a strong ongoing connection.

Talk as candidly as possible about your relationship and how it's working for each of you. Be prepared to hear, without defensiveness, problems they have with you and your group. Be willing to admit errors and misjudgments. The words *I'm sorry* or *I was wrong—I need to learn* may seem trite by themselves. At the right moment, though, they can be transformational.

Avoid unhealthy rivalry. Many managers tend to see relationships as opportunities for competition. Some of that can be constructive, especially if aimed at achieving mutual goals. But take care that interactions with others don't become primarily about winning. Too often, we fall into an "us versus them" attitude. Instead, find ways everyone can achieve their goals, at least in the long run.

Forming and Using Networks Takes Time and Effort

We recognize that many features of work and the workplace today make it difficult to devote the time needed to build and maintain networks.

In a task-focused culture, it's hard to find time for what many managers, whose responsibilities are constantly growing, consider socializing or politicking. Even if you recognize its importance, time for something that, at the moment, rarely feels urgent can be limited.

Organizational and workplace features make networking difficult too. The rapid formation and dissolution of task teams, fast-changing organizational structures, a constantly shifting marketplace, and the need to deal with distant colleagues make it unclear who should be in your network.

No wonder we tend to form haphazard networks focused on today's problems.

In spite of these difficulties and negative predispositions, effective managers create the kinds of networks we're describing. Studies of senior managers who recently took over major business units clearly revealed that establishing a strong network was one of their most urgent priorities.[5]

How do they find the time? Here are some guidelines in the form of questions.

Do You Build Networking into Your Daily Work?

As we said in chapter 1, effective managers use their daily work and interactions to make and build relationships. They're opportunistic. They place themselves in positions, like meetings with outside groups, that allow such contacts. They build networks through hundreds of little steps fitted into their schedules. Not all of it can be done this way, of course, but more than you might think, particularly after you've identified those you want in your networks.

Do You Understand the Power of Weak Ties?

Managers adept at creating networks recognize that not all connections need to be close and deep. If you spend most of your time building such ties, your world will be limited to those you work with regularly, and you will miss the opportunities of a diverse network that includes what are called "weak" ties.[6]

Weak ties are network relationships with individuals who are usually on the periphery of your daily work that connect you with worlds different from your own and extend your reach to provide access to unique information and other resources. A key virtue of weaker ties is that they require less effort to maintain and demand less reciprocity.

Thus, the relationships in your network should include a core of strong ties surrounded by many diverse weak ties. Because they extend your reach, weak ties are especially useful for scanning the environment inside and outside your organization to identify coming challenges and opportunities. You can use them to solve problems, gather information, and find new ideas. On the other hand, strong ties are important for doing actual work and for the coalition building often needed to implement new ideas.

Do You Use Software Tools That Facilitate Networking and Collaboration?

Social networking and similar software can make networking much easier. We strongly suggest that you investigate tools on the Web or within your company. Wikis and other collaboration platforms are useful for building and maintaining strong ties. Social networking sites can help maintain weak ties. They make the maintenance of contacts and the exchange of updates easier. Blogging or the creation of wikis can be useful ways to seek information, involve others in ongoing discussions around issues of mutual interest, and collaboratively develop documents, such as plans, spreadsheets, and presentations. These tools are almost essential for a network or team spread over many locations.

Encourage your firm to make such tools available. They will significantly extend your ability to network while reducing the time required.

Have You Found a Networking Style That Works for You?

Develop a networking style that you're comfortable using. If you're more introverted, then take advantage of work-related activities like conferences that expose you to a broad range of people in a setting with built-in opportunities to talk about business matters of mutual interest. If you're more extroverted, you may be able to strike up useful relationships in the gym or at social networking functions the company offers.

What Creating a Network Requires of You

Building and sustaining multiple relationships will reveal who you are, your motives and aspirations. Ask yourself two critical questions:

Do my colleagues trust me?

Do people like to deal with me?

It's important that you understand what is meant by each and that you answer yes to both questions.

Do Your Colleagues Trust You?

We asked a similar question regarding your relationships with subordinates in chapter 4. In the same way, trust is the foundation of influence in a network.

As with subordinates, trust means that others believe they can count on you to do the right thing, and it's based on two components: your competence and your character.

Competence. Your network colleagues' trust is built on their perceptions of your technical, operational, and political know-how, along with your track record of accomplishment. It's their belief that you know both *what* to do and *how* to get it done.

But the context here is different than it is with your subordinates, who assess your individual competence as their manager. Your colleagues will take a broader view, evaluating you based not only on your personal knowledge and know-how but also on the competence of your group. You will not be considered able if they think your group inept and unable to deliver what they need.

Character. Much the same standards apply here as with your direct reports. Your intentions—your values and standards—are as important as your capabilities. People assess you not just by what you do and say but by *who* you are and *what* you intend. You need to demonstrate a dependable internal compass that leads you consistently to deal with people honestly and respectfully.

In a network context, colleagues expect you to be a team player, someone who can balance the needs of others and the organization as a whole against your own. They expect you to be on their side and not just your own. That means you're concerned about them and their success too. You help them look good. You help them achieve their own goals and carry out their plans. You share your network and its resources with them. Colleagues also expect you to keep your people in line and require them, by example and precept, to be team players too.

Working with colleagues isn't always easy. They're not always team players, and a few can even be bullies. It's important when you encounter someone like this that you step back and try to see the world from their point of view. Don't automatically jump to the conclusion that "they're jerks" and you cannot work with them. It will help if you can understand their priorities and, especially, the pressures on them. That insight can then guide the way you approach them and what you propose.

Unfortunately, in a few cases, you'll conclude they *are* jerks and bullies looking out only for themselves and not the best interests of the whole enterprise. When this happens, the best approach is usually to confront them calmly and professionally and let them know their behavior or demands aren't acceptable. Point out your own efforts to work for the good of the firm, and express your continuing interest in finding a way forward that serves all needs. This obviously involves some risk that they will escalate the conflict or agree superficially but continue to oppose you behind the scenes. In the end, you may need to take such struggles to a higher level in the organization. In any case, avoidance and passive aggression are almost never the solution.

Do Your Colleagues Like to Interact with You?

"Like to interact or deal with you" is not the same as "Do people like you?" This is not about being merely pleasant or likable. It's about the experience of dealing with you. Are colleagues confident that dealings with you will be consistently constructive?

Here's the key question to ask yourself: How do people experience me? When someone deals with me, do they go away feeling generally more positive, more negative, or the same as they felt before the encounter? To some extent, the answer for any given interaction will depend on the context, the issues discussed, and the outcome—but not entirely. There's an underlying quality of interaction, apart from the specific matters discussed, and that quality is what concerns us now.

We all know people who are unpleasant to deal with. They approach every interaction with an attitude—angry, competitive, sarcastic, or constantly fault-finding. Each time you deal with them you get a jab in the eye, so to speak, or they rant about someone or something. They may routinely imply, in demeanor or tone of voice, that whatever you say is silly or stupid. They're impatient or critical. You're always on guard because it feels as if everything you say will be attacked. You leave an interaction depressed and tired. We say working with such people carries high "transaction costs," or they're "high maintenance." Their competence doesn't compensate for these faults, for research shows that such "competent jerks" can find themselves marginalized because others avoid working with them.

We heard one example of this at a small meeting. As it extended into late morning, someone asked, "Should we stop for lunch?" Without thinking, someone else glanced at his watch, to which the first person smirked, "Ah. Another mechanical man. Can't tell if you're hungry without checking the time." From some, this might have been a funny remark, instantly forgotten. From this fellow, his voice loaded with sarcasm, it was a gratuitous put-down not forgotten by the person who suffered it. The one who made the remark later complained about feeling isolated. No one wanted him around, in spite of the fact he was smart and very knowledgeable.

How you interact matters. Research shows that if people have a choice, they will elect not to work with a difficult person, *even when the person is competent.*[7] Guess how much influence difficult people have on others?

You must ask yourself, What is it like to deal with me? Do people leave an encounter feeling down, beat up, sucked dry—even in small ways? Don't assume it doesn't matter if you're truly good technically. Expertise is critical, but it won't compensate for poor interpersonal skills.

We've described in detail how to create a network, because it's fundamental to your success and because so many managers fail to do it. It takes precious time, rarely feels urgent, and can make all but the most gregarious of us uncomfortable at times. Without putting in the effort to create your network, however, you will lack the influence you need in your organization to function effectively as a boss.

Set your mind to engaging others, approach it with the right attitude, use any social tools available, find a style you're comfortable with, and then work at it systematically and diligently. That's why we outlined the specific steps involved.

Building a network will help you exercise more influence, improve your chances of success, and make progress on your journey. For all the effort and, sometimes, discomfort involved, you'll discover how rewarding work can be when you build it around a rich web of relationships.

7

DON'T FORGET YOUR BOSS

Make the Most of this Critical Relationship

11:20 a.m. Jason notices his boss, Ray Sanchez, is online, and places a video call to him. "We could use more time to put together a budget," Jason says. "Is that possible?" Sanchez looks harried.

"What's the problem?"

Jason recalls the long list of problems he compiled that morning. How much does Sanchez want to know?

"No problem," Jason finally says. "A lot going on. I'm still trying to get my arms around it. And I'm waiting for some analysis from Barry."

"Wish I could help," Sanchez says, "but finance says the deadlines are set in concrete, and Fred backs them up." Fred is Fred Whitelaw, Reynolds Ed CEO.

"I can give you better numbers next week."

"Look," Sanchez says, "everybody's in the same boat. What's wrong with the pro forma numbers in the original Project Emerge proposal?"

"We're looking at those," Jason says. He wonders how far to go down this road. "I'm just doing some due diligence, making sure they still make sense."

"We're counting on you to make them make sense," Sanchez says.

So, Jason thinks, I'll survive only if I hit the original numbers. "I'm working on it," he says.

"How are you otherwise?" Sanchez asks. "Everything is fine? You're settling in?"

"I'm . . . fine," Jason says. He decides to push the issue. "I'm going to talk to Gena and other publishers about using their material."

"Good. You need to work that out. Those people are already unhappy enough as it is."

"Where do you stand on it?" Jason asks. "I'm sure Gena's already talked to you."

"Oh, an earful," Sanchez says. "Listen, I want you two on the same side. Make that work. It's important. You're the glorious future, but they still pay the rent."

It's not the ringing expression of support Jason wanted. Another standard, he thinks: produce the original numbers *and* make everybody happy, especially those who think you're stealing their material and locking them out of a promising market.

"One more thing," Jason says. "Can you help with Jack Cavit? He still hasn't named the sales team for Project Emerge, and we need time at Sales Conference to orient those people."

"If I get involved every time a publisher wants something from sales, I wouldn't have time for anything else. You guys have to fight your battles," Sanchez says.

"I'm hoping you might make an exception for this," Jason says. "Cavit is one of the reasons I have questions about the numbers. It looks like he's not doing what he committed to do."

On the laptop screen, Sanchez's face goes immobile, his eyes half shut. Several times his lips move but no words emerge, until he finally says, "Okay, let's do it this way. You talk to Cavit. Then tell me if you can't get what you need."

So, Jason thinks, all I have to do is talk to the elusive Mr. Cavit. No small feat all by itself.

One member of your network deserves special attention: your boss. Managers at all levels too often neglect or mishandle this critical relationship and so fail to make the most of it.

Managing *up* is important because your boss plays a pivotal role in your success—or your failure. You can leverage your boss's influence in the organization on your behalf in several ways—for example, by obtaining valuable information, winning needed resources, and securing important support for your personal development and career. When you face difficult trade-offs and must make decisions that create both beneficial and painful consequences for others, your boss's advice, insight, knowledge of the organization, and access to higher management can be invaluable. As your organization shifts and changes shape in an uncertain market, a good relationship here becomes a necessity for navigating through the turmoil. The penalties of a poor relationship are many: less influence, little information or advice, fewer resources, and limited personal development and career support. Worst case, you can find yourself isolated, ignored, pushed out—your journey stalled, your career derailed.

Why Is It Often an Uneasy Relationship?

This relationship can be problematic for two reasons. First, a boss plays conflicting roles: supporter and evaluator, which can create confusion. Second, people often bring their past experience with authority into the relationship, which can create unnecessary complications.

This is another area where being a star as an individual contributor may not have prepared you for management. As an exceptional performer, you probably had minimal interaction with your boss. If so, you most likely didn't develop the skills of managing up that you need now.

Do You See Your Boss as Coach and Developer or as Evaluator and Judge?

You're caught in a difficult dilemma, one that can feel personally threatening. The boss is not only a potential source of great help, in both your job and your career, but also the one who evaluates your performance. To get help from her as a developer, particularly with your personal development, you must reveal your shortcomings. But if you do, she in her role as evaluator may interpret your weaknesses as serious faults. Many managers handle this dilemma by striving to appear capable and in control even when they're not. They see their boss more as threat than ally and lose the potential benefits of her help.

Are you confused by your boss's dual role? Do you tend to see your boss as primarily a judge? Does that attitude seem safer to you? That's understandable, but it's not always the most helpful point of view.

What can you do? Don't presume your boss is always one or the other, judge or coach. Instead, think of his dual roles as extremes between which he moves back and forth depending on the situation. At first, in small ways that aren't risky, test his willingness to provide support. That way, you can see when, where, and how he's likely to focus on development rather than evaluation. Learn his feelings about what's important in management—such as careful planning, decisiveness, building consensus—and make sure you develop and display those qualities.

Do You See Past Bosses in Your Current Boss?

In chapter 4 we discussed the possibility that some subordinates will bring to their relationship with you already-formed negative attitudes about authority figures. Now that possibility is reversed, and you must examine your own attitudes.

How do you feel about your current boss? How do you respond to authority in general and to those who have it? If most of your bosses have frustrated you and fallen short of your expectations, you and they may be victims of the emotional baggage you carry forward from past experience. Reflect on your own history and the feelings it's created in you. That history may lead you to perceive your current boss not as who she is but as an amalgam of past authority figures, with all the positive and negative feelings that flow from that past. Unless you're aware of these feelings, you'll be at their mercy.

On the other hand, you may respond to authority with overde-pendence, rather than resistance. Extreme deference and auto-matic, unquestioning compliance don't work well either. Those who react this way never disagree or push back, even when they're right or it's in their best interest.

Both antagonism to authority and too much deference will keep you from seeing your boss clearly and realistically and pre-vent you from securing the work and personal benefits available from a good relationship.

What Should Your Relationship with Your Boss Be?

Do you realize that your relationship is actually one of *mutual dependence*? Your boss depends on you and needs your commit-ment and support to succeed. Just as you may wrestle with your reliance on your people, he probably struggles with his depen-dence on you and his other direct reports.

Think of the relationship as a partnership in which the partners depend on each other to succeed and are able to influence each other in ways that improve the performance of each. It's not a relationship of equals, certainly, but it's not entirely one-way either. You usually do have some room to negotiate and create the relationship that works for both of you.

Take Stock of Your Current Relationship

Is your current relationship a partnership? Are you and your boss able to have a normal, constructive discussion about work? If not, why not?

Don't assume you can make significant differences in how your boss thinks or operates. Most likely, the best you can do is nudge her in directions that work better for you. That's certainly worth doing. But you're unlikely to create large changes.

With that in mind, use the following questions to assess and improve your relationship. They focus on actions you can take.

Are You Meeting Expectations?

By far, the key factor in a good relationship is your ability to perform as expected.

Results. Performance targets create the foundation for your ongoing relationship. Unless you and your group produce the results expected, you're unlikely to enjoy much of a partnership. And it's not just the results you attain but *how* you attain them. If you hit your numbers but your boss hears complaints all day about how you railroad other groups, he probably won't consider you someone who "meets expectations."

Information. But results aren't the only expectation. Do you keep your boss informed? Reach explicit agreement about how often and in what way you will report progress. Develop a sense of what your boss wants to know. Some prefer to know a great deal; others much less. In general, no boss likes to be surprised or seem ignorant of something she should know. If you must err, do it on the side of overinforming. Many bosses actually want more information than they say, so discover the right balance through experience. Find out as well how your boss wants information delivered: written reports via e-mail, in person if that's possible, or by video call.

Support and loyalty. Your goal is to make the relationship work for both of you, and that requires some degree of support and loyalty. Just as you want your boss to care about you, and your people want you to care about them, your boss wants your care and concern too.

Be generous and assume the best intentions, even when you disagree. Express disagreement as your opinion offered in support of your boss's success. Some people bridle at the word *loyalty*. We don't mean blind loyalty, but loyal people earn the right to question and disagree on occasion. Those who speak up only when they disagree will usually enjoy less influence than those who have demonstrated prior support. So on those occasions when you do honestly agree with your boss, say so clearly and explicitly.

You cannot succeed in this relationship at the expense of your boss; you will rise or fall together. Your task is to make *both of you* effective. Help your boss build on her strengths, and overcome or bypass her limitations.

Does Your Boss Trust You?

The foundation of all network relationships is trust, and the relationship with your boss is no different. Can he count on you to do the right thing? If you feel micromanaged, the reason may be that you've neglected to establish real trust. The essence of building trust is to negotiate what you both mean by "do the right thing."

Do you both see the current situation the same way? Make sure you share a common understanding of the challenges your group faces and what needs to be done. If you see the need for fundamental change and your boss wants to stay the course, you must resolve this difference right away.

Do you agree about where you and your group are going? Once again, a plan is critical. Do you have one? Have you reviewed it with your boss? Does it make clear what's to be done and when? Make sure your boss knows your goals and plans and agrees with them. Ideally, she had a hand in creating them.

Do you negotiate expectations when you're given an assignment? Don't let your relationship be one in which you simply accept whatever is passed down without discussion. If the expectations are unrealistic, you will have no one to blame but yourself when your team fails. Reach agreement on the results you're expected to produce—what will happen by when. Do this at the beginning, and update expectations periodically. Warn your boss of potential risks, and play out various scenarios of how you might handle them.

Do You See and Understand Your Boss as a Person?

It's easy to forget that beneath your boss's mantle of authority there's a person just like you. He has hopes, aspirations, frustrations, strengths, weaknesses, and fears. He's the product of his background, training, and experience. He has a personal life—a family and family history, religious beliefs, social organizations, political views, and hobbies. Do you know enough that you're able to see the world through his eyes?

Do You Understand Your Boss as a Manager?

Your boss has goals, plans, and pressures, as well as managerial strengths and weaknesses, preferences, and foibles. Do you know them? What's your boss on the line for? What's her boss telling her to do?

Do you know how your boss prefers to make decisions, and do you work within that pattern? Does he prefer lots of analysis and data? Does he need time to reach a conclusion? Does he want everyone's opinion before deciding? If you must depart from these preferences, do you first negotiate explicitly what you will do?

Do you know and respect the ways your boss prefers to work? Some bosses want written analyses before a discussion, while others prefer the discussion or presentation first, followed by a written summary. Some want lots of data; others want the highlights. Some want to be intimately involved in every detail; others prefer regular reports but nothing more unless there's a problem.

When you approach your boss, do you expect guidance or answers? We know a manager whose boss always responded to questions with questions of her own. Finally, this manager realized: "I had to come in with some ideas about how I would handle the situation, and then she would talk about them with me. She would spend all the time in the world with me."

Do you present a problem and expect your boss to solve it? Many bosses resist that approach. Instead, try going in with a problem, an analysis, alternatives, and a recommendation he can react to.

Can You Identify Your Boss's Strengths?

This stumps many managers we know. They focus on their boss's weaknesses and can talk at length about them—and often do with their peers. But they seldom look for strengths. That's a shame because your boss's strengths are what you must leverage, and you cannot leverage what you don't recognize or appreciate. Whatever your boss's weaknesses, identify what she does well. There must be something. Don't fall back on something like "She knows how to play the organizational game." There's something there. What is it, and how can you use it to learn and do your work more effectively?

Are You Clear About What You Need and Expect?

Negotiate what you need from your boss. Don't make him guess. What can he do to help you? Provide resources, support from other groups, relief from distracting responsibilities, clearer direction?

In addition, think about the way you prefer to work and what you need from a superior, such as specific goals, help and ongoing guidance, or a certain degree of autonomy. Be sure you know where the boundaries are. Test how negotiable they are. Where your needs and your boss's way of managing diverge, talk through the differences. Where differences involve high stakes, talk sooner than later. It's easy to underestimate the risks of conflict avoidance and the cost of the passive aggression that often accompanies it. Your nonverbal communications—expression, manner, body language, tone—often reveal your true feelings about your boss and can slowly corrode this critical relationship.

Have You Discussed with Your Boss Your Own Growth, Development, and Aspirations?

How can your boss help you grow and develop? She's not responsible for your career and personal development, but it's in her best interest for you to improve in ways that will help you (and her) succeed. From your boss you can get advice and guidance; feedback about your performance, strengths, and weaknesses; insight into what others think of you; developmental assignments; and access to training programs and other learning opportunities.

To obtain these, you must first communicate your desire to learn. Then, you must agree about *how* and *where* you want to grow—what competencies you need to develop, such as building a network, making a plan, managing performance, or assessing subordinates. Have reasonable expectations. Take responsibility for your own development. Besides, your boss probably has no more time and no less pressure than you, and many bosses, unfortunately, are uncomfortable in this role. The more specific the requests you make, the better—to attend a training course, for example, or advice about a specific problem.

Do You and Your Boss Come from Different Cultures?

Be aware that cultures differ in their expectations and treatment of people with authority.[1] In some, the boss is expected to be participative; in others, directive. In some, proactive and assertive; in others, humble and modest. Compare the characteristics of both your cultures. Where your assumptions and expectations differ, be prepared to talk about them explicitly.

Have You Figured Out How to Work with Multiple Bosses?

If you report to more than one boss, take care to nurture both relationships. Realize that both depend on you to do your job. Almost certainly, neither can accomplish their agendas without you and your group. Accept that their goals will differ; they are probably paid to focus on different priorities. You are being paid to negotiate the trade-offs required by their different agendas in order to serve the best interests of the enterprise. If your relationship with one of your bosses is a dotted line, that doesn't mean you can ignore the relationship or wait for that boss to approach you. We know a manager who suffered an unforeseen sting in his performance review because he ignored his dotted line to the manager of global strategy, who was located five time zones away. Our acquaintance mistakenly thought this boss would make clear what he wanted, but, in fact, the boss expected him to take the initiative.

If necessary, schedule regular contact with the distant manager(s). If possible, give each the same periodic reports that quickly summarize your recent and upcoming work for each and all. That way, all your bosses can see everything you're doing. If individual bosses want more detail, you can provide it in separate reports.

Managing multiple bosses will require more time and effort, but the benefit is that they represent a larger set of resources. Be forthright with all of them about your multiple relationships and whatever trade-offs they might require. In talking with them, it can be helpful to offer specifics. For example, walk them through the logic behind decisions you have made that reflect those trade-offs. See whether they agree with your judgment calls. If possible, try to align their expectations of you so that you're not constantly faced with conflicting direction. If differences of sub-stance exist between or among your bosses, bring them together in person or in videoconference and suggest ways to resolve the problems. Don't let such differences go unsettled. You must take responsibility for creating the conditions for your own success, and you're expected to do what is necessary for the good of the enterprise. They count on you to balance and manage the multi-ple relationships.

Surviving a Problematic Boss

What we've said so far may sound fine to you—in theory. But you may have a boss who presents problems.[a] Perhaps he's absent, physically or psychologically. Perhaps she's overly focused on herself and her own success. Perhaps he's simply incompetent; he doesn't understand the work and what's important in it. Perhaps she's totally results driven and doesn't care about you or anyone else. Perhaps he's powerless and cannot obtain the resources your team desperately needs because his web of relationships is impoverished.

Absentee bosses simply aren't available. They're located far away, they rarely talk to subordinates or make themselves avail-able, or they're consumed with other demands. We know manag-ers who have so many direct reports they have virtually no time for any one of them.

There are various strategies for dealing with this situation.[3] Get their attention by framing your communications around *their* concerns and priorities. Be prepared and efficient with the time you do have together. Keep them informed with regular, brief reports in writing or e-mail, along with short, heads-up notes when something important arises. Get to know the boss's support staff; often you can ask a question and get a response through them. If you know the boss's schedule, you can intercept her between meetings.

Some bosses are problematic because they focus only on their own needs. This approach may be so ingrained they're unaware of it. But they're insecure and view all relationships in personal terms. "Are they for me or against me?" is the first question they ask about those around them. They're terrified of being embarrassed or failing.

To deal with such self-absorbed people, you must understand the world as they see it: a hostile place full of personal danger. Don't expect empathy or personal support. Give praise for genuine achievements and accomplishments. Look for ways to offer real empathy. Support clearly and vocally his good ideas. To persuade him to change course, couch your reasons in terms of either buttressing his reputation or protecting him from embarrassment. Don't expect praise or credit for your knowledge, good ideas, or accomplishments; almost certainly you won't get any, and he may even take credit for them. Be careful if he asks for your "real opinion." It's unlikely he wants criticism of any kind.

Though often well meaning, technically incompetent bosses present different challenges. They can be helped if they know they lack knowledge or understanding. But overconfidence and ignorance often go together. You may need to work with peers and colleagues to deal with problems here while continuing to inform and educate such a boss along the way.

A completely goal-driven boss may need reminding on occasion of organizational or people issues. She may simply overlook human costs or consequences. Raise and negotiate such issues. However, nothing is likely to dissuade her from the single-minded, frantic achievement of whatever goal she's trying to achieve. You'll probably have more success if you embrace the goal too while raising reasonable suggestions and alternatives along the way.

Of course, those are short-term ways of coping. Weigh the benefits of such a relationship against the costs. Long-term, you'll probably need to work out some other options. If you're lucky, you won't have to deal with a bad boss very often.

For all other more or less typical bosses, work hard to build a productive relationship. Initiate the kinds of discussions we've suggested. It's difficult to succeed without his support, and impossible in the face of his opposition. Always remember that your reports face these same issues with you. Let your experience in each relationship—with your boss and with your people—guide you in the other.

Don't make the mistake, as many managers do, of ignoring such a potentially powerful source of help and support. Take responsibility for, and play an active role in, making it a partnership that benefits both of you. Avoid seeing yourself as a passive, powerless subordinate. Don't assume it cannot be a positive, mutually helpful relationship until you've tested the possibilities on several occasions. It's too important—to your ability to exercise influence and thus to your journey—to merely let it be whatever it will be.

Where Are You on Your Journey?

Imperative 2: Manage Your Network

What have you learned about yourself? Are you ready and able to develop the network of relationships you need if your team is to succeed?

The following questions both summarize the key ideas in part II and help you assess where you stand now in regard to them and where you need to improve.

Do You Identify Those Who Should Be in Your Network?

Do you *systematically* identify the people and groups inside and outside your organization on whom you and your team depend to achieve your goals, or who depend on you to reach theirs?

1	2	3	4	5

No, I don't
do any of this
well

Yes, I'm
consistently
good at all this

Do you constantly reevaluate your networks and your relationships within them to keep up with changes in the organization, in the world around you, and in your purpose, goals, and plans?

1	2	3	4	5

No, I don't
do any of this
well

Yes, I'm
consistently
good at all this

Do You Proactively Build and Maintain Your Operational Network?

Do you consciously and systematically reach out to create and sustain ongoing relationships—including both strong and weak ties—with those you identify as members of your operational network—*the people you need to do your group's everyday work?*

1	2	3	4	5

No, I haven't consciously created an operational network

Yes, I consciously created and sustain an operational network

Do you actively and consistently seek to understand and support the needs of members of your *operational* network?

1	2	3	4	5

No, I don't actively work to support these members

Yes, I'm consistently careful to support these members

Do you consistently seize opportunities to connect with *operational network* members?

1	2	3	4	5

No, I don't consciously seize such opportunities

Yes, I always look for and seize these opportunities

Do You Proactively Build and Maintain Your Strategic Network?

Do you consciously and systematically reach out to create and sustain ongoing relationships—including both strong and weak ties—with those you identify as members of your strategic network—*the people you need or will need to help you and your group achieve your longer-term goals?*

1	2	3	4	5

No, I haven't consciously created a strategic network

Yes, I consciously created and sustain a strategic network

Do you actively and consistently seek to understand and support the needs of members of your *strategic* network?

1	2	3	4	5
No, I don't actively work to support these members				Yes, I'm consistently careful to support these members

Do you consistently seize opportunities to connect with *strategic* members?

1	2	3	4	5
No, I don't consciously seize such opportunities				Yes, I always look for and seize these opportunities

Do You Use Your Network to Provide the Protection and Resources Your Team Needs?

Do you protect your team from distractions and misunderstandings, proactively speak for and represent it and its needs, and actively resolve problems inside and outside the team as necessary?

1	2	3	4	5
No, I need to be much better at this				Yes, I do this consistently well

Do you use your networks to secure the funds, people, information, support, and other resources your team needs?

1	2	3	4	5
No, I need to be much better at this				Yes, I do this consistently well

Do You Proactively Use Your Network to Accomplish Your Team's Goals?

Do you seek help and cooperation from your network in building the future you've defined with your team? In particular, do you build coalitions of network members in support of your team's purpose, goals, and plans?

1	2	3	4	5

No, I need to be much better at this

Yes, I do this consistently well

Do you actively help others in your networks achieve *their* goals?

1	2	3	4	5

No, I need to be much better at this

Yes, I do this consistently well

Do your network colleagues trust you—do they believe your competence and character will lead you to do the right thing for all of you?

1	2	3	4	5

No (or I don't know)

Yes (I have real data)

Part Three

MANAGE YOUR TEAM

ARE THOSE WHO WORK for you a real team or merely a group of people who coordinate their individual efforts?

Too many managers overlook the management possibilities of using a team to influence their people. Instead, they focus on building the most effective relationships they can with each person who works for them. They may call their group a team and put up posters extolling teamwork, but they spend their time managing individuals and pay little attention to the collective performance of their people. They rarely use their groups for diagnosis and problem solving, and all too often handle, one-on-one, many problems that clearly affect their people as a whole.

In taking this approach, they're wasting the powerful influence that the social dynamics of a real team can have on the behavior and performance of its members.

What makes a team different, and why should you want your group to be a team? If *team* is more than just another word for a group, what is it?

A team is a group of people who do collective work and are mutually committed to a common team purpose and challenging goals related to that purpose.

Collective work and mutual commitment are the key characteristics. Collective work requires joint effort beyond simple cooperation and coordination. It produces an outcome that is more than the sum of individual efforts. Mutual commitment means members hold themselves *and each other* jointly accountable for the team's performance. Not only do they think and act collectively, but the social, emotional bonds among them are strong. They share a genuine conviction that all will succeed or fail together, and that no one can succeed while the team fails.

Mutual commitment springs from the two pillars noted in the definition: first, a common, worthwhile purpose, a sense of *doing something important together*; and second, *specific and challenging team goals* based on that purpose.[1] A team says both, "We *do* something important," and, "We're *going* someplace important."

Without purpose and goals, you cannot create a team. But they're not enough. Clarity about roles, how the work is done, and how members interact matter too. Members need to know what's required of them collectively and individually, and how they're expected to work together—what kind of conflict is acceptable and unacceptable, for example, or how they should communicate.

Creating and sustaining a team requires strong management—it rarely happens spontaneously—but it's worth the effort. For doing collective work that requires a complex mix of varied skills, experience, and knowledge, teams are more creative and productive than groups of individuals who merely cooperate.

Through purpose, goals, and clarity, groups become teams—communities that exert strong influence on members' attitudes and behaviors. That's why the ability to transform a group of people into a real team and to sustain the team in the face of potent forces that work to pull it apart can make you a more influential and effective manager.

One manager we know who discovered this feature of teams called it a "mystic new power." Yet another was happily surprised when he learned how committed people could become to a team and its work once they felt part of it and, through it, part of something larger than themselves.

These managers came to appreciate the possibilities of *managing a group as a whole*. They learned to rely more and more on building commitment through the team, on using the "subtle pressure" of team goals and values to stretch performance. They found they could influence individual behavior much more effectively this way because all of us are social creatures who want to do something important and who, especially, want to fit in and be accepted as "part of the team."

The Four Elements of Building and Sustaining a Real Team

What it takes to create and manage a team can be summarized in four tasks, each of which is explored in the four chapters of this section.

Chapter 8, Define the Future. Does your team know where it's going? Can you and your people describe the future you're trying to create? Above all, does your team have a compelling common purpose and specific, challenging goals focused on that purpose? By *purpose* we mean not the work your group has been given but the benefits it provides to others, the role it plays in the larger scheme of things, the reason it matters in the organization and the world.

Chapter 9, Be Clear About How Your Team Works. Besides purpose and goals, team members need clarity about who does what, how work gets done, and how people work together. Purpose, goals, and team culture—the values, assumptions, beliefs, and practices shared by all members—are what can make a group into a real team

Chapter 10, Your Team Members Are Individuals Too. For all the emphasis on creating a team, you cannot ignore the individuals involved. Here we consider the basics of managing people—hiring, managing performance, developing—but always in the context of the team.

Chapter 11, Manage Through Your Daily Work. Virtually all management work comes down to what you do every day, day after day. This is where you create and manage your team. It's where you "do" management, where you actually practice your purpose and pursue your goals. Effective managers use the daily work—the fragmented, unplanned problems and opportunities that come at them every day—to make progress toward achieving their goals.

Many managers think of chapter 11, managing the daily work, as the heart of what they do because it focuses on their day-to-day activities. But the topics covered in all four chapters are part of creating and sustaining a productive team.

The burden of putting all these pieces in place and maintaining them in a tumultuous world falls on you. Most teams underperform. Too many forces, especially those we described in chapter 1 around the paradoxes, work to pull them apart. Management does make the difference.

Notice here that we're shifting our focus. Until now, in parts I and II, we've focused on the *interpersonal* aspects of management—exerting influence through your one-on-one relationships with others as a boss and a colleague. But here in part III, we go further because effective management requires more than personal interaction. It requires impersonal *systems through which you influence others*, including purpose, goals, roles, standard practices, values and expectations, feedback systems, and many more.

Effective teams are built around such systems, not on the interpersonal relationships between manager and members. Systems lift management from the mere supervision of moment-by-moment activity, allow bosses to manage large groups, and create the boundaries within which subordinates can act with autonomy. To create and manage a team, you must learn to develop and use such systems.

Systems provide an important benefit personal interaction cannot. They help you influence those on your team who report not to you directly but to one of your direct reports. Because you don't deal as personally and regularly with these people, you have fewer opportunities to influence them directly. Management systems let you influence the work of everyone on your team, not just those who work for you personally. Without them, you'll never be able to lead a team with more people than you can deal with face-to-face. Systems let you manage large groups, including large organizations.

As you make progress and take on larger groups and more responsibility, your ability to influence your *in*direct reports through management systems will become increasingly important.

As an organizational and management device, teams are growing more and more important. They offer a more flexible response to the challenges posed by technology, globalization, and competition. No wonder the ability to create and manage a true team is a crucial management skill—*the* key management skill, some would argue—whether you manage a permanent group of direct reports or a virtual, highly diverse, widely dispersed, temporary team created to deal with a specific problem or opportunity. In fact, these are the characteristics any group, even those without a designated leader, must possess to become an effective team: a mutual sense of why it exists and where it's going, a strong team culture, and some way for each member to satisfy his or her individual needs through participation in the team.

Teams are so important now that inability to build and lead an effective team is becoming a key derailer of high-potential managers.[2]

What about the group of people you manage? Is it a real team or just a group of people who work together?

8

DEFINE THE FUTURE

Manage for a World of Change

12:15 p.m.   Jason sits eating lunch with Roberto Lujan in a pub down the street from the office. It's the first lunch out Jason has taken all week. This is an important conversation with a new key player.

Roberto is an Argentinean whose work with the IFTE a few years ago and UNESCO more recently brought him in daily contact with hundreds of schools in emerging economies around the world. He joined Project Emerge only a week before Jason arrived.

As manager of school relations, he's in charge of the day-to-day working relationships with schools that offer Project Emerge courses—the administration, testing, certifying, and tutorial parts of each course. His arrival was timed to coincide with launching the program to sign up schools for the coming fall term. Working with Laraba Sule in marketing and the IT department, he's designing a series of Web-based procedures to support schools and their students.

After they chat about their backgrounds and families, Jason asks Roberto, "Do you have any questions? I'm still new, but I'll do my best to answer them."

"I do have questions," he says, "based on impressions from my two weeks. The first is this: is Project Emerge an important project?"

It's not the question Jason expected.

"Yes, of course," Jason says. "It's important for the company because it will be a more advanced line of product for us and it will open a significant new market for Reynolds, a market we haven't been able to reach easily or well through traditional ways of doing business." He's quoting now from the original proposal for Project Emerge. "In fact, it's expected to provide over 30 percent of the company's growth, maybe more, over the next few years."

Jason tries to read Roberto's face to see whether he's answering his question. But Roberto remains silent, and so Jason continues.

"You understand better than the rest of us what's driving this: the growing need in emerging markets for learning and education, a demand that local schools can't handle, especially in technical areas. Those economies need skilled, knowledgeable people to develop the technical and social infrastructures that advance prosperity and all the other good things that come with it: health, stability, literacy. In a sense, we're helping those societies lift themselves out of poverty."

Jason feels like he's delivering a speech. Yet Roberto listens attentively. Jason believes what he's saying, but he's not sure it needs saying outright. Isn't it understood? Of all people, doesn't Roberto know this already?

"Thank you," Roberto says finally. "Now I have one more question."

"What's that?"

"I've talked to many people as part of my orientation and my work in the two weeks since I joined Project Emerge. No one has ever talked about the importance of what we do, for the company or for schools and students in the developing world. Nor do I read of these things in the documents I see—except for the original project proposal, which now seems to sit on people's shelves no longer read."

From his folder, Roberto pulls a document Jason recognizes as that proposal. Roberto opens it and reads:

"To build a successful business by fostering the growth and development of emerging economies through partnering with local institutions to provide world-class, easily accessible, inexpensive technical education."

"Why," he continues, "do we not hear more of this? It seems that everyone focuses entirely on doing their jobs of signing up schools and finishing the first course."

"You're right," Jason says. "No one spoke to me about those things either."

"No one I talked to," Roberto says, "ever described what we do in that context. No one seemed to see themselves connected to those great commercial and social purposes. Isn't it better when we do our work in the conscious awareness of where we're all going together and why? Perhaps people would get along better if we did."

Do you and your group know where you're going? Have you defined and communicated the future you want and the steps that will take you there? Are you pursuing a clear purpose and related goals? Do you talk about such things?

It's important to do this. Yet many managers say they're simply carried along by events. They don't act or make decisions in conscious pursuit of some longer-term goal. They just respond as best they can, moment to moment, problem to problem, to keep the work flowing.[1]

No question, preparing for the future is difficult. Seeing what's ahead and making accurate forecasts is nearly impossible. Time for planning and implementation eludes most managers. The pressures of today almost always trump the needs of tomorrow.

This chapter is about how you prepare for the future as a manager: why you have no choice but to look ahead, the benefits of defining where you're going, the key elements of a plan (a road map for getting to the future you want), some guidelines, and how to guide your group through the kind of difficult change the future often brings.

Why Must You Worry About the Future?

Some managers are slow to realize that their responsibilities go beyond simply keeping their groups running smoothly today. They're also responsible for the future and the results they produce there.

Do you feel responsible for the future? Pay attention, because it will inevitably be different from today—for three reasons:

You want it to be different. You and your group aspire to be better—faster, cheaper, higher quality. Or you want to grow. Or you want to innovate.

Your organization wants it to be different. It's pursuing a new strategy. Or the people you serve and depend on, who make up your network, are changing.

Outside forces are changing the world around you no matter what you want. Even if you continue doing the same work, the context in which you operate is constantly shifting, and you must adapt. Your only choice is to move forward or lose ground.

Preparing for these changes is called "making a plan," which, too often for many managers, consists of a document in a notebook identifying steps they will take next month, next year, sometime in the future.

But a plan is more than a to-do list with dates. It's about defining and proactively creating the future you want—what many refer to as thinking strategically, not just tactically. Strategic thinking focuses on the longer range and what's important if you want to achieve your goals not just now but into the future. It's about asking such basic questions as, "What are we really trying to do?" or "Should we change the way we do our work in some basic way—is there a better way?" or "What will we be doing in the future and how will that differ from our work now?" On the other hand, tactical thinking is about the short term and focuses on accomplishing today's work on time, on budget, and per specification.

Some people will tell you that strategic thinking is the province of only senior managers and executives. We disagree. All managers at all levels must concern themselves with both the short term and the long term, the tactical and the strategic, within the context of the groups they run. That's why your plan needs to be much more than a schedule of near-term activities.

Done well, a plan defines the meaning and context of the work you and your team do, identifies the forces shaping your world, and describes both the future you want and your strategies for creating it. In short, it's the foundation for virtually everything you do as a manager. When we refer to *planning* or your *plan*, we're referring to all those elements, not that notebook gathering dust in your bookcase.

What Are the Benefits of Defining the Future?

The benefits are many.

Defining the Future Fosters Commitment Within Your Team by Imbuing Its Work with Purpose

It makes explicit that you're all *doing* something worthwhile together, and so it fosters that sense of shared purpose, that sense of "we" common to every effective team.

People relate to worthwhile purposes and goals. Most of us want to feel part of something larger and more important than ourselves. When workers were asked how important it was that their lives be meaningful, 83 percent said "very important" and another 15 percent said "fairly important."[2] That's an astounding 98 percent to whom it was at least "important." Is it important to you and those who work for you? Most likely, it is.

The same survey revealed that less than half of all employees in every industry studied felt strongly connected to their company's purpose. Most organizations—whether a small group or a large company—are missing a great opportunity by not focusing more on why they do what they do and why they matter in the world.

"Well," we sometimes hear managers say, "it's easy to find real purpose in some lines of work—like health care or education. But it's not easy in most." When someone says that, we think of a story we heard about employees in a pet food plant who were asked to write a mission statement, a description of their fundamental purpose. What they produced didn't mention "excellence" or talk about making the "best" pet food. It began, "Pets are important to people." Those workers didn't just make pet food. They contributed to the happiness of people who owned pets.

Purpose is possible in any field. The survey just cited also revealed that at least 25 percent of workers in retail, finance, and chemical manufacturing—not fields known for their inherent "good of mankind" motives—strongly felt their work was important because of their company's purpose. Almost all work, directly or indirectly, immediately or ultimately, provides benefit for someone or some group. Identify that customer or ultimate user, and the benefit, and you're well on your way to finding a compelling purpose.

We know a hospital administrator who discovered, when he told everyone that janitors were members of the infectious disease control staff, the janitors felt more pride in what they did and the quality of their work improved. They were part of something important: protecting patients and staff from infection.

No job is meaningless. Identifying purpose and making it explicit can transform a job into a calling instead of a career stepping-stone or just a way to pay the rent.

In a virtual workplace, where members of a group rarely gather face-to-face, a strong sense of purpose can be the glue that holds them all together.

Defining the Future Gives Everyone on Your Team a Common Goal and Direction

Specific goals and objectives anchor purpose in tangible reality and satisfy people's desire to strive toward something both challenging and meaningful. Clear goals foster that sense of "we" at the heart of every real team by helping team members pull together toward the same destination. In a study of group performance, only those groups with a challenging goal were able to create the internal bonds that convert a collection of people into a true team.[3]

A related benefit is that a plan, especially the process of developing it, can help surface any cultural or generational differences that group members bring to their collective work. Once surfaced, such issues can be worked through and resolved. In the same way, having a clear plan can foster cooperation between different groups.

Defining the Future Keeps You, Your Team, and Your Network Focused on What's Important

A plan gives you perspective for making decisions. It provides a framework, a set of guidelines, for how to assign resources and make choices. It will help all concerned concentrate on what will produce the results you want, even in the midst of daily crises and chaos. It will tell you, as manager, where to focus special attention, where to stay involved, and even where you may need to immerse yourself in the ongoing details. Being "managerial" or "strategic" doesn't mean staying above everything. It means staying in close touch with the right things, the strategies and initiatives that truly matter, without doing the work yourself or micromanaging those who do.

Defining the Future Is a Source of Trust and Influence

Justifying your needs in terms of where you're going is a powerful argument. How is your boss likely to respond if you say, "We need another person," versus "With another person, we can reach our goal of increasing output 50 percent next year." People and groups who know where they're going have more influence than other groups, especially when their plans are in sync with the larger organization.

Defining the Future Will Reduce Conflict

We pointed out in chapter 5 how organizations tend to generate conflict that can be both destructive and constructive. Defining the future around a worthwhile purpose and related challenging goals can help minimize the destructive conflict and "politics" that can sap a firm's vitality. If every group in an organization feels united by an overall purpose, that sense of common cause can serve as the social glue that overcomes their differences. Conversely, the lack of a uniting purpose will only foster the sense of "maximize me, minimize you" that leads to destructive political conflict.

Defining the Future Is the Basis for Your Strategic Network

Without a plan, you cannot define your future needs and priorities and how they'll differ from today's. Without that knowledge, you cannot identify the individuals and groups who may not be important to you today but will be tomorrow.

Defining the Future Will Help You Center Your Relationships with Your People Around the Work

In part I we discussed the need to keep relationships with your people centered on the work. A plan makes that work real and specific, especially as it defines the responsibilities of each team member. Carrying out the plan is what the relationship is about. At the same time, your plan can serve as a key component of the trust you need from your people. Pulling together a compelling plan helps demonstrate and define the competence and character that generate trust in you. A manager with a plan is far more likely to be trusted than one who stumbles from crisis to crisis.

Defining the Future Will Help You Deal with Unforeseen Change

Paradoxically, making a plan is worthwhile even if conditions change and you cannot pursue it as intended. Planning *is* worthwhile because the process of thinking about the future will prepare you for contingencies. Dwight Eisenhower, allied commander and later U.S. president, led the landings in Normandy on D-day in 1944 that turned the course of World War II in Europe. After all the planning required by that immensely complicated operation, he concluded, "Plans are nothing. Planning is everything."[4] Few plans survive contact with reality completely intact. If you've prepared a plan thoughtfully, and considered alternatives and contingencies carefully, you'll be better positioned to deal with whatever arises.

Defining the Future Is Crucial to the Success of Virtual Teams

For virtual teams, that sense of shared purpose and goals can form bonds among members, even when they lack the daily interaction that creates ties among members of colocated teams.[5] In short, defining the future creates the context for virtually all you do as a manager. It helps you create the right relationships with your people and assess daily problems so emergencies are less likely to supplant what's truly important. Not only will a plan help you identify who should be in your network, it will help you use your network more effectively. A plan creates a context for delegation by making clear what activities are most important and should be delegated with greater care. A plan also creates a framework for making ethical judgments by helping you weigh the conflicting needs of stakeholders—in short, by helping define *a greater good*.

If you're a producing manager, a plan will help you balance your dual responsibilities for both personal accomplishment and management.[6] It's easy for producing managers to slight their management duties because the pressure to produce as individuals always feels more tangible and urgent than the requirements of being a boss.

So never think of your plan as a mere document in a notebook you put on the shelf. It should be something you and your people live and breathe every day as a way to focus effort, screen activities, and manage time. A good plan invests everything you do with vital meaning and provides a framework for dealing with whatever arises.

Have you and your group defined the future you want? Do you have a plan? Does it play the key roles just outlined?

Written and Unwritten Plans

Too many managers and organizations think of a plan only as a written document, frozen in time, a rigid view of the future. Indeed, we strongly suggest you write it down because that will encourage you to communicate your goals and involve others. But don't think of that written document as your "plan." It's only a part, an out-come or artifact, of something bigger: your unwritten plan.

Your unwritten plan is far broader than your written plan. Your unwritten plan exists in your mind as a living, evolving under-standing of *what* you do, *where* you're going, *why* you're going there, and *how* you're going to get there.

As these elements become clear and you're confident enough to share them with others and to commit to them publically, you will write them down in a formal document called "your plan." That document may seem complete and final, but it will always be only a part of your thinking about the future. That sum total of your thinking about what's ahead we're calling your *unwritten plan*, for lack of a better term, to distinguish it from the formal, written plan documents you periodically prepare.

Think of your written plan as a partial snapshot of your unwrit-ten plan at a given moment. That written plan will differ from your broader, more fluid, and more disorganized unwritten plan in key ways.

Your written plan will cover the near future—say, one year—and may even look out a few years. *Your unwritten plan, however, antic-ipates what is coming over the distant horizon, where things are still out of focus.* Even if you cannot see clearly, you still need to look out as far as possible to discern thunderclouds or clearing skies on the distant horizon. As that hazy future comes closer and more into focus, you can incorporate what you see in your written plans.

Your written plan will include specific objectives, milestones, action steps, and clear assumptions. *Your unwritten plan tends much more to include gut feel, fuzzy goals, general direction, and broad priorities.* Over time, as you persistently gather information and test ideas and approaches, you'll move many of these elements from fuzzy to focused, vague to specific, unspoken to written.

Your unwritten plan will include your evolving evaluation of the people on your team. As manager, you must constantly assess your people's ability to carry out their present and future responsibili-ties. Some of this you will write down and some you will not.

Your unwritten plan also includes your evolving thoughts about your network and its ability to support your current and future plans. What will you need from your colleagues? What new demands will they place on you? How will your plans change your network, who's in it, and how it works? Who might oppose your plans and why? Some of this thinking may find its way into your written plans, but much will not.

Your Unwritten Plan Exists at Two Levels

First, it's unwritten and unspoken. Here it comprises a set of thoughts, ideas, possibilities, potential goals and priorities, bits of information, hunches, and opinions that exist only in your mind (or in notes and disjointed fragments you've written down) because they haven't yet congealed into something you can express and discuss coherently. Nonetheless, this is a critical stage, one that you need to feed with a constant stream of new information of all kinds—hard data, opinions, impressions, gossip, and so on— from many places. This is one reason you need a strategic network.

The second level of your unwritten plan is still unwritten but now it's spoken. It consists of ideas developed enough that you put them out for discussion with others in your group or network. Here you may start informally writing them down in order to share them, though they're still semiformed and perhaps even inconsistent and somewhat incoherent. But they're formed enough that you can explore them with others.

Important: encourage others to reveal the ideas and hunches forming inside their minds. The best plans *emerge* through a rich exchange of ideas and input from a diversity of sources.[7] As they emerge, they constantly change through a never-ending process that's partly rational and partly unconscious, messy, murky, and creative. Software platforms that ease the sharing of ideas, encourage collaborative development, and foster the process of emergence can be invaluable for this purpose.

In sum, a written plan covers only those portions of your thinking that are clear, specific, focused, thought through, and ready to go public as a formal (and often official) document bearing the title "Plan." Unwritten plans consist of your and your group's thoughts—ranging from vague hunches to roughly written ideas—about the future and how all of you will create it. Formal, written plans are prepared at key points, while unwritten plans are living, dynamic possibilities that constantly change as you learn more from experience and carry on discussions with your people and network. Gradually, much of your unwritten plan will find its way into some official, public written plan, but not all of it.

We will focus here on your written plan. But remember that it's only an artifact of the forward thinking that should always be going on inside your head or in discussion with others.

The Three Key Elements of a Written Plan

Every organization makes plans, ranging from simple one-year budgets to elaborate strategic forecasts. And every organization has its own planning process. Consequently, instead of explaining how to plan, we describe three core elements of defining the future that you can apply to whatever planning your organization does. If some of this information is not formally required by your organization, prepare it nonetheless for yourself, your team, and your network colleagues.

Here are the key elements of a written plan:

1. Be clear about where you are now.

2. Define where you want to be in the future.

3. Identify how you will get from the present to that future.

Most likely, you will perform these steps in sequence, but be aware that they're a perpetual loop of activity. As you act and get feedback on each step, you will adapt and revise your plans.

1. Be Clear About Where You Are Now

Most organizations neglect or undervalue this step on the optimistic assumption that everyone knows where they are. That's a mistake. Begin your plan with a clear statement of where you are now, being sure to include not only what you do but for whom and why you do it. This is the first step in creating a plan driven by a sense of purpose.

Use these questions as guides in defining where you and your team are now:

What do you do? What work does your group literally and physically perform? Describe your team's work, including critical tasks and metrics, such as sales, costs, and other performance indicators, that define your current work.

For whom do you do it? Who's your customer, whether internal or external? Who depends on and benefits from what you do? Who's not your customer? What benefits aren't you going to provide to your customers?

Why do you do it—what fundamental purpose do you serve? What value, what benefits, do you add? Why is what you do important? How do your efforts fit into the larger organization and contribute to its overall goals? Take care with this answer; it gets at something critical: your purpose. If you disappeared today, how and for whom would the world be different tomorrow? Why do you matter?

How do you do what you do? How are you organized? How do you divide up responsibilities within your group? Are there other ways to do it? Why have you chosen the path you are pursuing?

What key problems do you face? What challenges keep you from performing as well as you could? How are you currently addressing them?

Do you know the answers to these questions? Would everyone you work with agree with your responses? The process of documenting and sharing them with others is a first step in getting people involved and committed. If you're in a new managerial position, working through these questions will help you learn as well.

Try to see your group as outsiders see it. Not everyone will view you in the same way, and few, if any, will perceive you as you do. For every outside stakeholder, ask the critical question raised above: how would their world be different tomorrow if your group disappeared today?

2. Define Where You Want to Be in the Future

Take a proactive view of your future. What would you like your future to be? Obviously, what actually happens will be a result of both your own actions and forces outside your control, but you needn't be the victim of those forces. Your actions can make a significant difference.

Don't plan by viewing the future as a series of steps starting from where you are now. That will make the future you envision merely an extension of the present and the way you do things now. You'll be trapped by the way you see the world today. Instead, in your imagination, leap to the future you want and describe that world. Then figure out how to get from here to there.

Think of the future not merely in terms of what will be expected of you and your group then. Think about what your group *could* do, the opportunities available, if it were operating at the highest level it's capable of attaining.

When you imagine the future, focus on two different time periods: one year and the distant horizon. Three years makes sense for most businesses, though the nature of some businesses requires longer leaps. For those two future points—one year and three or more years out—answer the following questions:

What forces will shape the future? What trends and forces in your team, organization, industry, and market will create change in your world? Is the market shifting? Is your organization changing? What are customers doing and how are they changing? Competitors? You cannot define the future with great clarity. Instead, the goal is to define it enough to provide direction—to determine "this way, not that." Consider both problems and opportunities. Do scenario planning around the key forces at work. What is the best and worst case for you around these forces, and how would you react to each? If you're in an industry dependent on oil, for example, consider the consequences of oil prices at the high and low extremes. Pay particular attention to where your company or organization is going and the effects of that on your goals, strategies, and plans. Your strategic network, particularly your weak ties with those whose worlds extend beyond yours, will be invaluable as you scan the horizon for the forces that will shape your world.

What will you do in that new world? Given all those ways the world will be different, combined with your aspirations to perform differently or better, define the future you and your group want. In that future, what will your group literally and physically do? As best you can, describe your work in the future, including estimates for the performance indicators used in describing current work. Add new indicators if necessary.

Why and for whom will you do what you do? Will your purpose change? Who will be your customer or ultimate user? Who will depend on you and benefit from your work? What value will you add for your future customer? Why will your work be important to that user? Will your customers remain the same but have different needs, or will you be serving new customers?

How will you do it? What will be the key activities in your work? How will they be divided among your group? If nothing specific will force you to change, then ask yourself, If we were starting over, would we work the way we do now?

How will your future work fit into the larger organization? How will you contribute to the overall purpose and goals of your organization as it evolves and changes?

What key problems will you face? What challenges in the future might keep you from performing well? How might forces beyond your control present obstacles? How will you deal with them?

What key opportunities are likely to appear? Are there major shifts or developments ahead that you can seize and take advantage of? Technical innovations, legal or regulatory changes, or industry consolidations, for example?

If your view of the future were a photograph, some parts of the picture would be in focus, and others fuzzy. No one can divine the future in detail, and when your work is inherently innovative, you may not even be able to forecast the exact direction the future will take. Here the definition of purpose—describing how and why your work will matter in the future—can play an important role.

Defining the future you want is at the heart of your management responsibilities. Both your organization and your team count on you to look ahead, imagine the possibilities, discern the threats, alert your team (and others), mobilize it to respond, and manage the tensions between staying the course and making significant change.

3. Identify How You Will Get from the Present to the Future

Only after you define the future can you consider how to move from here to there.

What can you do to create that future? Are there forces at work that create opportunities for you? How will you deal with the forces working against you?

This "how to get there" will become your actual plan—the strategies, milestones, and activities that will take you there.

The line between this step and the previous—where you're going and how you'll get there—is often blurred. In fact, a useful way to proceed is to move back and forth between the two steps by conducting experiments or even by simply letting people try a variety of different things.

Take small actions. Identify the assumptions behind your thinking and test them. Test ideas. Talk to ten customers or end users. Make trial runs. Create mockups and show them to users. Try something on a small scale, improvise, and see what happens. Allow others to do the same. Too much chaos is a bad thing, but so is rigidity that ignores a changing world.

It's another paradox that management and planning require both chaos and order, and your job is to understand when one versus the other is the right course. Above all, don't try to figure out what to do by sitting in a room and "planning." Instead, as Andy Grove, former head of Intel, the premier computer chip maker, said, "Let chaos reign, then rein in chaos."[8]

To map your route into the future, ask these kinds of questions:

Given how you identified the future you want, how would you summarize the key ways your future work will differ from your current work? Identify where change will be necessary. Will the work itself be different? Will you serve new customers? Will you deliver your work in different ways? Estimate future performance metrics. Will sales increase? By how much? Costs? Don't ignore aspects of work that can't be easily measured, such as your basic purpose or the benefits your work provides to others.

What are the key strategies, the critical activities, that will produce the change you want? Great success seldom comes from doing twenty things right. More often, it's the result of focusing on the right one, two, or three big things. What are those? Where will increased sales come from, if that's your goal? Will you sell more to current customers? Or will you develop new products or services that appeal to whole new groups of buyers? These are your strategies, levers, or priorities where everyone must concentrate their efforts.

To create strategies, you must look behind a flurry of discrete facts, results, impressions, and ideas and synthesize what you see and know. What we said about plans in general applies in particular here. Strategies often emerge. After the fact, managers like to think they consciously and carefully figured everything out in the beginning. More likely, the approaches they chose emerged from trying lots of different options and paying careful attention to the outcomes.

For each strategy, what are the key action steps and milestones? These will help you determine whether you are making progress, need to make corrections, or even should rethink targets and strategies.

What is the role each member of your team will play? Relate everyone's role to the targets, key changes, and strategies you've identified. You want everyone to see the connection between their work, the work of the group, and the work required to create the future you want.

What new competencies will you need, and where will you get them? Almost certainly your group will need new knowledge, skills, and perhaps even new values. Where will you find them? You have two choices: hire new team members or develop current members. Probably you'll pursue some combination of the two.

Look at the current competencies of your team members, and then look at the competencies needed to carry out your strategies and plans. The gap between the two will tell you where you need to develop or find new capabilities.

Once you've taken these steps, you should be able to ask any member of your team the following question and receive the same answer: *what are the key targets we're trying to achieve, and what are the few key strategies or areas of focus that will get us there?*

Your Plan and Your Company Plan

Most companies require all managers to create some sort of plan. In our experience, such plans often fall short of what we've defined above. Company plans typically focus on the financial aspects of the business—they're budgets, in other words—because they're aimed at helping the company hit its financial targets, with too little attention given to what will produce the numbers. In our approach, numbers—metrics—are critical but aren't necessarily ends in themselves; instead, they're a way of expressing a reality you're trying to create. Focus on the reality behind the numbers and what will create it.

If your organization's plans are mostly financial, you still must understand the goals and strategies behind the numbers, even if they're not widely communicated. They're the context for what you do. You may need to uncover them by talking to your boss, using your network (again, the value of far-flung weak ties), studying company Web sites and documents, and looking at commentary by outside analysts.

Prepare a written plan as we've described it for your group and your network, including your boss. Most likely, it can serve as the basis for whatever plan your company requires. If your company also requires information or elements we've not included, you must include them, of course.

How Do You Define the Future?

Based on the experience of seasoned managers, here are some further questions that embody suggestions for thinking about the future.

Do You Involve Others in Planning?

Don't plan by going off alone and returning with a plan engraved in stone. Your plans and goals must fit within and serve the larger organization. You're not free to wander off on your own. Thinking about the future needs to incorporate the ideas of others. Working as a team, and with others in your network, means you develop a view of the future that all members find appealing and can strive toward together. Work hard to include distant team and network members.

Involve your boss in your planning—not just the development of a written plan but also the unwritten plan that's constantly evolving in your mind. Make him a partner, an influential ally, and a valuable source of information, guidance, and evolving ideas about the future.

Involve your network, too, as you make plans. Share with network colleagues the future you want to create, and talk to them about their plans, both written and unwritten.

Do You Use Technology to Help with the Planning Process?

Technology can play a key role in creating both your unwritten and written plans. If possible in your organization, set up and use social networking tools and collaboration platforms to develop the plan and manage around it, starting with the development and sharing of thoughts and ideas about the future and then going on to reach consensus about your current work, outlining a more definitive view of the future you want, and making plans for creating that future—strategies, plans, milestones, roles, and priorities. You can also use such technology for tracking progress against plans and overall for keeping the discussion open as to where you're going, how, and why.

Do You Stay Open to New Information and the Possibility of Change?

You should be gathering new information, testing assumptions, trying alternatives, looking for oncoming problems and opportunities all the time. Remain open to anything new that touches your world. Remain skeptical of even your own assumptions about the future. Test and confirm them again and again. We're certainly not suggesting change for the sake of change—remaining steadfast is often the right course—but that you remain open to the possibility of change.

Are You Aware of Cultural Differences That Can Affect Planning?

If the group you manage is multicultural, consider how diverse cultural attitudes may influence your plans and their implementation. Cultures can differ in their fundamental beliefs about how much we control our futures, the importance of deadlines, the need to establish social relationships before team members can work together, tolerance for uncertainty and ambiguity, and even whether change is inherently positive or negative. Learn the cultural attitudes that your team members are likely to bring to their work, never forgetting that individuals' attitudes within a culture can vary widely. Talk explicitly about such matters and manage expectations carefully. If a deadline is truly important, for example, you may need to manage it closely.

Do You Focus on Opportunities and Strengths More Than Problems and Weaknesses?

Too many managers we've seen define themselves primarily as problem solvers and perfection seekers. While you do need to solve problems and perfection is an ideal, they are not where you should focus. Your most important job is to achieve results now and in the future. You do that by identifying and exploiting opportunities and strengths. These might include ways to grow, grow faster, cut expenses, develop new markets, and so on. To repeat a critical point: success almost invariably comes from finding the few opportunities that are truly important and then using strengths to take advantage of them. Do identify weaknesses that can harm you and your group, do keep them from derailing you, but don't fool yourself that removing all weakness is the goal or that resolving problems by itself will produce the future you want.[9]

Getting to the Future—Guiding Your Group Through Difficult Change

Your plans will inevitably call for changes in your group and its work. Some changes, even those that are technically challenging, will be possible to make using your group's current knowledge, roles, skills, and values, but some will require far more difficult adaptations. For these, the group will need to develop new knowledge and skills, take on new roles, alter basic patterns of work, and adopt new values, all while giving up familiar approaches that no longer work. Guiding your people through change of all kinds is a key part of creating the future you want, but guiding them through the changes that require more fundamental adaptations can present special challenges.

The challenges arise from what's required of the people involved. Change does generate resistance, but not because people automatically resist it. They don't. How many of us wear the same clothes and eat the same food every day, if we have a choice, and how many of us would refuse a lottery jackpot simply because that much money would change our lives?

People fear *loss*, and they resist change because of the losses they fear it will bring—in the influence they wield; in the value of the knowledge, skills, and competencies they've worked so hard to develop; in key relationships; in rewards; and even in the loyalties they feel to people (colleagues, friends, family, a valued mentor) and groups (ethnic, religious, corporate) with which they identify. Fostering change that threatens to create such losses will test your management skills. That is the kind of change we focus on now.

Suppose sales of a key service your team provides are suddenly down significantly. Some initial inquiries reveal a new competitor is drawing away buyers because it offers similar services at a price 20 percent below yours. You bring it up with your team. At first, some members express disbelief or skepticism. How can anyone offer quality service at that price? Others are shaken. How can we meet or beat that price? Some even rant a bit about customer loyalty and maintaining quality standards. What's potentially at stake here is the way you do business. What may be required is more than minor adjustments.

Here is where you must understand the dynamics of change and how to help a group move from a status quo that's no longer tenable to a different future.

The Dynamics of Change

Successful change contains three components:

A change process. Change occurs through a series of steps that include events, decisions, policies, meetings, other forms of communication, actions, and practices. Think of these steps as a process guided by you that unites the other elements and ultimately leads to a good outcome.

Dissatisfaction. People involved will rarely change unless they're unhappy and uncomfortable with the status quo. This is why it often requires a crisis to bring about dramatic change. But the costs of a crisis are usually high, and so it's better to build dissatisfaction before a situation turns critical. A general sense of unhappiness, however, isn't enough. Unless people see the connection between their actions and the status quo they dislike, the problem will belong to someone else in their eyes, and they're unlikely to feel any need for personal change.

Identification of a better way. To change, people also need to see a better world in the future. Where dissatisfaction *pushes* them away from the status quo, a better world *pulls* them toward something different and attractive. Difficult change requires both.

Now it's clear why formal authority cannot bring about change. You cannot order people to ignore the losses they fear. You cannot demand that they be dissatisfied with the current state of affairs. And you cannot dictate a new world they will find attractive. You can only encourage these things. For change to happen, the people involved must reach their own conclusions.

Do You Know How to Foster Dissatisfaction?

Short of a genuine crisis, the key ways to create dissatisfaction are through information and discussion.[10]

In the previous example, you and your team might study the competitive offering in some detail, talk to former customers who now use it, and do some additional market research. That will let you determine whether the problem is real. If it is, the data will help to convince your group that it must do something because the situation cries out for change. Use your authority not to decree a problem—people may or may not accept your assessment—but to focus people's time and attention on activities, like market research, that will let them discover the problem themselves.

You can also foster dissatisfaction through instilling a culture of continuous improvement or instituting ongoing practices like benchmarking, where you constantly compare your group's performance with that of others. Such steps can get people's attention or create dissatisfaction when business is good. We know of a manager in a mining company with record profits, but the profits came from an unprecedented spike in commodity prices, not from exceptional productivity or superb efficiency. This manager reframed the goal by changing his message from "increasing profits" to "reducing costs." When his group compared their costs to those of competitors, they could see for themselves the necessity of improvement.

Still, some team members are likely to resist. Regarding the example above, for example, they might say the problem's not so serious—the competitor will soon have to raise prices, or past customers will stick with you because of loyalty and quality, or the research you did was flawed and the data is wrong.

Recognize that you, the one pushing the need to change, will attract controversy and people's negativity. Sooner or later, some team members will turn to you and demand to know how you, the authority figure, are going to solve this problem. Their dissatisfaction will settle on you. After all, solving problems is your job, isn't it? Some will even say, "Our problem's not the competition. It's a lack of leadership." You may even be tempted to buy this point of view if you conceive of your role as the one who solves all problems. This is a serious trap. If you let it, the problem will soon become you, not the competition.

When people resist in these ways, it's critical to keep the discussion going, which is why process is important. You need forums where analysis and discussion can continue. As you talk, your task is to keep the group focused on the problem and its reality, not on you or some other easy way of avoiding the need to change. Your persistent message must be, "What we face is real. It won't go away. We must deal with it. We can solve it if *together* we face it and work to find a solution." Holding fast, not letting the group find some easy way out, can require great endurance and fortitude.

You will know people are sufficiently dissatisfied when they say, "There *is* a problem, it's *our* problem, and *we* have to find a solution." At this point, they will be ready to sit down and talk seriously about what they need to do.

Do You Know How to Identify a Better Way?

The common name for "a better way" is vision. Conventional wisdom about change and management says that you, the person in charge, are supposed to develop a vision and sell its glittering promise to your people. You're the one who cries out, "Follow me! I know the way!"

For many challenges and changes, this approach works fine. When the challenge is straightforward and well understood, when your group already possesses the necessary knowledge, skills, values, and practices, then you and your people can quickly agree on an approach, set goals, make plans, marshal resources, and move forward quickly.

However, other challenges—like the need for your group to deal with a low-price competitor—are more difficult. The solution isn't clear. There's no obvious way forward. To find a way, you must involve all stakeholders, including your team, networks, and, not least, your boss—each of which will bring different experience, expertise, needs, and goals to the issue. At this stage, these players recognize and accept responsibility for the problem. Now your challenge is to continue the discussion and develop jointly a shared vision.

The goal is both to define a new, better world where the challenge you face will be resolved, and to define how you will get there. Obviously, you cannot define a future world in great detail, but you need a collective vision that not only is attractive and provides useful guidance but also leaves room for new ideas and learning and can accommodate a changing world.

These discussions about how to move forward will inevitably create conflict, and that's good. People will propose vastly different approaches and defend their positions vehemently because they fear the loss of something important, such as jobs, status, relationships, or the status that comes from knowledge and competence built up through years of experience. Only through creative and constructive disagreement can good ideas surface and be thoroughly examined. So foster the expression of ideas and full discussion, however difficult.

Keep the team focused on resolving the challenge. Manage conflict to keep it creative and task related, rather than personal and destructive.[11] The more painful the process becomes, the more people will try to avoid it, leap to quick, short-term solutions, or throw it back on you. Again, don't let yourself become the problem.

A vision of the future—the solution to the problem, how it will work, how you'll implement it, and the expected outcome—is important. But it must emerge from the group and its deliberations. Only then will it be a shared vision that all are committed to implementing, however difficult.

Do You Pay Enough Attention to the Change Process?

Real change is unlikely without a change process. Whatever the series of specific steps your process comprises, it should be *transparent* to all involved by making clear in advance how and when information will be gathered; what analysis will be done and when; where and how people will have an opportunity to express and test their ideas, opinions, and feelings; and how and when decisions will be made.

Focus on communication, communication, communication. Change and the process for deciding on change often emerges. You cannot define a detailed process in advance. But you can communicate at all stages what's being done and, better yet, involve others. Too often, managers remain silent because "we haven't decided yet—there's nothing to report." Keep people informed of both the process and any progress. Silence is quickly interpreted, right or wrong, as lack of concern, incompetence, and even malevolence.

Involve others. Throughout this discussion, we've stressed the importance of involving stakeholders at every step of the process. They include all the people involved or affected by the change: your people, network members, even outsiders in some cases, and certainly your boss. You may not include your boss in every discussion, but it's critical that she agree with your analysis of the problem and the need to act. She may even have thoughts about the changes required, which you will need to respect and somehow accommodate. Keep her informed, and think of her as a partner. Call on her as needed for help with her superiors and other parts of the organization.

Include your networks to create coalitions. If the change involves more than your group, involve your networks in assessing the problem, identifying options, and generating support for a new approach. You create support by building coalitions—groups of like-minded colleagues who all agree about the need for change and how it should be done.[12]

The ability to guide your people through this kind of difficult change—change that entails loss for stakeholders—is a critical skill for creating the future you want. Too many managers see themselves as the implementers or objects—the victims, even—of change instigated or imposed by others. To manage, be an agent of change.

Nothing you do as a manager will be more important than developing and pursuing a view of the future that you and your group want to create. Planning, defining that future, is a way of thinking, not just an occasional activity that produces a formal document called a "plan." Such a document should be a periodic artifact of a process that never ends. A clear sense of the future—where you, your group, and your organization are trying to go—is the framework for virtually all you do as a manager.

BE CLEAR ABOUT HOW YOUR TEAM WORKS

Foster the Right Team Culture

1:45 p.m. After lunch, Jason takes a short walk to think about his conversation with Roberto. *Why don't we talk more about Project Emerge's purpose? What we're doing is good for everyone.*

Now, as he returns, he again stops by Cavit's office in hopes of talking about getting salespeople assigned to Project Emerge and time allotted at Sales Conference. Cavit is there but unavailable. Jason stays a few minutes and chats with Cavit's assistant about finding a school for his children when (*if*, he thinks) they eventually move to London.

2:00 p.m. An e-mail arrives from Kathy Wu, the Project Emerge assistant editor in Boston. She wants to set a time to talk next week. Jason reads the two-line message three times. Setting up a formal phone appointment feels ominous. It crosses his mind she may be planning to quit because of her disagreements with Sumantra, who insists Jason is her boss because he's senior editor. Jason replies and offers some possible times.

2:06 p.m. He picks up the information from Sumantra about the IFTE and begins to look through it.

2:09 p.m.   Cavit's assistant calls and says, "Don't tell Jack I told you, but if you go to the smoking area behind the building, you'll find him there around 4:30. A word to the wise: let him have a puff or two before you interrupt him. He'll be much friendlier if you do."

2:14 p.m.   Jason hears raised voices somewhere across the open office area. He gets up to see what's going on.

The noise is coming from Laraba Sule's cubicle, where a small cluster of people is gathered around her computer: Laraba, Sumantra, Jay, Roberto, and Kim. As he approaches from behind them, he hears Jay's raised voice, followed by Sumantra's.

"You *cannot* use this content," says Sumantra, Project Emerge senior editor. "They have not allowed it. How can we work with the other imprints when you simply steal their content?"

"It's a *promotion* piece, Sumantra," says Jay, the online production manager. "We're not selling it. Nobody's paying for it. It's just information about the course." His rising anger and frustration are unmistakable.

"It's only an orientation piece, Sumantra," Laraba says, her voice both pleading and conciliatory. "It's not the course itself. Why would anyone care? This was due to the Web people yesterday. They're already angry at us, and if we don't give it to them now, we'll miss the revisions they're making in the company site. Why can't we use it?"

"Because in describing the Introduction to Programming course it shows content that we do not have permission to use. It describes a course we cannot offer in the form we're showing it."

"All right, Sumantra," says Jay. "Why don't you tell us why we can't use that content."

"The imprints that own it haven't given their permission."

"And why haven't they?" Jay asks belligerently.

"I don't . . . I suppose they wish to use the content themselves."

"What's stopping them? If we use the content, so what?"

"They think we are competing with them," Sumantra says.

"Really? Our course will only be available to students at schools in developing countries. That's not their market."

"They think we are preventing them from seeking that mar—"

"Look, Sumantra," Jay says, "I'll tell you the real problem. The real problem is you—you won't do your job. You're supposed to design the course *and* secure the material, but you don't have the courage—"

"Stop!" Jason calls out as he steps into the cubicle. Everyone turns and looks at him. "Jay, that's over the line."

Jay's face is flushed, his mouth set, eyes glaring. Sumantra looks at the floor, shocked. Laraba, mouth agape, looks from Jay to Jason and back.

"This discussion is over," Jason says. "Jay, bring the promo and come with me to room A. Sumantra, come to room A in fifteen minutes. The rest of you—please join us in about twenty minutes, and tell the others who aren't here to come too."

Jason stands and waits. Kim and Roberto step away silently. Sumantra slips away without looking at anyone. Laraba turns to her e-mail. Jay follows Jason to the meeting room.

Who can do good work in the midst of confusion about who does what, how the work gets done, how members work with each other, and how the team is doing?

These issues may not seem momentous—purpose and goals may seem more important and are certainly more glamorous—but they matter profoundly because they constitute the culture of your team.[1] Without the right culture, team members are unlikely to take responsibility for their work or commit themselves to it and the purpose and goals around it.

Think of culture as the infrastructure of a team, like the infrastructure of a society—the transport systems (roads, railroads, airports, canals), the education system, laws and regulations, governance structures (government, police, courts), trade agreements, and so on—that guides how that society functions. Infrastructure does nothing productive itself, but it makes everything else possible. Team culture, like infrastructure, *enables* productive work. If you get the culture wrong, nothing else your team does is likely to work well.

Culture is crucial to the trust that links team members because it defines what they expect of each other. Remember, we said trust is counting on someone to do the right thing. Culture defines "the right thing" within a group.

The right culture can reduce conflict and keep it productive. Culture defines how to handle many of the management paradoxes we outlined in chapter 1 that can create conflict—tension between individual and group, for example, or disagreement over work practices.

It can lift from your shoulders the burden of trying to manage by telling people what to do. With the right culture, you can motivate group members through group expectations, values, and practices. Instead of saying, "Do this because I'm telling you to do it," you say, in effect, "Do this because *the team expects it of you.*" Culture is a key system that makes management more than personal interaction between you and those who work for you.

As a management tool that doesn't depend on personal interaction, *culture is a useful way to manage team members who don't report directly to you.* It's a powerful tool of *indirect* influence that extends your influence beyond those in your immediate circle.

But understand that culture is about performance, not keeping team members happy. It's about doing good work. The right culture makes a team more effective at what it does. In fact, the members of an effective team may or may not be "happy" with the group all the time, but they care deeply about its performance and want to contribute to its success.

The Importance of Clarity

There are four critical elements of culture needed to create and sustain a team. You cannot impose on your team the culture you want, but you can influence it strongly. Most importantly, you can make sure the key components of culture are clear. As manager, you must ensure:

Clarity about individual roles—who does what and how each role contributes to the team's purpose and goals

Clarity about how the team does its work—work systems, practices, and processes

Clarity about how team members work together—the values and norms for collaboration that prescribe and guide interaction among group members

Clarity about progress—feedback for the team as a whole and for individual members about both work results and how well the group is functioning as a team

Clarity seldom happens or holds for long by itself. Group relationships and roles, especially in organizations passing through rapid change, tend to move toward confusion. It's no surprise that teams often underperform in spite of the advantages they offer. Preventing that slippage, ensuring ongoing clarity, is an important part of your job.

Clarity is challenging because it embodies another paradox: the need to be clear—"here's how we do what we do"—while remaining flexible in the midst of rapid change. It's a never-ending struggle to strike the right balance between order, stability, and predictability on one hand and flexibility and adaptation on the other.

A team's purpose and goals, the future it's trying to create, are the foundation of culture and must be clear. A team's plan defines the roles needed to do current and future work. Indeed, it defines the work itself and the values and beliefs needed to do it well. And much of the feedback you provide will be about progress against the plan. In working with your team to create and clarify the right culture, refer to the plan often, for team culture and plan cannot be separated.

Team Members Need Clarity About Their Roles

Each of your people needs to know:

What do I do? How can anyone feel responsible and work hard if they're confused about what they do, what results are expected of them, and how much freedom they have to act or make decisions?

How does my work support the purpose and work of the team? Making this connection is critical to ensuring each person feels like an essential and valued team member.

How does my work relate to the work of others on the team? To work effectively, members must understand their colleagues' roles, how their different roles fit together within the team, and what they can expect of each other.

You cannot eliminate all ambiguity or foresee all circumstances that might create role confusion. Nor should you strive for rigid, detailed job descriptions, because you want people willing on occasion to share roles or step outside their regular responsibilities.

Questions to Determine Whether a Job Is Engaging

As you divide the team's work among members, give some thought to the kinds of jobs you create. It's possible to structure a job so it encourages the jobholder to engage personally with the work, feel committed to it, and devote extra effort to doing it well. Here are some questions you can ask:[2]

- Is there a *clear link* between the job and the team's overall purpose and goals?

- Does the work *challenge* the jobholder to use and grow his skills?

- Does the job involve a *whole, natural piece of work*, with a beginning and an end, and an identifiable final product the person can point to and say, "I did that. It's my contribution to the team"?

- Is the jobholder able to *have contact with the "customer,"* the one who will use the product or service produced?

- Does the job allow the person to *exercise some control* over her work—its planning, scheduling, pacing, and so on?

- Does the person have the performance targets and feedback data he needs to *track his own performance*?

- Does the job offer some *opportunity for advancement*?

How do the jobs on your team stand up to these criteria?

Team Members Need Clarity About How the Team Does Its Work

This aspect of team culture concerns how work gets done. It includes all those activities that occur, or should occur, regularly, such as meetings, updates, written reports, plans, analyses, reviews, standard practices, recurring events, work flows, who gets to make what decisions, and processes, such as gathering and analyzing information.

Make these recurring "ways of working" into an explicit but flexible system of activities clear to everyone.

Such a system can help ensure consistency and avoid confusion and conflict. How should customer complaints be handled? How do we communicate changes in project scope to make sure everyone affected knows about them? If team members know, they won't have to figure out the best way to proceed every time, and they can be comfortable knowing what to expect from others.

A system will also ensure that important work actually gets done. Too often, such important but rarely urgent activities as planning and analysis are pushed aside by pressing but ultimately less important problems. Add these activities to your "system" and treat them as urgent.

Which work you standardize will depend on what you do. Resist the impulse to standardize everything. Review and question the system and its various pieces frequently. Take care not to adhere rigidly to processes that need to change or don't apply to the situation at hand.

Have You Identified the Information You and Your Team Need?

Regular reports, analyses, and updates can provide important information and guidance. Identify those your team needs, who will do them, when, and how (what information, how presented).

Do You Hold Regular Meetings?

No group can function as a team unless it routinely convenes, in person or virtually, and members address issues of common concern. Studies of effective managers show that both individual interaction and group meetings are an important part of how they manage their teams. Neither is sufficient by itself.

Do You and Your Team Make Decisions in an Open, Systematic Way?

A good decision is more than a good response to a dilemma. It's also a choice the people involved are willing to implement, and that often depends on not only the decision itself but *how* it was made.

For that reason, your decision-making process is an important part of how your team does its work. *How* has two components: *who's* involved and *what steps* make up the process.

Are Decision Rights Clear in Your Team?

Do people know and agree about who gets to make what decisions? Which do you make? Which do others get to make, under what circumstances? Are there guidelines or limits on what kinds of decisions people can make?

Do You Involve Others When You Make Decisions?

You and your team can make decisions in a variety of ways:

- *Autonomous decisions* are made by you alone, as head of the team, without consulting or involving anyone else.

- *Consultative decisions* are made by you but after you consult team members and others.

- *Joint decisions* are made by you and team members together by arriving at consensus—that is, everyone involved is willing to support the decision though it may not be everyone's first choice.

- *Delegated decisions* are made by a team member or the team as a whole without your involvement, except that you have specified parameters or boundaries—for example, that cost cannot exceed a certain amount or a new product must retain certain features.

How do you and your team make decisions? If you tend to make autonomous decisions, remember the benefits of inclusion: *better diagnosis* of the problem or opportunity; *early identification* of assumptions, perceptions, and misunderstandings that are best addressed in the beginning; *more trust* in the outcome because those involved feel a greater sense of control; and, not least, *greater commitment* to the final choice and its implementation.[3]

Does Your Team Follow a Reality-Based Decision-Making Process?

People dislike arbitrary decisions. They want to know that a transparent, data-based process will be followed in making important team choices. Such a process might include these steps:

1. *Discuss and define the problem* within the team. Identify stakeholders—people who have something to gain or lose.

2. *Explore the issue* through data gathering, analysis, and discussion that involves key stakeholders.

3. *Generate possible solutions* by discussing, refining, critiquing, and, if possible, testing them. Identify the consequences of each option for stakeholders.

4. *Make a decision*, ideally through one of the more open approaches noted above—consultative, joint, or delegated.

5. *Implement the decision*, taking steps, if possible, to mitigate any consequential harm to stakeholders.

6. *Review/critique the outcome* after some time has passed. What can you learn from the results? How might you do it differently next time? Take the time to debrief disappointing *and* successful outcomes.

Rarely does the process unfold in reality as neatly as it appears here. Steps overlap, get repeated, loop back. But having a process and striving to follow it will improve your decisions. And it will help you avoid the trap of leaping to the first plausible choice without exploring alternatives that may be better.

Talk explicitly in the team about this process, especially in virtual or cross-cultural teams, where it's particularly important to be clear about such things. Follow the process consistently. Expect team members to use it themselves.

Team Members Need Clarity About How They Work Together as a Team

How team members "work together" is about shared values, norms, beliefs, and expectations that guide team members as they interact. These values and norms are the social glue that keeps their interactions productive and any conflict constructive.[4]

Consider, for example, group norms that might develop around attendance and participation at meetings ("Everybody attends, listens, participates, and treats others with respect"), team priorities ("Team goals before personal goals—no competing within the team"), how to disagree and confront colleagues constructively ("Focus on the work, not the person"), quality of work expected ("Are you proud of it?"), expected contribution ("Everybody pulls their weight"), and many other such considerations.

No group can work as a team unless members agree on such "rules of the road." How much would you care about the group and its work if you thought your colleagues cared less than you about the quality and importance of your joint work?

How Do Members of Your Team Work Together?

When you take over an existing group, you need to understand the culture you've inherited. The roles, rules, values, and norms already in place are your starting point. Identify them by watching how people do the work and work together. What's more important to members: the team or individual work? Who has influence and who's ignored? Is disagreement allowed? How do people treat each other when they disagree? What's expected of individual members?

Pay attention because in every team a distinctive culture will emerge quickly and spontaneously. Early gatherings of a new group—or the initial meeting after you take over an existing group—are especially important. These early moments are the right time to set out the purpose and goals of the team, establish how you will function as boss, and begin to define how members will work with and treat each other.

Do you ever think about these issues? Unfortunately, many managers don't. If you're one of them, you're overlooking a potent management tool that lets you influence members *through* the social dynamics of the group.

Are You Doing What You Can to Foster the Emergence of the Right Team Culture?

You cannot impose culture. It will emerge no matter what you do. But you can and should try to shape it. That will be more or less difficult, depending on the group's existing culture, members' expectations, whether the culture you want matches the culture of the broader organization, and whether members trust you.

Team members do want to know where you stand. Because you're the authority figure, they will look to you for guidance, at least initially. You can foster the values, norms, assumptions, and practices you want by:

Suggesting or *espousing* those you believe will make the team more effective.

Focusing attention and discussion on them (discussion is critical).

Asking for agreement on them.

Expecting team members to follow them.

Enforcing them when they're ignored, abused, or forgotten.

Reminding team members to expect them of each other.

Coaching the team as a group about how to apply them.

Hiring, promoting, rewarding, and recognizing those who exemplify the values, beliefs, and norms you want.

Modeling the standards, beliefs, and norms you want in all your actions and decisions. This is perhaps the most important way you influence culture: you *show* it. It does no good to expect others to accept criticism if you can't receive it yourself. Show what you want not only by your actions but by taking action *visibly*. People need to see that you walk the talk.

Are There Clear Standards Around the Work That You Consistently Enforce?

In an effective team, members want everyone to do the work assigned to them. They expect each other to do their best and, on occasion, to make extraordinary efforts to produce good work. Members need to feel that they and all their colleagues are committed to quality and that a lack of it anywhere reflects on everyone. The team should expect results, not mere effort, and focus relentlessly on team purpose, plans, goals, and priorities.

Members expect you to enforce team standards rigorously. Nothing can destroy a team as quickly as a member who falls short of team standards while you condone his shortcomings. How hard would you work if you thought others were held to lower standards?

Are There Clear Norms About How Team Members Treat Each Other?

Espouse and enforce a culture that encourages everyone to participate, expects members to treat each other with respect, values personal differences, and fosters recognition of each member's contribution. No one can contribute fully if she doesn't feel valuable or valued.

Group values and standards become particularly apparent when members gather, and so it's important to set norms around meetings—both face-to-face and virtual. Expect people to attend, arrive on time, come prepared, participate, allow and encourage others to talk, listen, keep confidential matters confidential, always treat each other with respect, and accept and respond to disagreement about work issues calmly and impersonally.

Participation is important for two reasons. First, research makes clear that the more frequently an idea is stated, the more likely it is to be adopted. Good but rarely expressed ideas tend to be ignored. Be sure the team hears and considers everyone's opinions. Second, members who rarely participate can become angry or frustrated and feel less committed. "People should speak up," you may say. Perhaps they tried and felt they were cut off or ignored, and so they've given up. Some people simply don't assert themselves; they believe saying something once should be enough. That's naive, but it's still your job to get all ideas and opinions on the table and fully considered.

Cultural and language differences can influence the work of a group as well. We know of one international marketing team charged with the introduction of a new line of personal care products throughout Europe. In all the team's videoconferences, the Spanish member said little because he was uncomfortable speaking English, the group language. The manager didn't draw him out during or after meetings. When the line was launched, it quickly became clear the group's plans had ignored some important features of the fastest-growing market for such products in Europe: Spain.

Do You Make Sure the Group Allows, Even Encourages, Constructive Disagreement and Conflict?

Watch for constructive conflict.[5] You want it. If there's none in your group, good ideas are likely to be missed. If that's happening, talk about it and encourage people to express differing points of view.

In group discussions, two actions will encourage constructive disagreement. First, allow questioners and dissenters in the team to speak their minds. These are people inclined to step back and ask fundamental questions: Why are we doing this at all? Why are we *still* doing it? What if we did it a different way? Group members often try to silence such questions as matters already settled or too troublesome to address. Though often irritating, questioners can lead to real innovation.

Second, to foster useful conflict, press adversaries to *inquire* rather than *advocate*. People who disagree often simply repeat their respective positions more and more loudly, ferociously advocating their own points of view. Encourage them instead to make inquiries of each other. Why do you believe that? What evidence do you have? How did you arrive at that conclusion? Encourage a spirit of curiosity. Of course, it will help if you yourself inquire rather than advocate when you disagree with someone.

Do You Talk About Team Culture Explicitly and Often?

Too often, the values and standards that make up team culture are considered off-limits for explicit discussion. But if they can't be expressed, they can't be clarified, understood, modified, or dropped. Talk about them frankly in meetings and general discussions. Be clear and forthright about your expectations. Encourage people to express their opinions about them.

Do You Coach Your Team?

Don't assume that all members know how to function well in a team. For some, it may be a new experience, and so they won't understand even the basics: how to listen, participate, disagree, or deal constructively with disagreement. And don't assume that coaching individuals on the team is the same as coaching the team as a whole. From the beginning and at every opportunity, coach your group *as a team* in the values, norms, and behaviors you support and expect. Talk about such things in team meetings. Your role is pivotal, but be patient. You will need time to encourage the right standards and values. Groups don't become real teams overnight.

Team Members Need Clarity About How They're Doing

Feedback about performance is the fourth type of clarity a team needs. Because real teams serve a compelling purpose and strive toward challenging goals, members want current, concrete information about progress.

Do You Conduct Frequent Reviews of Team and Individual Performance?

Embed the idea of frequent reviews in team practice and culture. In reviews, it's important to cover *team* performance and make clear it's *everyone's* responsibility. Members need to hold each other accountable.

If your team's purpose is to carry out a specific mandate with a deadline, or your team has launched an important initiative, conduct a thorough review of performance and plans at roughly the midpoint. By this time, plans and direction will be taking shape, but it won't be too late to make significant course corrections.

For ongoing work, alternate quick reviews and in-depth reviews. For example, every month, look for problems that need immediate attention, and then, every quarter, do a detailed review of progress against goals and plans.

Do You Use Performance Metrics?

Numbers—sales, costs, volume—are useful. They lift the answer to "How are we doing?" above the realm of personal opinion. They focus on results rather than effort. They help define where you need to go. Looking at what drives them can provide useful ideas for improvement.

It can be harder to come up with useful metrics in not-for-profit and government work because simple measures, such as sales and profits, are harder to find for the complex problems these organizations address—such as reducing poverty or improving education. But growing evidence in all sectors of society supports the mantra that you only get what you measure.[6]

Use metrics whenever you can, but beware of their limitations, two in particular: first, understand what drives them, because they rarely tell the whole story. Costs are up? Why? A one-off cause is one thing, a chronic problem something else. Second, not everything important can be measured. Don't ignore, for example, team culture and whether the team is living up to its own standards. Also, some goals in your plan may lack numbers because they're still too general, half-baked, or far out in the future. In these cases, judgment is the only yardstick. Don't hesitate to apply it and ask for others' opinions.

Measure the right things. Many metrics—such as sales and costs—only measure current activity and usually reflect the result of steps taken in the past. They don't let you see what's coming in the future. Find other measures—leading indicators—that let you look ahead. For example, if you track customer satisfaction or competitive pricing, a drop might foretell a coming decline in your sales if you don't respond. Identify such measures that are appropriate for your group and track them too.

Do You Encourage Your Team to Evaluate Itself and Make Self-Corrections?

Providing feedback needn't be a case of your telling the team how it's doing. If purpose, goals, and work standards are clear, particularly if you use key metrics, team members should be able to assess themselves. If they can, your role is to lead a discussion that pinpoints problems, uncovers root causes, identifies possible solutions and lessons, and lays out plans for responding. Also, take time to discuss with the team how it will handle reasonable mistakes or failures. Remember that innovation rarely happens without risk taking and missteps. Develop a team habit of debriefing both successes and failures to identify lessons learned.

Do You Include Yourself and Your Performance in Your Reviews?

How are *you* doing? You're not perfect. Where are you trying to improve as team head? What mistakes have you made? What are you doing to improve your performance as boss? Ask team members for feedback about ways you can make the team more productive. You may find this kind of discussion uncomfortable. But it's important. Don't force your people to carry the burden of your making the same mistakes over and over.

Are You Careful to Note and Recognize
Good Performance?

It's too easy to focus on problems and take good performance for granted—"Well, that's what you're supposed to do." When you see it, stop and take note of praiseworthy work, recognize the people involved, and thank them—all within the context of the team and its work as a whole. Recognition is particularly important when results are down, the organization is going through tough times, the future is uncertain, and you must focus on retaining people's commitment.

The Challenges of Managing
Virtual Teams

Virtual work groups, including groups whose members are both colocated and dispersed, present challenges. Here are some questions that can help you deal with them.

Are You Explicit About Purpose, Goals,
and Team Culture?

Much of what's required by virtual teams mirrors what we've already suggested for all teams, virtual or not—being clear about what the team does, its purpose and goals, and team culture, how members work with each other.[7]

Get agreement early about purpose and goals, the future you're trying to create, and return to those topics regularly to remind members of the significance and context of their work. Talk about how the group will do its work and how group members are expected to interact. Then talk regularly about how the group is functioning. Ask for members' opinions, both in group discussions and in one-on-ones. Confirm everything—understandings, conclusions, decisions, assignments, deadlines, and schedules. It often makes sense to write out the key elements of team culture, just as you write down key elements of your plans.

Do You Understand How Virtual Team Members Come to Trust Each Other?

Trust among members is a key characteristic of any effective team, and you need to understand that virtual work groups seem to develop it differently than do colocated groups. When there's little face-to-face contact, members base trust on task dependability rather than social interaction. They trust members who are reliable, consistent, and responsive, who meet deadlines, answer quickly, and do what they say they'll do—in short, who perform predictably. These are qualities you may want to stress and incorporate explicitly in the norms for your virtual team.[8]

Do You, If Possible, Bring the Team Together Physically, at Least in the Beginning for a Launch Meeting?

Even if trust can develop without much in-person contact, work groups still benefit from meeting physically—company-sponsored events are often a good venue for this—especially in the early days of the team or of your tenure as its manager. If you do gather, allow time for socializing. Don't spend the entire time on work. Have each member present pertinent biographical and other background information, as well as any potentially relevant expertise and experience they may bring to the group.

If possible, it's also useful to meet midway through a major initiative—the work has taken shape but it's not too late to make major changes—and at the end of an initiative for a debriefing.

Are You Careful to Foster Interaction Among All Virtual Team Members?

Pay particular attention to member participation and interaction. Make sure all members are engaged and contributing. If some members seem reluctant to express themselves fully in group discussions, follow up one-on-one to obtain ideas or reactions they may have withheld in the group setting. Never assume that silence means agreement.

Be sensitive to the "out-of-sight, out-of-mind" danger for members who work apart. As team manager, maintain some regular one-on-one contact with each member by phone or video. It's your job to keep all members connected and contributing.

Don't hesitate to give members feedback about their performance. However, for such one-on-one discussions, use some form of interactive media, video ideally, that allows real discussion and give-and-take, as well as problem solving and counseling.

When Hiring or Selecting Team Members, Do You Look for Interpersonal Team Skills?

It's a common—and fatal—assumption to think that since virtual team members interact less, their interpersonal skills don't matter, and they only need appropriate technical skills. Organizations with extensive experience in using virtual teams have found the opposite—interpersonal skills, including the desire to connect productively with others, are if anything even more important in virtual groups. So when selecting members, look for evidence of interpersonal competence, such as a desire to share information and carry on useful discussions. Give candidates a clear idea of the conditions—working at a distance—that they will find.

Dealing with Differences Among Team Members in Global Work Groups

Just as work groups possess their own values and attitudes, so do different societies. These differences can affect how well a team functions. National and regional cultures differ in their attitudes about formal authority, in their views of the purpose and conduct of meetings, in their styles of communication, in members' need for context and explanation, in their predispositions toward change, in their handling of conflict, and even in what constitutes an individual's identity.

How should you approach such differences? You cannot ignore them, because they can easily prevent your group from working to its full potential. Here are some general but important considerations.

Are You Aware of Specific Cultural Differences?

It's not enough to understand that "cultures are different." If you manage a multicultural group, learn something about the *specific* cultures and cultural predispositions of group members.

In Spite of General Cultural Differences, Are You Careful to Understand and Deal with the Individuals Involved?

There is often as much diversity among individuals within a culture as there is between people from different cultures. The danger is that we treat useful generalizations about cultures—for example, "hierarchy is important in Indian society"—as stereotypes with which we label and prejudge individuals. Use cultural characteristics only as preliminary guides for exploring and determining the actual values and attitudes of the individuals you work with.

Are You Aware of Your Own Cultural Predispositions?

You grew up in a particular culture that shaped your thinking and feeling. Understand it and how it compares with the other cultures in your group. Beware the tendency to view your own culture as the standard from which others deviate. Remember that others will measure you against their own cultures.

Do You Avoid the Subtle Trap of Thinking That Cultural Differences Are Good or Bad, or Right or Wrong?

Don't pass judgment on such differences. One point of view or predisposition isn't better than another. Some work better toward some ends, and others work better toward other ends. Someone is late producing a report. You consider deadlines important and tardiness a sign of laziness or lack of discipline. But the person may hold a less stringent view of deadlines and feel it's more important to devote time to other matters. Consider this not a character flaw but a different way of looking at the world that is neither good nor bad in principle. It's simply a difference you need to recognize and accommodate. If a deadline truly is critical, you will need to make that crystal clear and manage it closely.

Do You Talk Explicitly in Your Team About Cultural Predispositions and All Aspects of Group Process?

Many teams and team managers are reluctant to be explicit about team purpose, goals, standards, roles, and values or about how such differences might affect the way the group functions. Don't be. Talk about them without judging differences or the people involved. Being explicit is good for all groups, but for multicultural groups, it's essential.

You Must Protect Your Team from the Weaknesses Inherent in All Teams

Teams are not perfect. They can fall into subtle but common traps. Here are some to look for.

Is Your Team Insular?

There is a dark side to strong team cultures. They can feed the human tendency to see the world as "us versus them," where "them" is any other group, even groups within the same organization. When this happens, the team shuts itself off from the interests, points of view, and legitimate concerns of others. Your team needs to see itself as part of a larger organization, with its broader purpose and goals. Part of your job is to protect your team from distraction and unnecessary interruption, but you do a disservice to all involved if you always press your team's interests over those of the organization and other groups. Protect your group—but not too much.

Does Your Team Discourage Dissent and Disagreement?

A team that avoids disagreement will discourage new ideas and innovation, which are often the result of constructive conflict. It's a paradox of teams that you must foster both mutual support and constructive confrontation among members.

Has Your Team Fallen Prey to Groupthink?

Here is another aspect of the dark side of a strong culture. *Groupthink* is group pressure to conform to the way group members are "supposed" to think.[9] It's a more insidious way team culture can stifle new ideas and approaches. In groupthink, innovation isn't openly or obviously suppressed, but nothing new ever comes up because members censor themselves without realizing they've all adopted the same way of thinking. Combat it by recognizing it—you can fall victim to and even encourage it yourself—and proactively fostering new ideas and approaches. Pay attention to how often someone inside the team challenges what it's doing. As you hire new team members, seek people who share your group's values but also bring different perspectives.

Has Your Team Split into Subgroups?

Work will inevitably bring some team members into frequent, close contact and foster the formation of subgroups that can easily become warring factions. Shared personal interests or backgrounds can create subgroups too. Obviously, problems arise when people see themselves as members of a subgroup rather than the full team. So encourage full contact among all members. Create assignments that partner members who normally don't work together. Be alert to the influence of subgroups when the full team meets. This is a particular problem for far-flung teams whose members work in different locations, especially where those locations also represent different cultures.

Creating a team, sustaining it over time, and managing through it is no easy task. Few teams actually match the ideal characteristics we've described here for long periods of time. Too many destructive forces pull constantly on them, not least the tendency for conflict to turn personal, the ongoing struggle between teams and individual members, or the myriad traps just described. Maintaining a team, providing the direction, clarity, protection, and resources it needs, will require from you constant effort and vigilance. It means understanding the social dynamics that can make the whole far more (or less) than the sum of its members.

Once again, management makes the difference between group dysfunction and a high-commitment, high-performance team.

10

YOUR TEAM MEMBERS ARE INDIVIDUALS TOO

Manage Both Teams and People

2:25 p.m.   Jason follows Jay into room A, an enclosed meeting room, and shuts the door. Jay sets up his laptop to show the promotion piece.

"Wait," Jason says. "Before you do that, Jay, I have to tell you that what you said to Sumantra was unacceptable. We cannot have people attacking each other personally."

"Okay, okay." Jay shrugs. "I mouthed off. I got carried away. Sorry. You know me."

"That's not good enough," Jason says. "And it doesn't matter if I know you or not. You went too far and made it personal, and I'm calling you on it. When everyone else comes in, I expect you to apologize—sincerely—to Sumantra. Since you attacked him in public, you need to apologize in public."

Jay looks at Jason as if the thought were ludicrous. "I was right," he says. "Sumantra thinks he's going back to his buddies in editorial when Project Emerge tanks. Don't burn your—"

"Now you're doing it all over again," Jason says. "Stop it. You don't know what Sumantra thinks. And your approach doesn't change anything. It just lets you vent your frustration."

"I'm not the problem," Jay says, in a more subdued tone. "Believe me, I'm not the problem."

"Look," Jason says, "I'm going to work with you on this but be clear: if you attack someone personally again, we're going to have a talk about your future here."

Jay looks surprised. "All right," he says. "I hear you."

"Good. I mean it."

"Can I show you the promo?"

"Sure."

Jason watches the seven-minute piece in silence. It's what a school official will see when visiting the Reynolds Ed site for more information. And it's truly good—interesting, engaging, and informative. It not only describes how the whole process works for all involved, it also conveys a strong sense of how the course will look and feel and how the student will experience it. Jason couldn't have hoped for anything more appealing. He was vastly relieved. Maybe, he thinks, Jay does have the development process under control.

"It's good, Jay. Good work," Jason says when it's done.

"It's not just *good*," Jay says, "it's outstanding. It's wonderful. It's beautiful. It brings tears to your eyes, and it's a programming course, for heaven's sake!"

"It's extremely good. I enjoyed watching it. I think it does the job."

"It does, doesn't it? I'm glad you think so. I had to push and push eMedia, but they finally got it. And I'll tell you a secret. On Monday we get the first version of the actual course for review and testing. We're right on schedule. And it's beautiful. Just like the promo."

"That's great news, Jay," says Jason. "I'm relieved to hear that, and I'm eager to see it. I suppose it uses the content you sponged that I've been hearing about."

"Absolutely," says Jay with a grin.

"Don't be so pleased with yourself," Jason says. "This isn't an 'us against them' game. You're aggravating a problem that was tough enough already. You act like we only have to do this one course, when the ultimate goal is to create a business that makes many courses. And for every course, we need to be partners with the groups that provide the content we use. That's the only way Project Emerge can succeed."

Manage your people as a team, but never lose sight of this reality: team members are people who still want to be seen and cared about as individuals. It's human nature—and the paradox of teams. Most of us want to belong to a group. That's a powerful urge. But, simultaneously, we each want recognition for our personal contribution.

The way to deal with the paradox is to keep in mind the context of the team when managing individual team members. Recognize each for their contributions to the team, for their faithful compliance with team standards and expectations, and, not least, for their constructive disagreement within the team when that occurs.

Don't let team rules and expectations become so restrictive that they allow no individual latitude. Make the team a place where both sets of needs—individual and team—can work in partnership, where individual needs can be met through the team.

How Well Do You Interact with Your People?

Much of management consists of simple interaction with others—making contact, engaging in positive, respectful give-and-take, and connecting as both a professional and a human being.[1] You've probably worked with managers so focused on their work that they walked the halls with a quick stride, head down, ignoring everyone else. How did people feel about them?

Do You Have Lots of Varied Dealings with Your People?

Effective relationships require frequent contact. In fact, good managers spend most of their time interacting with their direct reports and others. Management is a contact sport. How much of your time do you spend engaging with others? It should be substantial.

A significant portion of people's trust will be based on their day-to-day interactions with you.

Are You Open and Accessible?

In effective relationships, both parties initiate contact. Is a substantial portion of your contacts initiated by others? This requires that you make yourself accessible. For example, is your office door mostly open, and are you frequently where people can approach you? Are you psychologically available? Are your body language, demeanor, and other nonverbal cues welcoming and positive? Some bosses exude an aura that says, "Don't bother me."

Would People Say You're Honest and Forthright in All Your Dealings?

Do you strive to be truthful? When you say something, can people believe you and count on you to do what you say?

Would People Say They Know Where You Stand?

Clarity and candor not only help people work together but also are signs of respect. Do you let people know when and why you're displeased? Equally important, do you let them know when you're pleased and why?

In Your Contacts, Do You Fully Engage the Other Person?

Do you make a real human connection in every interaction? When a direct report talks to you, no matter the subject, are you fully focused? Do you listen and ask questions? Is there genuine give-and-take, a real dialogue, with both of you contributing substantially, if not always equally? Remember what we noted earlier: real listening means you're willing to change your mind based on what you hear. Or are you always telling and selling?

Your people bring all of themselves to work, and you'll sometimes find yourself listening to people's personal problems. You need not resolve or take responsibility for these problems, and you may sometimes have to limit the time spent on them. But you do need to listen, recognize and respect people's feelings, treat them confidentially, and when relevant and appropriate, take them into account.

Do You Pay Attention to All Your People?

Those who work for you know how and with whom you spend your time. They watch. Those left out know they're on the outside. So be aware of how much and with whom you interact. Keep contact time roughly equitable over a period of time. *Equitable* does not mean *equal*. Events and problems will lead you at times to focus on some people more than others. Besides, some people want lots of contact, while others don't. The goal is to give each person what she or he needs.

What About Distant Team Members?

It's easy to overlook people who aren't physically present every day because they're located elsewhere or they telecommute. Since you and they won't have the spontaneous give-and-take that creates any strong relationship, you'll need to be proactive and systematic in contacting them. Talk regularly on the phone or by videophone to review work, solicit ideas and opinions, get to know them, share your thoughts, and generally stay in touch. Arrange to meet them whenever possible. Take responsibility for keeping them connected.

What About Older, More Experienced Team Members?

Younger managers are often intimidated by older, experienced people and avoid them. Or they consider them intractable dinosaurs. Get to know them each as individuals; find out what they have done, know, and can do. Be willing to learn from them, seek their help and advice, and ask what they need. Ask them too, if appropriate, to mentor younger team members. Even if they know more about the work than you and have done it longer, they still look to you for support, resources, and information, as well as political and strategic guidance. Perhaps you're being fast tracked, and they're plateaued in their career growth. Remember, they also hope and deserve to keep learning and have access to appropriate opportunities. If you neglect their development, they will become the resistant dinosaurs you at first—mistakenly—assumed them to be.

If they do seem uncomfortable with your role as their boss, you might need to have an explicit conversation with them about their reservations. Avoiding the subject will not make it go away. If you do confront them, do it in a way that's not accusatory or threatening—by saying, for example, "I get the impression, I could be wrong, you're not comfortable with me as your leader. How can I help you? What can I do to help make this situation work?"

What About Your Steady but Not Star Team Members?

Most managers focus on team members at the extremes—the high and low performers, who do need attention. But in most groups the bulk of work is done by the majority of people in between—competent, steady, dependable B players who know and do their jobs but don't stand out. They plug away and rarely ask for much. If you were a star performer, beware the trap of undervaluing such "merely competent" people. Don't accuse them of lacking motivation or skill. It's easy to overlook them—until they leave. Then you'll discover how much you depend on them.[2]

What About Individuals You Don't Like or Understand?

This is the acid test of your interpersonal maturity as a manager. If you rely on your gut to drive your relationships, you'll only feel comfortable with people similar and familiar to you. Human chemistry guarantees that you'll like some people and dislike others. Those you dislike are the ones you avoid when you walk around the office. Perhaps they remind you of someone in your past, but the reason doesn't matter, except that knowing it may help you get over it. Find some way to interact or even work with those you need but dislike. Get to know them. Most negative feelings diminish with familiarity. They probably don't like you either. Take responsibility for making the relationship what it should be.

What About People on Your Team Who Don't Report to You Directly?

Of course, most of your interactions will probably be with the direct reports you pick to help you build and run your part of the organization. Don't forget, however, that you're responsible for your entire group, including those who work for the people who report to you directly. You must find ways to build connections with *all* those who work for you, both direct and indirect reports.[3]

Find ways to have contact, including real interaction, with your indirect reports without undermining the authority of their bosses who report to you. You need to know what's happening on the front lines. It's too easy to become isolated and hear only what intermediaries want you to know. You need rich sources of timely and critical information about the big picture, priorities, key opportunities, and challenges. You also want to recognize achievements throughout your group.

Use the many tools, such as social media, that encourage people to share their ideas and thoughts. But don't let them replace real face-to-face contact. Walk around. Get on a plane and visit distant group members as often as your company permits. Get to know names, the day-to-day realities of working with customers, and something personal about all your people.

Some companies we know require managers to hold town halls or meet at least once a year for extended, informal chats with people down the line. It's not a bad idea. Ask your direct reports to include their people in meetings, as appropriate. Put your indirect reports on subgroups or task forces. Attend gatherings where you can chat with them or be around where they work. Give them assignments (coordinate this with their bosses, your direct reports). Keep in mind: these are likely successors if one of your direct reports leaves. Contact with them will help you learn firsthand their strengths and weaknesses. It will also help you find out whether team purpose, goals, strategies, and culture are permeating the entire group, and it will provide the firsthand data necessary to make succession decisions.

Do these questions help you develop some sense of what it's like to deal with you? This is a question we raise again and again because it's so important. How do people experience you? How does dealing with you make them feel about themselves?

Think about your interactions as if you were the other person. What was she looking for? Did he get it from you? Do you think she came away feeling more able or positive about whatever you discussed or about herself? Was he more able and willing to do the work, or to work with you, because of your interaction?

If you're not sure how to answer, think about how you can gain some insight. Think about asking your human resource department to help you conduct an appropriate 360-degree survey of those you work with. Taking that step requires courage because it involves some risk—you may hear painful things—but the feedback can make you a much more effective manager.

All this requires time and effort you surely feel you don't have. The issue is not so much the amount of time you spend with others but the quality of interaction. A short, focused connection is better than a long but distracted interaction. As much as possible, build ongoing connections into the nooks and crannies of your days. Take advantage of hallway meetings and chance encounters. The challenge of virtual groups is that you need to be much more thoughtful and deliberate about making connections.

How Well Do You Know Your People?

If you don't know your people, you cannot make intelligent decisions about assignments for them, and you cannot capture their commitment or decide how much to trust and delegate to them. Nor can you fairly assess and weigh their interests as you make difficult choices that involve them.

Use the following questions as rough guides to assess what you know or need to find out.

What is this person's *generation*, and what does that say about her approach to life and work? Knowing her generation—preboomer, boomer, Gen X, Gen Y/Millennial—can provide clues about her attitudes toward life and work. Try to understand how her generation differs from yours. The Web makes this information easy to find.

What are this person's *career aspirations*? What does he hope to accomplish, and where does he want to be in five or ten years? How can his current work help him achieve these goals?

What is this person's *life stage*, and what does that tell you about his needs and concerns? Single, single with children, married with no children, raising a young family, empty nester, putting children through college? Life stage and generation were once related, but the stage of life when people marry and bring up families now varies so much, it's sometimes hard to correlate the two.

In what *culture* was this person raised? The national or ethnic cultures in which she grew up can have an enormous impact on the attitudes, values, and assumptions she brings to work and to life in general.

What are this person's *outside interests*? Does he devote time and effort to activities outside work? Church? Community? Education? Such interests can be revealing. We know someone who does clerical work in the office, but outside she organized and ran a successful $200,000 building campaign for her local community center. People's real talents aren't always recognized or utilized at work.

What is this person's unique *life history*? Where did she grow up? Under what circumstances? What key life experiences made her the person she is?

What are this person's *strengths* as a person and as a team member? Most managers have no trouble identifying someone's weaknesses. They interpret their role as evaluators to mean they must focus there and devote far less attention to people's strengths. Yet people's strengths are what will take your team where it needs to go.[4] If you cannot immediately identify each team member's strengths, perhaps you're too focused on weaknesses.

Do You Know Your People Well Enough to Empathize with Them?

You need empathy, the ability to see the world as others see it without being captured by their point of view. This is the only way to understand truly why people think and feel as they do. Unless you can put yourself in their place, you won't be able to manage them well. Develop the mental habit, when dealing with someone, of pausing three seconds and trying to step into their shoes.

Empathy is possible only if you realize that others are fundamentally different from you. Yes, you know others look, dress, act, and talk differently. But do you understand that they think and feel differently too? They have different goals, fears, needs, sources of satisfaction, and ways of looking at the world. You cannot put yourself in their place unless you appreciate how profound these differences are.

Understand what real empathy is. It's not simply understanding how *you* would feel in someone else's position but how *that person* feels, given who they are. It often requires that we accept and understand feelings quite different from our own. This is why you need to know each of your people as unique individuals.

Ultimate empathy, of course, is the ability to see not just the world but *yourself* as others do.

Do You Delegate?

Are you good at delegating? It's a key way you work with the individuals who work for you. You'll never get the best from others or leverage yourself as a manager if you cannot let go of the notion that you must guide and oversee every step your people take.

Delegating well requires making judgments person by person about current skill levels, whom to trust, the importance of the work at hand, the consequences of failure, and the level of involvement to maintain. It can be risky, but you cannot succeed without doing it.

Some first-level managers who were stars as individual contributors are good enough that they can successfully micromanage all their people. They can succeed without delegating. The trap here is twofold: they limit the effectiveness of their current group, and they set themselves up for future failure. At some point, as they advance, they physically and mentally won't be able to micromanage all the work. Delegation is a skill that requires experience to learn. Better to begin learning from the start.

Delegation is *not* abdication. It's not a binary choice between close guidance versus no involvement. There are many steps in between, and managers willing to learn eventually discover there are levels of delegation, depending on the subordinate's readiness, motivation, and the task at hand.

Don't hide behind the excuse many managers offer: they justify themselves by warning of the consequences. We know a German manager who, when told to delegate more, told his boss, "There is, of course, a danger that we will become a bit sluggish . . . and . . . make mistakes or miss opportunities."

That may be an adequate reason for not delegating if you've just taken over a group. But if you use it after managing for a time, then you're failing. It's your responsibility to make sure you have people to whom you can give responsibility and authority. Nothing will hold back your career more than a reputation as someone who cannot delegate or manage people's performance.

Do You Know How to Develop People and Improve Their Performance?

Everyone recognizes the benefits when your people learn and grow. They become more able and motivated, and they produce better results. Creating the future you want, reaching the goals you've set, will depend on the ability of your people to increase the knowledge and skills they already have, develop new competencies, and overcome debilitating weaknesses.

Developing people is also a way to engage them. All of us are more likely to commit to managers and organizations that help us improve in our work and move ahead in our careers. Most of us like to get better and we even like to be pushed moderately. It's not unusual for organizations to discover in exit interviews that people leave because they weren't growing or learning.

What is your role as manager in your people's development? You cannot "develop" someone else. In the end, all development is *self*-development. Yet your role is crucial. In a nutshell, it is this: people learn by trying, learning, and trying again. Your job is to provide new challenges—opportunities where the consequences of failure are minor—followed by feedback, coaching, and the ability to try again.

How well do you foster the growth of your people? Are you setting the expectations, providing the opportunities, along with the coaching and other help people need to take charge of their own development?

Do You Know How Each of Your People Needs to Grow?

The ability of your team to carry out its plans and reach its goals will depend on the knowledge, values, and skills of individual team members. Hence, preparing plans for the personal development of each member should be part of defining and preparing for the future you and your group want.

Prepare a written *individual development plan* with each team member. In it, identify his current set of competencies (knowledge, skills, values) and compare them with (a) what his role *currently* requires and (b) what it will require *in the future*. The gap between actual and needed competencies both now and in the future becomes the basis of that member's plan. Specify what needs developing and how it will happen—developmental assignments, a company course, mentoring by a more experienced team member, and so on. In each plan include the person's own career hopes and plans. The needs of the group should take precedence, but the more you incorporate a team member's aspirations, the better. In fact, a good way to begin an individual development plan is to ask the individual to prepare a first draft that includes the elements just noted, along with any personal hopes and aspirations.

Do You Encourage Team Values That Foster and Expect Personal Growth?

A team can be a motivating environment for continuous development. What better reason to grow than the prospect of making a greater contribution to the team and its purpose? Team members are far more likely to work at getting better if colleagues expect each other to strive for improvement. You cannot impose this value, but it's one you can express, encourage, and reward.

Do You Coach People Every Day?

Do you think coaching is something you do only occasionally or as problems arise?[5] If so, you should broaden your thinking. Virtually every interaction you have is an opportunity to assess, explain, show, or encourage someone. Coaching involves talking someone through an activity, either before or after they do it, in order to improve their performance. It involves explaining, asking questions, demonstrating, role playing, and critiquing what you observed—whatever's appropriate for helping someone do better. It's usually best done quietly, person to person. The test of a good coaching session is that the person you're coaching leaves it both more able and more confident.

In the preparatory discussion before an activity, talk about goals, ideal outcomes, boundaries, and guidelines. People often don't know how to be different, and so merely describing what's needed is often not enough. You may need to show them or demonstrate what you want. In the review discussion, begin with the person's self-evaluation and lessons learned based on the preparatory coaching. Expand on the person's own insights, if necessary, followed by what might be done differently next time. In giving feedback, be descriptive, not judgmental, and as specific and concrete as possible.

We know a rising star in a leading investment bank who was recognized for his outstanding ability to bring in business. But he was also known for his impatience with colleagues who didn't, to use his words, "get with the program right away." He seemed to have a gift for leaving associates feeling battered and bruised. He knew of these problems because in his formal annual review his manager had told him of his effect on others. But little changed until he got a new boss who day by day—not once a year—pointed out his misbehaviors *as they occurred* and specifically coached him each time on better approaches.

Think back over the past two or three workdays. On how many of those days did you give people specific performance feedback and coaching? You should be doing it every day, even several times a day. *Use every possible opportunity, day by day and incident by incident, to review, critique, praise, and coach.* If you're not doing it every day, you're missing opportunities.

Do You Discourage Upward Delegation?

How often do you end a discussion with one of your people and discover that the next step is yours to do? It happens all the time, and it can act as a major drag on your time—not to mention the loss of an opportunity for your subordinate to learn. At the end of every interaction, ask, "What happens next and who's responsible?" If you're responsible, ask whether progress really must depend on you. Sometimes there's no way around it. But when that's not the case, find some way to keep responsibility where it almost always belongs: on your subordinate's shoulders.[6]

Do You Help People Evaluate Themselves?

In many cases, those who lack knowledge and skill cannot recognize their own strengths and weaknesses, precisely because of their ignorance. It's your job as manager to help them assess themselves accurately. If people don't know where they're good and where they're not, they won't know what to emphasize and where to get better.

Do You Use the Talent on Your Team to Help People Develop?

Teams contain a mix of talent, expertise, and experience that members can draw upon. If you partner experienced and inexperienced team members to carry out a task, you can both accomplish essential work and simultaneously make the inexperienced member more proficient.

Do You Make Clear Your Willingness to Help?

Do people see you primarily as judge and jury of their performance? They will, out of caution, unless you make clear your willingness to coach, teach, counsel, provide learning opportunities, make corporate resources available (such as courses), create developmental assignments, and remove obstacles that might be blocking progress. You cannot abdicate either role of developer or evaluator, but you can make clear you play both roles, not just that of judge. Ask people to let you know how you can help them improve.

Do You Know How to Conduct a Performance Appraisal?

A performance appraisal differs from a coaching session. Where coaching focuses on one aspect of performance and is often done on the fly, a performance appraisal is a dedicated discussion that touches on *all or most aspects* of someone's performance. It may include coaching but also involves much more. Many companies require such an appraisal every year, but that isn't often enough. You should talk frequently with people about how they're doing—identifying strengths, praising good performance, pointing out problematic weaknesses, coaching for specific behaviors, and counseling. As we described earlier, use individual development plans as the basis for these discussions, and keep the plans updated by noting progress or problems.

As you review performance, keep these guidelines in mind.

Always discuss a person's performance in the context of the team— its purpose, goals, strategies, and plans. Here, *how* they do their work is important their ability and willingness to function as team members—not just *what* they do. Recognize individual performance, even when team performance falls short, but avoid the impression that individuals can win while the team is losing.

Remember: the only purpose of an appraisal discussion is to improve future results. Review the past only to the extent such information will lead to better future results. Most of all, an appraisal is not an opportunity to vent frustration you feel about someone's past performance. Keep your personal feelings out of it. Be candid. Be clear about consequences. But don't be angry. And never treat anyone with disrespect. In giving feedback:

- Cover the positive, not just the negative.

- Give specific, concrete, recent examples of both.

- Describe rather than evaluate, conclude, and judge.

- Focus on the problem, not the person.

- Have a discussion in which you listen as well as talk; avoid declarations and pronouncements.

- Avoid criticism of general personality traits—"You're not assertive enough!"—because it's irritating and not helpful.

- Always end the appraisal with next steps—an action plan for building strengths and overcoming serious weaknesses.

Be prepared for disagreement. When someone disagrees with your assessment, stick with metrics, data, and concrete examples. Explore an issue rather than argue about it, and never allow the discussion to become personal. If the two of you cannot reach agreement, identify ways to watch for the behavior in question. When you see it reappear, discuss the incident as soon as possible. Be clear about what new information or evidence will lead either of you to change your mind.

Don't withhold important negative feedback for fear of conflict or upsetting the person. More than one manager has let someone's performance deteriorate to the point where she must be disciplined or fired. Such outcomes are grossly unfair if they come as a surprise, especially if an earlier discussion might have set the person straight.[7]

Do You Know How to Deal with Poor Performance?

Disciplining or firing an employee requires care, skill, and humanity. They are the hardest parts of being a boss, but they're unavoidable.

Many managers struggle with the fact that they're dealing with people's lives. Being fired is more than a setback, a personal bump in the road. It's a blow to ego and self-esteem, not only at work but at home and socially. Spouses, partners, and children are often directly affected too. No wonder many managers spend sleepless nights going over and over what they could or should do. By the time they fire someone, they've usually devoted a great deal of time to the person, had a number of tough conversations, and gotten to know the person professionally and personally. They often consider a termination a personal failure, particularly if they hired the person.

These feelings are normal and good, a sign of your compassion and humanity. But they cannot stop you from taking necessary action. Even if you were part of the problem, poor performers cannot stay on the team.

A manager we knew conducted an informal and unscientific poll of experienced managers. "When you look back over your experience," he asked, "what do you think you could have done better?" What he heard most often matched his own experience: "I didn't face up to people decisions fast enough. I usually knew someone wasn't going to make it well before I actually did anything about it. I wish I'd faced those issues quicker, resolved them, and gone on. Everyone would have been better off."

When someone's performance is obviously unacceptable and everyone knows it, including the person herself, it's easier to take action, especially if the person has had every opportunity to improve. But some situations are not so easy. They will test you as a manager.

Consider the situation of a person whose performance was acceptable but is no longer. This occurs at times of change when some people cannot adopt the new values, skills, relationships, or thinking needed.

A second situation may be even harder. This is one in which you must terminate an employee who's good but not good enough to help the group reach the future it wants. This can happen with longtime employees whose level of work has been adequate so far but won't be sufficient to help the team grow and attain more ambitious goals.

In both situations, you should make every effort to find alternative work for the person. But if you cannot, you must—with all possible humanity and care—let them go. It will be a severe test of your managerial will.

When you're dealing with a poor performer whose job is in danger, consider these questions.

Do You Understand That Disciplining and Firing Are Multistep Processes That Need to Be Followed Systematically?

Disciplining and firing should include not only what we suggest here but also the policies and practices of your organization. As soon as you realize an employee is a "poor performer," let your boss know, and contact your firm's HR department for guidance.

Do You Start by Trying to Understand the Reasons for Poor Performance? (It's Not Always the Person)

We tend to assume that responsibility for poor performance rests with the individual. Either they lack motivation or knowledge and skill. However, there are other possible reasons. The job may be poorly designed. Look at it and the work involved. Some jobs are failure traps. Given the realities of the organization and the work, no one is likely to succeed in them. Or the job may be fine, but the fit between the job and the person is poor; it doesn't use the strengths of the person, or it calls on him to perform activities he doesn't like or value. In these situations, consider modifying the job if appropriate—"job sculpting" is becoming more common—or moving the person to a position that makes better use of his skills and interests.

Are You Careful Not to Set People Up for Failure?

Have you been clear and forthright about the work and what you expect? Is there any chance you've confused the person, and he's not sure what to do?

Sometimes managers create situations that lead inevitably to a person's failure.[8] You may have done this yourself. You conclude you don't want this person in his job. It may be something about his work or demeanor. Perhaps you inherited him from a previous manager, and you conclude, "He's not one of us." Having privately turned against him, you begin looking for evidence to justify the conclusion you've already reached.

Even if you say nothing of this to the person, he can sense it in your actions, words, tone of voice, and general treatment. Believing he's been written off, he becomes discouraged and his work suffers. He avoids you, hides or ignores problems, and may even steer clear of team colleagues, who then turn against him too. He enters a vicious, downward spiral, at the bottom of which his performance justifies firing him, though it didn't in the beginning.

Is this really a performance issue? Be aware of this downward spiral, aptly called the "set-up-to-fail syndrome," and recognize it early while there's still time to turn it into a straightforward, rational, and fair review process.

Do You Let People Know When They're in Trouble, and Help Them Improve?

If someone's job is in jeopardy, and you've satisfied yourself the person is responsible, she has a right to know she's at risk, why, and what she can do to salvage her performance. She also has a right to whatever help you can provide. Her team colleagues will expect, first, that you deal with her performance—a weak performer will drag down the whole group. Second, they will want you to deal with her fairly and forthrightly. Don't play games by telling her she's in trouble only after you've concluded she must leave.

When People Must Go, Do You Help Them Leave with Dignity?

Termination is a serious matter, never to be taken lightly. Some managers, distraught that they must fire someone, justify their action to others and to themselves by demonizing the person. We once heard a senior manager describe someone he was thinking of firing as not only inept but without *any* merit, personal or professional. We knew the person and understood why he had to leave, but we also knew the manager's description was extreme and unfair—so unfair, in fact, it diminished the manager in others' eyes.

It's important that you remain aware of your own feelings throughout this process. Don't let your own sense of dissonance— the conflict inside you between the "good" person you think you are and the necessity of doing such harm to someone—push you to demonize the person. Recognizing and managing your own feelings—emotional maturity—will help you treat the person with dignity through the difficult process of termination.

Treating any employee without respect, even when asking her to leave, is shameful and unnecessary. Unless she's being fired for cause—dealing drugs in the parking lot or physically attacking a fellow employee, for example—the details and explanation of her departure should be negotiated and handled as the painful but reasonable action it is. Help her leave with whatever separation benefits you can provide and with words of support and encouragement. Obviously, you must observe at all times your organization's policies and procedures.

Do You Know How to Select the Right People for Your Team?

Having described how to remove a team member, we want to end on a more positive note: how to add people. Managing individuals begins with hiring them.[9]

Nothing you do will be more important than finding the right people.

Hiring mistakes are difficult and painful to correct. The real danger is not that you hire people who are outright wrong, but that you add people who are adequate but not truly good or don't match well with the work. You can get everything else right and sabotage it all by hiring the wrong people.

But who are the right people?

Until you've clarified your team's purpose, goals, ways of working, standards, and values, you can't identify the right people. The right person is not just anyone talented but someone who's right for the job *and* for your team and its work.

Here are some guidelines.

Do You Start with a Candidate's Competence: What She Knows, Can Do, and Has Done?

However attractive a candidate may be in other ways, you need to satisfy minimum standards for the knowledge, skills, and experience the job requires. This may seem obvious, but we've seen too many managers find a candidate so attractive in other ways, they overlook glaring holes in what they know, can do, or have done. Other characteristics matter too, and some parts of the work can be learned on the job, but it's hard to make up for a lack of basic competence.

Do You Look for More Than Competence?

Competence is relatively straightforward to assess, and interpersonal skills can be uncovered, but character can be difficult to determine. Here are some ways to get at it.

Ask open-ended questions that aren't easy to answer briefly. Encourage the candidate to tell stories about his experience, including times when things didn't go particularly well. Stories can be much more revealing of character than answers to specific, detailed questions. And don't just accept the story as told. Ask for detail. Ask probing questions about what happened. Ask the candidate to tell the story from the point of view of someone else who was involved. Don't accept broad generalizations and clichés.

After asking open-ended questions, *be silent and let the candidate answer fully.* Even when she stops talking, say nothing for several moments. Some of the best information emerges when an interviewee feels compelled to fill the silence. An interview is not a conversation, and it's not your job to move things along briskly. Wait and listen.

Go beyond references. Do talk to the references provided by a candidate, but it's critical that you talk to others as well. Talk to former bosses, peers, and even subordinates—anyone who knows the candidate and his work. Ask for names of people who figured in a story the candidate told, and talk to them.

Have others interview promising candidates, including members of your team and people in your network who would deal with this person. Involve your boss for especially important and highly visible jobs. Never depend entirely on your own judgment.

Is the candidate genuinely and personally interested in what your group does? Describe your team's work to candidates, especially its purpose and goals. Paint a picture of the future you're trying to create and the way team members work together. Every candidate will say she's interested, but can you detect any sign of genuine connection? Does she spontaneously mention anything in her experience or even her life that resonates with your team's aspirations? It might be a hobby or volunteer work, anything to indicate the existence of genuine personal interest in the work and your goals. The ideal candidate is someone for whom the work will be more than a job.

Look for diversity. Hiring someone new is an opportunity to add different experience and a fresh outlook to your team. You want someone who fits in—whose basic values and interests mirror the team's—but not someone who simply blends in. This is a real danger because we're naturally attracted to people who are similar to us. This requires a delicate balance, but you and your team must embrace *both* collective purpose, goals, and priorities *and* individual diversity.

Pay special attention to a candidate's unique strengths. Is she analytical, good at explaining complex ideas, able to connect with others quickly and genuinely? Above all, look for strengths that match the needs of the job. You want the candidate, if hired, to enjoy exercising her unique skills. Will the job challenge her to develop and expand those skills?

Understand the candidate's weaknesses too, her lack of certain competencies or experience, as well as any parts of the work she dislikes doing. Make sure her weaknesses won't be fatal and can be balanced by you or colleagues. In sum: hire for strength, not to avoid weakness. Just make sure weaknesses won't be fatal.

Are You Willing to Hire People Who Are Better Than You or Who Compensate for Your Weaknesses?

Many managers say they try to find people who're smarter or more experienced or better than they, or who balance their weaknesses. But, in fact, the people they hire mostly fall short of those standards.

Do you have people who are better or smarter than you, or who provide some skills you're lacking? If not, why not? Think of the last batch of job candidates you reviewed. Did you find some reason not to hire the very best? If so, you may view your people as competition. Perhaps you're still judging yourself against the standards that applied when you were an individual producer. Perhaps you wrongly think of the boss as the one who's supposed to be the best on your team or who knows the most.

Do you have a successor? If you disappeared suddenly, could one of your people step into your shoes or grow into them with reasonable help? If you don't, why not? You're more likely to be promoted if your bosses know someone's ready to take your place.

To achieve the results you want, you need a team. But a team cannot function well if its members feel their individuality and contributions go unrecognized. This is one of the basic paradoxes of management. If you don't manage the constant tension here, these forces can weaken and eventually destroy the ability of a team to do its collective work well. Balance both sets of needs, always letting the team set the context.

11

MANAGE THROUGH YOUR
DAILY WORK

Bring the 3 Imperatives into
Your Everyday Activities

2:46 p.m. Jason is still in room A. Jay is gone and Sumantra has just come in. When Jason opened the door for him, people were already starting to gather, and Jason realized it would be their first group meeting in Project Emerge.

"Sumantra," Jason says, "nothing justifies the way Jay talked to you. People can disagree about work, but personal comments are out of bounds."

"I understand and agree," Sumantra says. "I know I frustrate him."

"But that aside," Jason says, "he has a point. I told you earlier that you cannot specify materials without helping to obtain them."

Sumantra looks taken aback. "Frank said not to bother."

"I understand. I think that was the wrong approach, but that's what he told you, and so you were simply—and willingly, it seems—following instructions."

"I prefer not to start a war," Sumantra says.

"What would you suggest, then? Project Emerge depends on using their material, but you won't approach them."

Silence. "I don't know," Sumantra finally says.

"Then let me be clear," Jason says. "If you specify materials for a course, it is part of your responsibility to obtain them. You must deal with the other publishing groups. Use me, if necessary, and I'll pull whatever other levers are needed. Is that clear?"

"Yes," Sumantra says hesitantly, almost inaudibly.

"What?"

"Yes," Sumantra says clearly, though he's obviously uncomfortable with the thought. "I don't know how to do that if they're so opposed."

"What if," Jason says, "you put the publishers who are so opposed on your editorial advisory board? They need to be involved, don't they? They should have been from the beginning. They have every reason to feel completely in the dark now—and suspicious."

"I will do that."

"Good. But first they need to be brought up to date. What if, when you invite them to join, you set up a meeting next week for a preliminary discussion with you, Jay, and me."

He nods as he writes a note to himself.

"Before we all meet," Jason says, "arrange a premeeting with you, Jay, and me to think about ways the other publishing groups can benefit directly from what we're doing. How can what we produce help them? For example, can they offer it in the markets where they sell their current products? In fact, draft some thoughts and put them in a wiki for all of us in Emerge to work on."

2:57 p.m. The rest of the group enters room A. Jason thanks everyone for coming on short notice and promises there will be regular meetings scheduled in advance, sometimes for the whole group and sometimes for those who report directly to him.

"We're meeting right now," Jason says, "because we have some immediate problems that need prompt action—by all of us working together. We need to talk about them and about who's doing what. There seems to be some confusion about that. But before we jump into that discussion, I want to raise two issues. The first is the incident that many of you just witnessed. If you weren't there, I'm sure you've heard about it. And then I want to talk about a very interesting question Roberto asked me at lunch concerning what we're really up to and why our work matters. All right?" Jason looks around. Everyone is waiting. "Okay," he says. "The incident. I want to say something about it and about how we're all expected to treat each other, but first, I think Jay has something he wants to say. Jay?"

How do you spend your time as a manager? Are your days under control? Do you carefully plan what you'll do and do what you planned?

Or do you find much of your time taken up with unplanned events, such as the incident above at Project Emerge, that take you in unexpected directions?

Perhaps you've discovered the reality of management—that it's inherently fragmented and reactive. Even general managers of major business units struggle to stay ahead of daily events.

But if that's the nature of management, how do you cope? How do you apply the 3 Imperatives—manage yourself, manage your network, manage your team—in such a chaotic, unpredictable landscape?

Effective managers have discovered how to do this. In this chapter, we'll cover what you might learn if you followed one and saw how she approached the daily tasks all managers must do.

Effective managers don't do the daily work *and* their work as managers. They don't wrest time from necessary but mundane activities to do what they "should" be doing. They *use* unplanned daily events, problems, and obligations as vehicles for doing managerial work. Moment by moment, they think about each daily task in the context of the 3 Imperatives and the purpose and goals they're pursuing.[1]

By taking this approach, they may attend a retirement party for someone in accounting and while there introduce themselves to the director of financial analysis because they know they'll be sending her an unusual capital request in next year's budget. As a learning experience, they may bring a junior team member to a client meeting where a problem will be discussed. They may take a few minutes at the end of a routine division marketing planning meeting to preview with colleagues some new thinking about customer service. They may share a market research report with a plant manager whose efforts to raise quality and cut costs were instrumental in producing the much improved customer satisfaction highlighted in the report. They may assign an urgent problem to two team members as a way of solving the problem *and* repairing their important working relationship, which was strained by a recent project that produced disappointing results.

Thus, effective managers accomplish much of their work in hundreds of little steps that eventually accomplish the work of management. Where such an approach proves inadequate—not all management work lends itself entirely to this tactic—managers create their own interruptions. They give assignments to people who will return and interrupt them when the assignment is done. They set up a meeting, or recurring meetings, to direct attention to some important topic. Waiting for spare time to appear is a fool's errand because it never will. And of course, they carefully review their activities and try to eliminate those they cannot use in some way to push their plans forward.

Do you consciously, systematically, routinely bend or extend everyday activities to accomplish management purposes?

The key is the way you think about and approach every task. Before dealing with a problem or request, before every event, pause briefly and ask, automatically and almost unconsciously, How can I use this to serve my needs and goals as a manager? Convert the activities that crowd your days into management tools for moving your team forward through an approach we call *prep-do-review*.

Prep-Do-Review

This simple action model will guide you to think of every activity not as one step—simply *doing* something—but as three steps: *preparing* to act, *acting*, and then *reviewing* the outcome.

Here's how it works.

Prep. Before acting, take literally a minute to prepare. Ask yourself, What am I about to do? Why am I going to do it? (That is, what goal, no matter how simple, are you trying to reach?) Who will be involved or affected, and what are their interests? And how am I going to do it?

Do. Perform the action you prepared to take in the prep step.

Review. Afterward, reflect on what was done and the outcome, including any expected or unexpected consequences. Identify the lessons to be learned. How would you perform the action differently in the future? This is probably the part most managers we know neglect. They assume that the right lesson is self-evident, but it rarely is.

Prep-do-review may sound simple and obvious. But too often we simply react to what's in front of us. We deal with what's there on its own terms, and our only goal is to solve it, resolve it, and move on. How often do we stop and consider the broader context or the consequences for all concerned? And how often do we pause for a moment, reflect on an event, and identify what we learned? Raise this approach—a way of thinking that usually takes no more than a few seconds—to the level of a practice that you follow in virtually everything you do.

How Good Are You at Asking Questions That Improve Performance and Help People Learn?

Prep-do-review will draw on a fundamental skill that, in our experience, all effective managers possess to a high degree. Think about any good bosses you've worked for, bosses who made you better and helped you learn. Most likely, they asked questions—not a few, not some, but many, all the time. What's the problem? Have you analyzed it? What are you going to do? Why? When? What if this or that happens? What happened? Why?

We know a highly successful senior manager in international publishing who was known for her questions. Here's how one of her people described her approach: "On the one hand, she was easygoing and fun. But she would ask and ask and ask to get to the bottom of something . . . Once she got information and knew what you were doing, you had to be consistent. She would say, 'You told me x; why are you doing y? I'm confused.' Then she would come on stronger . . . You were held accountable."[2]

A good manager's questions aren't aimed at catching people in mistakes or belittling them. They serve two purposes simultaneously: to guide people to the right actions or conclusions and to help people see a challenge in new and more productive ways. Good questions teach people how to think by demonstrating what questions to ask themselves.

Prep-do-review is the perfect format for asking great questions.

Use Prep-Do-Review to Apply the 3 Imperatives in Your Daily Work

Consider how prep-do-review can help you weave your management work into the fabric of everyday activities and problems.

How Can I Use This to Manage *Myself* Better?

Every Friday, many of your people gather after work for social hour. They invited you last week, and you spent a pleasant hour chatting socially. This week they invite you again, and after a moment's thought, you decline with thanks. You decide it's nice to do on occasion, especially if there's something to celebrate. But you don't want to create social relationships and be "one of the group." You are in fact a member of the team, but you're also not like other members. As you thought about it, you realized you need to keep a little distance.

Daily activities offer many opportunities to exercise authority, build the right relationships with your people, and demonstrate that people can count on your competence and character.

To find those opportunities, ask questions like these about daily events:

- What do people expect of me as the authority figure in this instance? Protection? Resources? Setting expectations and boundaries?

- Am I too concerned here with demonstrating that "I'm the boss"?

- How can I use this to create or reinforce the right relationships with people who work for me?

- How can I be caring without creating an inappropriate personal relationship?

- How can I use this to create trust—to demonstrate competence as a manager or to express my values and intentions?

How Can I Use This to *Manage My Network* Better?

After a meeting with production, you go online and order *The Goal*, a fictionalized story of a plant that turned itself around.[3] When the book arrives, you send it with a note to a new production manager you met at the meeting who, you discovered in chatting afterward, had always meant to read the book but hadn't ever gotten to it.

What you do every day presents many opportunities to create and connect with colleagues in your network. To find them, ask questions like these:

- Will this help me identify or connect with people who should be in my network?

- Will it help me reconnect with current members?

- Is this information I should pass on to a colleague?

- Will this help me collect information from my network?

- Will this help me learn more about the organization and the needs of other people and groups?

- Should I let my boss know about this—at least send an FYI? Is there some way she could be helpful through advice, support, or resources? Should I review the options with him in this matter before I take action? Is this something she would prefer to handle herself? Is there some way he could help me use this to develop myself?

How Can I Use This to *Manage My Team* Better?

This imperative has several facets.

How Can We Use This Event or Incident to Improve and Implement Our Plan?

You're called to a meeting in production planning to discuss a slowdown caused by equipment problems in an overseas plant. You, some colleagues, and the production people work out alternative plans. Then, during the social chat that ends the meeting, you take a couple of minutes, using a simple diagram you brought, to preview informally some changes in a key product that you and your team have begun to discuss. Out of that brief conversation come two ideas that lead to improvements.

To use events to pursue or improve your plans, unwritten and written, ask questions like these:

- Can we use this to gather information we need to define the future more clearly and improve our plans?

- Can we use this to make progress in implementing our plans?

- Can we use this to understand and make progress toward resolving a problem that's hindering our plans?

- Can this help us test the assumptions on which our plans are built?

- Can we use this to request help or build support for what we need to do?

- Can we use this to influence others in support of our plans, to raise awareness, and to build a sense of urgency?

How Can I Use This to Build and Strengthen Team Culture?

A new team member is a day late finishing an important analysis. You tell her, "You need to understand the effect on the team when you're late. Go spend five minutes with Randy, Hamilton, and Margaret. They're expecting you, and they're not going to criticize or blame you. They're just going to explain how they depend on and use what you do."

Daily events can often be used to define and reinforce how teams do their work and depend on each other. Ask questions like these:

- Can this help us talk or learn about our performance as a team, about how we work together, or about how we need to improve?

- Can this help us clarify or reinforce who does what on the team and how different team roles fit together and depend on each other?

- Can this help create or reinforce the values and work standards we apply to our work together?

- Can this help build and reinforce stronger ties among members or foster close cooperation among members who usually don't work together?

- Can we use this to encourage constructive, work-related disagreement or diminish interpersonal conflict?

How Can I Use This to Develop and Work Better with the People on My Team?

Your market researcher is running focus groups to assess preliminary print and online materials for an important marketing campaign. He will prepare a report afterward, and the session will be video recorded, but you know there's nothing like hearing and watching live customers. Usually, the sessions are attended by researchers and product developers only, but this time you ask your two key graphics designers to attend as well. They've never gone before, and you know they generally resent nondesigners who tell them how to do their work. But you suspect they lack a visceral sense of your new target customers. As it turns out, the designers go and hear customer comments, and are inspired to sketch a different approach on the spot and test it with the focus groups. As a result, they're able to make the materials much more effective.

Many managers think of developing their people as something desirable but separate from the daily work. They think development requires time away at a training course or coaching/ teaching sessions that produce no immediate results. Consequently, it's too often put off or ignored.

But to think of work *versus* development is a misconception of how people actually grow and learn. Courses and other "off-work" approaches have their place, especially for technical training, but the daily work should be where most learning and development occur. There it's rarely a matter of producing results *or* developing people. Instead, it involves using the work itself to develop people by the way you design, assign, and follow it up. With this approach, every task or problem is an opportunity for learning and growth that you can seize by asking questions like these:

- How can we use this to build the knowledge, skills, and self-confidence of people on the team?

- Is this an opportunity to recognize the contribution of a team member?

- Is this an opportunity to delegate? If so, to whom and how?

- Is there a performance issue here I must address?

- Can I use this to illustrate and clarify a performance problem?

- Can I use this to connect better with one of my people?

- Will this help me learn more about someone who works for me—background, goals, needs, and preferences?

Do You Use Prep-Do-Review as a Management Tool with Your People?

Prep-do-review will not only help you apply the 3 Imperatives in your daily work. It's also a great management tool in general that will improve how you manage your people. It will give you more ways to interact with others as a boss, improve outcomes, help people learn, and make you a better delegator.

The *prep* step provides an opportunity for you to preview people's plans and suggest changes, if necessary. Ask, *What* are you about to do? *Why* are you going to do it? *How* are you going to do it? How can you use this to *help the team make progress* on its goals and plans? *Who* should be involved or kept informed? How can this be used to *improve your knowledge and skills*? *What if* your assumptions are wrong or the unexpected happens?

Used this way, the prep step allows you to move the purpose, plans, and work of the team forward, to coach and develop others, and to delegate more confidently. It assures you that someone is well prepared and ready to act and that his actions will be consistent with the team's work in general.

With experienced subordinates doing routine work, you probably can skip this discussion. If you do have it, focus more on making sure the person has the necessary support and resources and understands any broader context.

For the *do* step, this approach helps you determine what role, if any, you should continue to play in the actual doing of the work.

Make a postaction *review* an automatic part of the updates people provide at staff meetings. Make it part of your one-on-one meetings. Model it when you describe something you did. What did we learn? What's the takeaway? If we were doing it again, what would we do differently? All the guidelines we noted in the previous chapter about appraising performance apply here.

Above all, always point out what went well. You can learn as much from success as failure. What really made something work? It's not always obvious. Even in failure, something probably was done right. Point it out. Reinforce it.

Managers sometimes tell us they avoid much praise because they don't want their people to let up. Does that mean then, we ask, that you sit in silence at a game when your team scores because you fear cheering will cause the players to stop striving? Of course not. Why is work different? People need encouragement.

Expect your team members to follow prep-do-review in their own work as well. Make it a part of team practice that members consciously adopt and apply. Coach them in its use. It will improve what they do, and help them use their daily activities to carry out the team's purpose, goals, and plans.

Use Prep-Do-Review to Delegate More Effectively

Some managers find that delegation goes against the grain. They must give up a comfortable identity as an accomplished individual performer. They fear that sharing authority will diminish their importance or control. They equate delegation with abdication.

If you share any of these fears and misconceptions, you will find prep-do-review a good approach. It makes clear how to delegate in levels or stages, depending on the current readiness (skill) and motivation (will) of the person involved.

Thinking about delegation this way helps you see how to reduce your involvement gradually. Your goal should be to reach a high level of delegation (low control) with all your people for normal, ongoing work.

Given this more detailed description of delegation, how do you do it? If your team comprises members at all levels of experience and skill, you should be delegating at all three levels. If, over time, you find yourself still delegating mostly at low and moderate levels (high and moderate control), you're probably not delegating enough.

Many managers think they're truly delegating at a high level, when their people would describe their efforts as moderate- or low-level. Talk to your people about how you delegate—the level you use most. If they think you're too controlling—or they want more supervision—they'll let you know, and you can negotiate how to proceed. The level of involvement is your call, but you need to know what your people think.

Remember that delegation doesn't mean you can't be involved. For tasks and initiatives critical to success, you need to stay connected and pay attention to detail. You can attend meetings as a participant, not the leader, ask for special reports and updates, talk to customers yourself, listen in on customer service lines,

Delegation level 1 Low delegation—high control	Delegation level 2 Moderate delegation—moderate control	Delegation level 3 High delegation—low control
Use with someone about to do work he's never or rarely done before.	**Use with** someone who has some experience, perhaps someone who's observed others and should be ready to act on her own.	**Use with** someone who has actually demonstrated competence.
Prep: Here the problem is more likely one of skill versus will, so describe how to do the work and coach him through the steps involved. Make clear the boundaries: budget, strategy, policy, and so on. If appropriate, take him through practice runs. If the problem is also one of will, set the activity in the context of the team's work and its purpose and goals. Make sure he understands the consequences of possible outcomes.	**Prep:** Ask her to describe her plan for doing the work and the various "What . . .?" questions. Satisfy yourself that she's well prepared and ready. Explain constraints or boundaries. Agree on what constitutes success. Coach as necessary. Make sure she understands the reason for doing the work and why it's important. See whether she can link to team purpose and goals.	**Prep:** Leave the prep to him. Involve yourself only if the work—say, a discussion he will have with an important prospective customer—is unusually important to team purpose and goals. If it is, ask for his preparatory thinking. Provide clear direction and boundaries. Agree on success. Here the issue may be more one of will than skill, and so make sure he understands the importance and consequences of the action.
Do: At first, you do the work as he observes. If the consequences of failure are low, you could observe while he performs the task.	**Do:** Let her do the work, perhaps with you present observing, perhaps alone, depending on the situation and your judgment of her readiness.	**Do:** He conducts the discussion without your involvement or presence.
Review: Walk through what you (or he) did. Answer questions. Identify lessons. Have him describe how he would do it next time.	**Review:** Ask for her self-assessment of how it went, in terms of both skill and will. What went well and what could be improved? Then, if you were present, give your assessment and discuss any differences. Identify lessons. Focus on tangible outcomes and specific behaviors. If you couldn't be present, ask others who were there. Reach agreement with her about what should be different or better next time.	**Review:** If this was routine work and it had a good or expected outcome, you won't have a review discussion except as part of a periodic general performance review. If it was more than routine work or the outcome was unexpected, ask for his self-assessment of what happened and what might be learned from it.

look at online comments from users, and discuss the work directly with those doing it. As with so much in management, you need judgment and skill to stay connected and involved with critical work without taking over.

The goal each time you use prep-do-review is that your team and its members emerge more able, confident, and willing. That will happen if you instill an atmosphere of thinking ahead, assessing outcomes, and improving all the time, for prep-do-review is a learning model. It mimics the way we learn best: by trying, evaluating the outcome, and trying again. It's how we take on any new skill or role. Using it will turn every activity into a learning experience.

In fact, this simple model is the fundamental cycle of activities by which effective managers manage: a perpetual loop of prep-do-review-prep-do-review. It's the way you convert mundane workday activities into management tools. It's crucial to making progress *through* the daily work. And it's the way you guide your people, produce results, and help them learn, without inserting yourself unnecessarily in what they do.

But it's not the magic elixir of success. Most—but not all—of your daily activities can be used to do managerial work. And not all managerial work can be done in this way. Some activities, such as making plans, will require your own or others' dedicated time and effort. Nonetheless, using prep-do-review as we suggest can save much time and make you and your team far more effective. If there's anything approaching a "secret" of management, this is it. It's the way you use the daily work to do your work as a manager. It's how you put the 3 Imperatives to work in all you do, every day.

Where Are You on Your Journey?

Imperative 3: Manage Your Team

Is the group you manage a real team? Does it have a strong sense of purpose? Have you defined the future? Is there a strong team culture that supports your purpose and goals and that constructively guides the work and interactions of your team?

How do you stand up to these standards as a boss? Use these questions to find out.

Do You Define and Constantly Refine the Future You and Your Team Are Trying to Create?

Do you have a plan, both written and unwritten, that defines your team's purpose; what you do now; where you want to be in the future; and the goals, strategies, and actions that will take you there?

1	2	3	4	5
No, I really need to work on this				I do this consistently and well

Are you constantly gathering information, discussing your view of the future with colleagues, and refining your plan?

1	2	3	4	5
No, I really need to work on this				I do this consistently and well

Do You Clarify the Roles, Work Rules, Team Culture, and Feedback About Performance That Turn a Group of People into a Genuine Team?

Do your people feel a strong sense of "we," a mutual belief that all are pulling together toward the same worthwhile purpose, and that all will succeed or fail together?

1	2	3	4	5
No, not really				Yes, they would all say they do

Do your people know their individual roles and how each role contributes to the team's purpose and goals? Would they agree with your answer?

1	2	3	4	5
No, not really				Yes, they would all say they do

Do your people know how the team does its work—recurring events, systems, and practices? Would they agree?

1	2	3	4	5
No, not really				Yes, they would all say they do

Do they know and share the values, beliefs, and expectations that guide how they work together? Would they agree?

1	2	3	4	5
No, not really				Yes, they would all say they do

Do they receive regular feedback as a team and as individuals?

1	2	3	4	5
No, not really				Yes, they would all say they do

Do you review and discuss all these issues regularly with your team?

1	2	3	4	5
No, not really				Yes, they would all say I do

Do You Know and Manage Your People as Individuals as Well as Team Members?

Do you know and interact actively and equitably with all team members as individuals?

1	2	3	4	5
No, not really				Yes, they would all say I do

Do you delegate to your people as much as possible?

1	2	3	4	5
No, not really				Yes, they would all say I do

Do you strive to help team members grow and develop?

1	2	3	4	5
No, not really				Yes, they would all say I do

Do you constantly assess people's performance?

1	2	3	4	5
No, not really				Yes, they would all say I do

Do you hire qualified people who both fit the team and bring diversity?

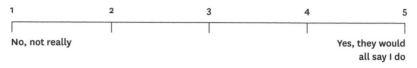

Do you deal with performance issues quickly, if necessary removing team members who cannot or will not perform?

Do You Use Daily Activities, Events, and Problems to Pursue the 3 Imperatives?

Do you approach all work thoughtfully—by using prep-do-review?

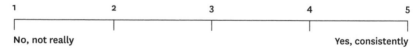

Do you consider how every problem, obligation, or event, planned or unplanned, can be used to make progress on your team's goals, to build the team, to develop people, and to strengthen your network?

Do you expect this approach of your people?

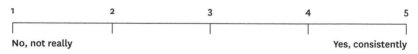

12

COMPLETING YOUR JOURNEY

Learn from Your Experiences and Relationships

3:55 p.m. The impromptu meeting is over. Everyone has spent the past hour discussing the problems that Project Emerge faces.

As people prepare to leave, Jason says, "A final comment. I need your help in a couple of ways. First, we need to keep the discussion going that started today. I'm going to set up a way to do this on our Project Emerge wiki so we can keep looking for solutions. All of you will have a chance to take part and contribute your ideas. You'll be hearing more about this soon. Second, my job in general is to make sure you succeed, to create a place where all of you as a group can do great work. If I'm not doing something that would help you . . . if I'm doing something that gets in your way . . . let me know. Just come up and tell me. Ask for five minutes and let me know. I'm not a mind reader. Even if I end up disagreeing with you, I'll always be glad to hear from you.

"In fact," Jason continues, "I need your help in a specific area. Every job gives us new challenges. Mine here at Project Emerge is to build bridges between us and the rest of the division, as well as outside groups, the IFTE in particular. Our success depends on

my ability to do that. Unfortunately, while it mattered in my previous work, I could get away with doing only a little of it, just the
things I had to do. It was certainly not something I was eager to
do or did naturally. So I'm going to be learning.

"Here's how you can help. All of you deal with other parts of
the company and with outside groups. Ask how we're doing. Tell
me what you hear. If there's a problem. If people don't understand what we're up to. If there's something we need to do for
others. If there's someone out there I should be talking to, let me
know. Believe me, I'm not looking for more things to do. But we
cannot succeed without the help and support of the rest of the
company. And I need your help with that challenge."

4:05 p.m.   Julia Morgan knocks on the open door of Jason's
office where Jason is making notes for his meeting with Cavit
about the presentation at Sales Conference.

"Thank you," she says, "it was good to meet and discuss those
things." She comes in, a worried look on her face. "I'm sorry to
bother you again, but I wonder if you've thought any more about
my request . . . for the cubicle with windows." She seems both
embarrassed and determined.

It had slipped Jason's mind entirely. "I'm sorry," he says.
"I know it's important to you. With everything else going on, I forgot. I should have raised it in the meeting."

"It's very important to me," she says. She looks troubled. "I get
so, uh, so sad this time of year. It's hard." She's fighting to hold
herself together.

"I'm sorry I didn't bring it up," Jason says. "Let me put out an
e-mail right now, give everyone through Monday to respond, and
then we'll settle it first thing Tuesday. I promise."

Return now to the question we asked in the beginning:
Where are you on your journey to management mastery?
How effective are you as a manager right now? How much further must you go to master the imperatives? Are you able to influence others to work together productively, not just those on your

team but others you depend on but don't control? Are you able to bring out the best your team is able to do?

Or have you stopped making progress? Have you become comfortable enough as a manager, have you learned enough to get by, so that making progress no longer seems important?

Progress will only come from your own work experience, from trying and learning, observing and interacting with others, experimenting and pushing yourself. Even if you're richly talented, there are no shortcuts, for you yourself are the subject. Management will provide endless opportunities to learn about yourself, your values, your goals and aspirations, your talents, your character under pressure.

Experience will not yield its lessons easily or quickly. Many work situations and outcomes are so complex they can seem to support conflicting conclusions. Only through broad and varied experience, with constant questioning and testing, will lessons emerge that carry you forward.

Do You Know Your Strengths and Where You Need to Improve?

All progress on your journey begins with a clear sense of where you are now. To help you develop that sense, we offer below a set of questions that both summarize the key areas of the 3 Imperatives and let you appraise yourself against those areas.

Rate your current strength in each area, based on how completely you match *all* elements of the descriptions. To merit a 5 in an area, for example, you must satisfy each aspect or dimension of the description.

The questions here are less detailed versions of those that appear in the summaries at the end of each part. Use these for a quick self-assessment or those in the summaries for a more detailed review of your strengths and the areas where you need to make progress.

Imperative 1: You're Able to Manage Yourself

You Use Your Formal Authority Effectively

This is a strength to the degree you consider your formal authority
a useful tool but not the primary way you influence others or the
key driver of relationships with your people. You exercise your
authority transparently—making clear what, how, and why you do
what you do—and even share it with others as possible and appropriate. You focus more on the duties and responsibilities that
come with authority than on the personal rights, privileges, and
perks it provides. You avoid creating relationships focused on
authority in which you think of people merely as instruments to
carry out your instructions.

1	2	3	4	5
Needs much work				Fully developed

You Create Human, Caring, but Not Personal Relationships with Your People

This is a strength to the degree you're able to create and maintain
relationships that are supportive and rich in human connections
but always focused on the purpose and goals of the team and the
organization. You avoid trying to influence people by making
friends of them—creating relationships that are close and personal in which the relationship itself is ultimately more important than the work it's meant to accomplish.

1	2	3	4	5
Needs much work				Fully developed

Others, Especially Your Own People, Trust You as a Manager

This is a strength to the degree others believe they can count on you
to do the right thing. They believe in your technical, operational,
and political *competence* and your *character*: your intentions,
values, and standards, as well as your emotional resilience and

maturity. And you have evidence of others' trust in you—your assessment is based on more than your personal opinion.

1	2	3	4	5

Needs much
work

Fully
developed

You Exercise Your Authority and Influence Ethically

This is a strength to the degree you consistently and systematically, before taking any important action, identify stakeholders and their interests, weigh those interests, and then, when acting, try to mitigate whatever harm may come to some because of what you do.

1	2	3	4	5

Needs much
work

Fully
developed

Imperative 2: You're Able to Manage Your Network

You Systematically Identify Those Inside and Outside Your Organization Who Should Be in Your Network

This is a strength to the degree you systematically identify the people and groups on whom you and your team depend to achieve your goals, or who depend on you to reach theirs. You constantly reevaluate your networks and your relationships within them to keep up with changes in the organization, the world around you, and your plans.

1	2	3	4	5

Needs much
work

Fully
developed

You Proactively Build and Maintain Your Operational Network

This is a strength to the degree you consciously and systematically reach out to create and sustain ongoing relationships with those you identify as members of your operational network: *the people you need to do your group's everyday work.* In it, you're building a combination of weak, wide-ranging ties and strong ties with those on whom you depend most. You actively seek to understand and support the needs of network members. You seize opportunities to connect with network members.

1	2	3	4	5
Needs much work				Fully developed

You Proactively Build and Maintain Your Strategic Network

This is a strength to the degree you consciously and systematically reach out to create and sustain ongoing relationships with those you identify as members of your strategic network: *the people you need or will need to help you and your group achieve your longer-term goals.* In it, you're building a combination of weak, wide-ranging ties and strong ties with those on whom you depend most. You actively seek to understand and support the needs of network members. You seize opportunities to connect with network members.

1	2	3	4	5
Needs much work				Fully developed

You Use Your Networks to Provide the Protection and Resources Your Team Needs

This is a strength to the degree you proactively speak for and represent your team and its needs. You protect your team from distractions and misunderstandings. You solve problems inside and outside the team as necessary. You use your networks to secure the funds, people, information, support, and other resources your team needs.

1	2	3	4	5
Needs much work				Fully developed

You Proactively Use Your Network to Accomplish Your Team's Goals

This is a strength to the degree you seek help and cooperation from your network in building the future you've defined with your team. You build coalitions of network members in support of your team's purpose, goals, and plans. You actively help others in your networks achieve their goals. Your network colleagues trust you—they believe your competence and character will lead you to do the right thing for all of you.

1	2	3	4	5

Needs much   Fully
work   developed

Imperative 3: You're Able to Create and Manage a Team

You Define and Constantly Refine the Future You and Your Team Are Trying to Create

This is a strength to the degree you have a plan, both written and unwritten, that defines your team's purpose; what you do now; where you want to be in the future; and the goals, strategies, and actions that will take you there. You're constantly gathering information, discussing your view of the future with colleagues, and refining your plan.

1	2	3	4	5

Needs much   Fully
work   developed

You Clarify the Roles, Work Rules, Team Culture, and Feedback About Performance That Turn a Group of People into a Genuine Team

This is a strength to the degree your people feel a strong sense of "we," a mutual belief that all are pulling together toward the same worthwhile purpose, and that all will succeed or fail together. Your people know their roles and how each role contributes to the team's purpose and goals. They know how the team does its work—recurring events, systems, and practices. They know and share the values, beliefs, and expectations that guide how they work together. They receive regular feedback as a team and as individuals. You review all these issues periodically with your team.

1	2	3	4	5

Needs much   Fully
work   developed

You Know and Manage Your People as Individuals as Well as Team Members

This is a strength to the degree you know and interact actively and equitably with all team members as individuals. You delegate as much as possible. You strive to help team members grow and develop. You constantly assess people's performance. You hire people who both fit the team and bring diversity. You deal with performance issues quickly, if necessary removing members who cannot or will not perform.

1	2	3	4	5
Needs much work				Fully developed

You Use Daily Activities, Events, and Problems to Pursue the 3 Imperatives

This is a strength to the degree you approach all work thoughtfully—by using prep-do-review. You consider how every problem, obligation, or event, planned or unplanned, can be used to make progress on your team's goals, to build the team, to develop people, and to strengthen your network. You expect this approach of your people.

1	2	3	4	5
Needs much work				Fully developed

How Did You Do?

Whether you answered the questions here or those that summarized each part, look back over your self-ratings. Is there a range—a few 1s, some 2s, several 3s, a few 4s, and perhaps one or two 5s? If you've rated yourself consistently 3 or above, you should be skeptical. Few bosses in our experience merit high ratings across the board, and it's only human for all of us to rate ourselves more highly than others might.

Don't be discouraged: no manager will meet all the standards implicit in the 3 Imperatives. They require precious time and much effort. Indeed, all managers are flawed, even the most successful and effective. As we've said more than once, the goal is not perfection. The goal is to develop the strengths you need to succeed, and eliminate or compensate only for those that can cause you to fail.

Here are some ways to think about your self-ratings:

Pay particular attention to your strengths. What do you do well now? Are there areas where you feel proficient? Have others identified them as your strong suits? Genuine strengths lead to opportunities—promotion or stretch assignments—that can help you develop new strengths.

Look at your strengths not by themselves but in the context of your organization's goals and strategies. What knowledge and skills does—will—it need? How can your strengths help the organization move forward? These are the strengths that can lead to the most opportunities and thus the most rapid progress. Use the needs of your organization to identify moderate strengths—3s— that you can grow to make yourself more likely to receive attractive assignments.

Do you know your *fatal* shortcomings? Look at areas where you rated yourself only a 1 or 2, and identify those that put you and your team in jeopardy. Focus there. Suppose your organization constantly looks into the future and makes plans, but planning is something you don't enjoy or do particularly well. Work on that right away by taking one or both of two possible approaches. Overcome it in yourself, if possible. Or work around it, say, by aligning with others—subordinates, colleagues, or even outsiders—who can help you compensate. Remember, however, that weaknesses not serious now can become fatal as you take on more responsibility. Assess yourself periodically to make sure you aren't caught by new needs required by a changing context.

Are you aware of your management preferences? Some aspects of the 3 Imperatives will excite you more than others. Knowing your preferences provides two insights. First, a strength combined with a preference is a potent combination. If you like developing people and are skilled at it, your chances of success rise in projects that require people to learn rapidly. Second, these are the parts of managing you'll gravitate toward because you prefer them, which means you may overemphasize them. Remember that strengths overdone can become weaknesses. For example, the ability to analyze data in highly creative ways, if taken to an extreme and used to browbeat or intimidate, will only irritate others without producing the agreement you want.

Do you know which parts of management you like least? Management is difficult in part because the 3 Imperatives can call on you to behave in ways that make you uncomfortable, at least initially. Giving people tough feedback is something many managers avoid. You cannot rely on your inclinations to pick and choose what you do. But if you recognize your dislikes, you can step back, think through the right course of action, seek the counsel of confidants, and evade the trap of unconsciously avoiding what makes you uncomfortable.

Can you see a connection between your strengths and weaknesses and your likes and dislikes? It's natural to like what you think you do well and dislike what you're not good at. But don't let your preferences drive your development. Remember, as you get better at some piece of management, your feelings about it are likely to change.

Have You Set Personal Goals?

If you work through your self-assessment as we suggest, you'll be able to set goals for self-development based on what will produce the greatest progress in your current journey. Write down your goals and keep them in mind all the time. Review and revise them periodically. They are the road map for your journey.

Do You Know How to Make Progress?

Now that you know where you need to make progress, do you know how to move ahead?

Do You Take Advantage of Company/Formal Training?

Don't overlook the formal training that may be available where you work. Besides the knowledge and skills they impart, these programs can help you understand the policies, procedures, practices, and culture of your organization—the context in which you work and gain experience. They can also introduce you to a broad range of colleagues, some of whom will become members of your networks.

Do You Use Your Daily Work to Develop Yourself?

Just as you use daily tasks to do your work as a manager, use them to develop yourself. This is where your most valuable learning will occur. Prep-do-review provides a useful approach.

Prep. Begin each morning with a quick preview of the coming day's events. For each, ask yourself how you can use it to develop as a manager and in particular how you can work on your specific learning goals. If delegation presents a challenge, consider delegating a task you would normally do yourself, and think about how you might do that—to whom, what questions you should ask, what boundaries or limits you should set, what preliminary coaching you might provide. Apply the same thinking during the day when a problem comes up unexpectedly. Before taking any action, step back for a second and consider how you can use it to become better.

Do. Planning to act in new and different ways isn't enough. You must carry through, not lose your resolve at the last moment. Stretch yourself. If you don't move outside familiar patterns, you're unlikely to make much progress. For example, if you tend to cut off conflict in a meeting, even constructive conflict, hold back and allow disagreement to be expressed and worked through—stepping in only if it turns personal or points of view are being stifled. The ideas that emerge may lead you to a better outcome.

Review. Reflection works best if you make it a regular practice. Set aside time toward the end of each day—perhaps on your commute home—to review the day's events and outcomes. What worked well? What might you have done differently? Replay conversations. Compare what you did or said with what you might have done if you were the manager you aspire to be. Where did you disappoint yourself and how did that happen?

Above all, ask yourself the fundamental questions we keep emphasizing: How did people experience you—what was it like to deal with you? How did people experience *themselves* when interacting with you? As you reflect on each interaction, think about whether others emerged from dealing with you more willing and able to do good work. If not, why not?

Finally, apply your own goals to the day's events. Did you practice any new behaviors or otherwise make progress on your own journey? How might you have used the day's events to move closer to the manager you want to become?

Some managers keep notes in a notebook or on the computer about how they spent their time, along with thoughts about what they learned. A CEO told us he began to record his reflections every Friday about the week past. Within six weeks, he said, he developed greater discipline to say no to anything "not on the critical path," which gave him time to spend with key regulators and jump-start the corporate globalization strategy.

Do You Seek Feedback?

Do you know how others react to you? One of your key challenges is to understand your real impact on others as boss, colleague, and subordinate.[1]

It's often not what you intended. Praise can be taken as implied criticism because it wasn't as specific or lavish as the recipient thought was deserved. We know of a U.S. manager who had performed badly, but he received such a calm and measured performance appraisal from his U.K. boss that he thought he'd escaped unscathed. In fact, he was about to be fired.

Time and again, research shows that many managers misconstrue, misinterpret, and misunderstand what people think of them as bosses.[2] Many managers believe they provide "clear vision and direction" or they delegate extensively, when their people say they do not. A manager we know stayed late for the several days her group was working after hours on a crash project. Her presence into the evenings wasn't required by the work, but she wanted to show solidarity. Only later, when she happened to ask, did someone reveal that people resented her presence because they took it to mean she didn't trust them.

This is why developing yourself through learning from experience requires that you *seek feedback, as well as help and advice, from others.* You need candid comments. The more honest they are, the more accurate your self-assessment is likely to be.

Are you able to ask other people's opinions of you? Getting this information isn't easy. Simply asking rarely produces the full, unvarnished truth. We all know people who say they want to know what others think, but they really don't want to hear anything negative. It's only natural for people to think you're one of those people, especially if they don't know you well. Over time, as people test your tolerance, you'll slowly earn a reputation for the ability to hear candid comments.

How good are you at receiving personal feedback, especially if it's not positive? Do you reject what you're hearing outright? Do you merely listen passively and apologize without taking the information to heart? Do you react by defending and justifying yourself?

Or are you able to respond in more positive ways? Do you communicate an attitude of trying to understand and learn from what you're hearing? Do you ask for examples? Do you request clarification and pose questions? This is tough to do, but you cannot deny the reality of other people's feelings, reactions, and perceptions. They're neither right nor wrong. Whatever they are, you must know them and deal with them.

Many companies conduct 360-reviews that provide candid feedback from those you work with. The results can be disconcerting, but enlightening and even life changing too. Also, corporate management programs often provide safe settings in which you can experiment with new ways of behaving, through role-playing and other exercises.

Have You Created a Developmental Network?

The best way to obtain such feedback is through your own network of personal supporters and confidants, your own personal board of directors.[3]

In chapter 6 we described two networks: an *operational network* of those involved in the daily work of your team, and a *strategic network* of those you need as your team pursues its longer-term goals. Now we describe a third; a *developmental network* of those who can help you make progress on your personal journey to management mastery. Think of this network as your own board of advisers.

You cannot make progress alone. You need not only candid feedback but also protection and sponsorship, help learning new skills, coaching about how to handle difficult problems, freedom to express your feelings without fear, and access to opportunities. The members of your developmental network are those from whom you can seek such assistance. They won't tell you what to do, but they can help you identify options, think through different alternatives, see yourself as others see you, make decisions that balance harm for some against a greater good, and handle the emotions that management arouses.

Because management is stressful—full of conflict, fragmentation, frustration, ambiguity, and the necessity of making decisions that touch people personally—a key function of your developmental network is to provide emotional support. For that, it should include confidants to whom you can express your feelings, fears, and shortcomings. These are people you trust personally, to whom you can risk exposing yourself and exploring personal and professional dilemmas, and whose experience and judgment you respect.

Because of its nature, this network will almost certainly be smaller than your others. It may share some members with them, but it should also include people who have little stake in your work that might color what they tell you. So choose its members carefully. Seek candor and honesty. Seek diversity too in order to obtain the different forms of help you will need on your journey. Avoid those whose personal and professional agendas may overwhelm their ability to focus on your best interests. Be willing to serve in the developmental networks of those who serve in yours.

Members in your developmental network can come from virtually anywhere, including your circle of personal friends, but certain groups or individuals are more likely to be involved than others.

Do You Include Your Peers?

This is the group that many managers feel most comfortable approaching for insight and help. Peers pose fewer issues of hierarchy and status to complicate things. Because many of them do work similar to yours, you can receive a different but empathetic point of view, discuss problems openly and freely, test ideas and approaches, and seek candid feedback about how they and others see you and your group. They can suggest new ways of thinking or good questions to consider. Little wonder peer relationships can be close, especially between those promoted to similar positions at the same time, and last a long time. For many managers, these are the closest personal relationships they have at work.

Yet peer relationships can be problematic too. Peers can be your competitors at work—for promotion, resources, and attention—which may limit their ability to give you unbiased help. That they work at the same level as you limits the depth and quality of what they can tell you, particularly about how to advance further.

For those reasons, and because you will need greater depth and diversity of advice as you make progress, your developmental networks must include more than peers.

Do You Include Your Boss?

Many managers view their bosses as threats, as opposed to allies, in their development. They only turn to superiors for help when there's a crisis of some sort. Fortunately, they're often surprised to receive a more supportive response than they expected. If you shoulder responsibility for your own development and take the initiative, you may find your boss a valuable source of feedback, information, and guidance.

Not all bosses can or want to play this role. So proceed slowly and test how far you can go at each stage—especially if you have a boss who is new to his position. He, too, will have his insecurities and will be learning how to be an effective coach.

Do You Include Those Who Work for You?

It's unlikely you will—or should—go to your subordinates for personal advice. But don't overlook them as an important source of feedback. These are the very people you're trying to influence, and you need to know the effects on them of your words and actions.

To get their real thoughts, you need their trust, which takes time to develop. It will help if you're open about your desire to improve and if you admit your own mistakes and shortcomings and how you plan to overcome them. Sometimes it's more fruitful to ask not for their personal opinions but what "people" in general think.

Many managers resist this approach. They're overly fearful of appearing weak, uncertain, and ineffectual. As we said before, there's a fine line here, and you must use your judgment, situation by situation, to stay on the positive side of it. But hollow confidence and misperception of your effect on others are hardly better and likely worse.

When seeking feedback, ask your people to identify ways you're fostering or hindering the ability of the team to do its best work. Use as a rough guide the self-assessment questions based on the 3 Imperatives that appeared at the start of the chapter. Seek to find out whether any of the areas covered there offer any opportunities, in your people's opinions, for you to do a better job.

Do You Learn from Role Models?

For all the skills needed to pursue the 3 Imperatives, there exists a vast gap between knowing *what* to do and knowing *how* to do it. To learn the *how*, find other managers you admire, who possess skills and expertise you lack. Learn by watching them actually do what you hope to do. Instead of simply mimicking others, experiment with different approaches until you find those that feel authentic and comfortable and produce the results you want.[4] In the end, you will blend example, advice, and insight from many sources into your own way of working.

Can You Endure the Discomfort of Learning?

Learning can be painful. You try and fall short, learn from the experience, and then try again and again, until you become proficient. It's painful because no one likes the feeling of incompetence those early efforts produce. Think about delegating. Your first efforts are likely to make you feel uneasy and may even produce poor results. It's easier, less discomforting, you may think, just to fall back on doing the task yourself.[5]

So you're caught in a dilemma. You can keep doing well what you're comfortable doing (do it yourself), even though it won't produce the results you want. Or you can do something new (delegate) that will eventually produce the results you want even though you do it poorly at first and it makes you uncomfortable. That's a difficult trade-off. Can you endure the feelings of incompetence and frustration generated by doing something not well initially, even if it's the right thing to do? You have to if you're to make any progress. Be patient.

To get past this hurdle, you will need emotional support, as well as feedback, guidance, and suggestions. This is one of the key roles your developmental network can play.

Do You Have Mentors or Other Advisers?

Much is made of finding a mentor at work—someone more senior who will give you wise counsel, protect you when necessary, open doors to opportunity, and generally act as your advocate.

Unfortunately, you cannot create or choose a true mentor. Such connections require some level of personal chemistry, develop slowly, and are difficult to maintain because they require effort and risk on both sides. A mentor who falls from grace can bring the protégé down too, and a protégé who performs badly or somehow stumbles can damage the mentor.

Instead of seeking an ideal mentor, develop several relationships with those inside and outside the organization who can help you learn and develop yourself. While you cannot force such things, you can make yourself available by behaving like the perfect protégé: someone who shares responsibility for the relationship by:

- Being eager to learn

- Making a genuine effort to apply what has been learned

- Being open to honest, even tough, feedback and advice

- Using the mentor's time and resources wisely

- Fulfilling requests made by the mentor

- Always acting in a way that reflects well on the mentor

- Minimizing any risks to the mentor

- Treating the relationship and what is said and done in it confidentially

- Being appreciative of help received

- Above all, making the mentor look good—usually by performing well and giving the mentor credit

Do You Seek Out New Developmental Experiences?

Besides learning from the events of your normal workday, you can actively seek out learning situations. This may mean you take on stretch assignments in your current work that broaden your experience, help you develop new ways of thinking and acting, and prepare you for advancement.

You needn't wait for such opportunities to appear. If you know where and how you need to develop, if you take a strategic, far-reaching view of your journey, you can propose or create opportunities and assignments. This approach works best when you combine your needs and goals with those of your organization so that your growth contributes to corporate objectives.

Create a self-reinforcing cycle of success by using your strengths to land or create growth assignments, which you then use to develop new strengths, which lead to more and more challenging growth assignments. In this way, your track record and reputation will grow, you'll acquire more influence and responsibility, your network will become wider and more influential, and your role in it will become more prominent—all of which will lead to even more opportunities for growth, advancement, and progress on your journey.

Have You Developed the Emotional Maturity
to Move Forward?

What we've said of those who work for you also applies to you: all development in the end is self-development. Take responsibility for your own journey.

That requires you to develop through experience and reflection, supported by your own developmental network, emotional maturity, competence, and resilience—the strong ego rather than the big ego that we described earlier. With a strong ego you'll be able to see your journey through.

EPILOGUE

The journey is difficult. It demands more of you than initiative and ambition, for the 3 Imperatives will inevitably call on you to act and speak in ways that may initially seem counterintuitive or out of character. You will need at times to cut against the grain of your own inclinations and even the expectations of others. Few people become effective managers by simply following their gut.

Thus, you will need not just self-awareness but self-control, personal discipline, determination, and resilience.

Constantly evaluating yourself and seeking feedback will open you to inevitable pain and risk. You will probably hear and discover things about yourself that differ from your cherished self-perceptions. You'll discover you're not always the person you think you are or the person you aspire to be. This kind of learning is particularly difficult for former stars unaccustomed to falling short and having to pick themselves up again.

Seeking help and advice can seem to imply weakness. Forgoing the illusion that you, the boss, know and control everything can be difficult. Hearing hurtful things and absorbing them without anger or defensiveness requires enormous maturity. Reaching out to others you may fear, including colleagues who aren't necessarily your allies and a boss who holds your future in his hands, isn't easy. To share your own shortcomings and need for growth is to make yourself vulnerable.

But there's no alternative. The journey requires you to grow beyond your initial strengths and develop new capabilities to meet the demands of increasingly complex and difficult work.

No wonder so many managers grow *less* inclined with experience to accept feedback and use it to improve themselves. No wonder so many give up their journey short of mastering the 3 Imperatives. No wonder fewer people today aspire to be managers at all.

So it's fair to ask, Why should you pursue something so difficult? Why push ahead on your journey?

Because of the satisfaction that can come to you if you do—satisfaction from at least three sources.

Satisfaction from the rewards you reap: recognition, advancement, income, status, and privilege. These may or may not motivate you, and we're not saying they should; but in a society that values such things, they are not nothing, especially when combined with other sources of fulfillment.

Satisfaction from the increasing positive impact you have on the work and lives of others. As you make progress on your journey, you will be given greater responsibility for larger groups of people. With that responsibility will come increasing impact on your organization, its success, and all the people in it. If you aspire to make a difference, to move beyond what you can accomplish as an individual, the journey will make that possible. Think beyond closing the *performance gap*: the difference between your group's current performance and its targets. That's important, but the real purpose of the journey is to close the *opportunity gap*: the difference between current performance and the best your group is capable of doing, which often is far more than the target. You demonstrate mastery when you're able to guide your group—whether a few people or an entire organization—to do the best work it can do. In addition, your effect on people and the quality of their lives can be profound. Those who work for you spend half their waking hours on the job, five days a week, a considerable chunk of their lives. It's in your power to shape not only their work but how they think of themselves in doing the work.

Finally, *satisfaction from doing something important for society*. Management isn't usually discussed in these terms, but without it, society cannot function. We depend on the ability of organizations, groups of people of all sizes and purposes, to function productively, and management is the critical difference. Management makes it possible for groups of people to do useful collective work. Without it, things fall apart—people put personal interests above collective needs, they operate at cross-purposes, and the political forces in all organizations eventually pull them apart. Without what you do, the institutions of society—commercial, military, governmental, social—cannot function productively for long. If you and enough other managers stop your journeys short of the destination, society and all in it will be the worse for it.

For your sake, for the sake of those around you, for the sake of all of us, we hope you will keep striving and moving forward. The effort required is great but so are the benefits and rewards.

We said the journey requires self-awareness, self-control, discipline, and resilience. To that list we must add one more quality: personal courage.

All of us are counting on you to be courageous.

Join us at http://www.hbr.org/beingtheboss where you'll find tools for the journey, additional information, a place to share your thoughts and experiences, a detailed bibliography, and more.

Reynolds Education Organization Chart and List of Characters

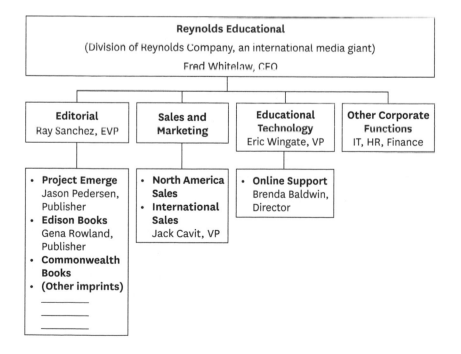

Reynolds Educational

(Division of Reynolds Company, an international media giant)

Fred Whitelaw, CEO

Editorial
Ray Sanchez, EVP

Sales and Marketing

Educational Technology
Eric Wingate, VP

Other Corporate Functions
IT, HR, Finance

- **Project Emerge**
  Jason Pedersen, Publisher
- **Edison Books**
  Gena Rowland, Publisher
- **Commonwealth Books**
- **(Other imprints)**
  _____
  _____
  _____

- **North America Sales**
- **International Sales**
  Jack Cavit, VP

- **Online Support**
  Brenda Baldwin, Director

Characters

Project Emerge

Jason Pedersen—publisher

Sumantra Tata—senior editor

Kathy Wu—assistant editor

Julia Morgan—editorial assistant

Laraba Sule—marketing manager

Jay Bradshaw—manager of online production

Roberto Lujan—manager of school relations

Barry Hultgrund—financial analyst (assigned to Project Emerge)

Kim Young—administrative assistant

Others—Reynolds Educational

Fred Whitelaw—CEO

Ray Sanchez—executive vice president, editorial

Eric Wingate—vice president, educational technology

Brenda Baldwin—director of online support, educational technology

Jack Cavit—vice president, international sales

Frank Rigby—former publisher of Project Emerge

Gena Rowland—publisher of Edison Books

International Fund for Technical Education (IFTE)

Jacques Levanger—senior manager, liaison for Project Emerge

Dr. Schmidt—member, board of directors, and member, Project Emerge editorial advisory board

NOTES

Introduction

1. See, for example, Patrick Barwise and Sean Meehan, "So You Think You're a Good Listener," *Harvard Business Review*, April 2008, 22–25; and Daniel Goleman, *Emotional Intelligence* (New York: Bantam Books, 1995).

2. Unless otherwise indicated, all quotations are taken from interviews conducted by Linda A. Hill in her research on how managers learn to manage and lead.

Chapter 1

1. See, for example, John P. Kotter, *The General Managers* (New York: Free Press, 1982); Henry Mintzberg, *Managing* (San Francisco: Berrett-Koehler, 2009), 19–25; Henry Mintzberg, *The Nature of Managerial Work* (New York: Harper & Row, 1973); Leonard Sayles, *Leadership: Managing in Real Organizations* (New York: McGraw-Hill, 1989); and Rosemary Stewart, *Choices for the Manager* (Englewood Cliffs, NJ: Prentice-Hall, 1982).

2. Mintzberg, *Managing*, 161.

3. For other examples of a discussion of the paradoxes of management, see David L. Bradford and Allan R. Cohen, *Managing for Excellence: The Guide to Developing High Performance in Contemporary Organizations* (New York: John Wiley, 1984); and Kenwyn K. Smith and David N. Berg, *Paradoxes of Group Life: Understanding Conflict, Paralysis, and Movement in Group Dynamics* (San Francisco: Jossey-Bass, 1987).

4. Joan Magretta, *What Management Is: How It Works and Why It's Everyone's Business* (New York: Free Press, 2002), 195.

5. See, for example, J. Richard Hackman, *Groups That Work (and Those That Don't): Creating Conditions for Effective Teamwork* (San Francisco: Jossey-Bass, 1990); J. Richard Hackman, *Leading Teams: Setting the Stage for Great Performances* (Boston: Harvard Business School Press, 2002); and Linda A. Hill, "A Note on Building and Leading Your Senior Team (A)," Case 9-402-037 (Boston: Harvard Business School, 2002).

6. See, for example, Warren G. Bennis, *On Becoming a Leader* (Reading, MA: Addison-Wesley, 1989).

7. See, for example, Joshua Margolis and Andrew Molinsky, "Navigating the Bind of Necessary Evils: Psychological Engagement and the Production of Interpersonally Sensitive Behavior," *Academy of Management Journal* 51, no. 5 (2008): 847–872.

8. Linda A. Hill, *Becoming a Manager*, 2nd ed. (Boston: Harvard Business School Press, 2003).

9. See, for example, Gary Hamel and Bill Breen, *The Future of Management* (Boston: Harvard Business School Press, 2007); Linda A. Hill et al., "Unlocking the Slices of Genius in Your Organization: Leading for Innovation," in *Handbook of Leadership Theory and Practice: An HBS Centennial Colloquium on Advancing Leadership*, eds. Nitin Nohria and Rakesh Khurana (Boston: Harvard Business Press, 2010); Linda A. Hill, "Where Will We Find Tomorrow's Leaders?" *Harvard Business Review*, January 2008, 123–129; and James O'Toole and Edward E. Lawler, *The New American Workplace* (New York: Palgrave Macmillan, 2006).

10. For the first use of the term *psychological contract*, see Chris Argyris, *Understanding Organizational Behavior* (Homewood, IL: Dorsey Press, 1960). For a review of the work on this topic, see Denise M. Rousseau and René Schalk, *Psychological Contracts in Employment: Cross-National Perspectives* (Thousand Oaks, CA: Sage Publications, 2000).

11. See, for example, Doug A. Ready, Linda A. Hill, and Jay A. Conger, "Winning the Race for Talent in Emerging Markets," *Harvard Business Review*, November 2008, 2–9.

12. Rosemary Stewart, *Choices for the Manager* (Englewood Cliffs, NJ: Prentice-Hall, 1982), 71–75.

13. Kotter, *The General Managers*, 91–92, 127; Mintzberg, *Managing*, 26–33; and Mintzberg, *The Nature of Managerial Work*, 50–51, 180–181.

Chapter 2

1. See, for example, David C. McClelland and David H. Burnham, "Power Is the Great Motivator," *Harvard Business Review*, March–April 1976, 100–110; and Scott Spreier, "Leadership Run Amok," *Harvard Business Review*, June 2006, 72–82.

2. See, for example, Ronald A. Heifetz, *Leadership Without Easy Answers* (Cambridge, MA: Belknap Press of Harvard University Press, 1994), 263–266; Joan Magretta, *What Management Is: How It Works and Why It's Everyone's Business* (New York: Free Press, 2002), 195; and Rodd Wagner and James K. Harter, *12: The Elements of Great Managing* (New York: Gallup Press, 2006), chap. 3.

3. Linda A. Hill, Tarun Khanna, and Emily A. Stecker, "HCL Technologies (A)," Case 9-408-004 (Boston: Harvard Business School, 2008).

4. Henry Mintzberg, *Managing* (San Francisco: Berrett-Koehler, 2009), 215.

5. See, for example, Adam G. Galinsky et al., "Power and Perspectives Not Taken," *Psychological Science* 17, no. 12 (2006): 1068–1074; David Kipnis, *The Powerholders* (Chicago: University of Chicago Press, 1976); and Joe C. Magee, "Leadership and the Psychology of Power," in *The Psychology of Leadership: New Perspectives and Research*, eds. David M. Messick and Roderick M. Kramer (Mahwah, NJ: Lawrence Erlbaum Associates, 2005).

6. McClelland and Burnham, "Power Is the Great Motivator," 100–110.

7. See, for example, Mary Gentile, *Giving Voice to Values: How to Speak Your Mind When You Know What's Right* (New Haven, CT: Yale University Press, 2010); and Lynn S. Paine, *Value Shift: Why Companies Must Merge Social and Financial Imperatives to Achieve Superior Performance* (New York: McGraw-Hill, 2003).

8. See, for example, Victor H. Vroom and Philip W. Yetton, *Leadership and Decision-Making* (Pittsburgh, PA: University of Pittsburgh Press, 1973).

9. Kenneth Thompson, "The Collected Papers of Mary Parker Follett," in *The Early Sociology of Administration: Management and Organizations*, eds. Henry Metcalf and Lyndall Urwick, vol. 3 (New York: Harper, 2003), 274.

Chapter 3

1. See, for example, Bruce J. Avolio and Fred Luthans, *The High Impact Leader* (New York: McGraw Hill, 2006); and Rodd Wagner and James K. Harter, *12: The Elements of Great Managing* (New York: Gallup Press, 2006).

2. See, for example, Kelin E. Gersick, *Generation to Generation: Life Cycles of the Family Business* (Boston: Harvard Business School Press, 1997).

Chapter 4

1. See, for example, John J. Gabarro, *The Dynamics of Taking Charge* (Boston: Harvard Business School Press, 1987).

2. See, for example, Thomas J. DeLong, John J. Gabarro, and Robert J. Lees, *When Professionals Have to Lead: A New Model for High Performance* (Boston: Harvard Business School Press, 2007); Jay W. Lorsch and Peter F. Mathias, "When Professionals Have to Manage," *Harvard Business Review*, July–August 1987, 78–83; and Jay W. Lorsch and Thomas J. Tierney, *Aligning the Stars: How to Succeed When Professionals Drive Results* (Boston: Harvard Business School Press, 2002).

3. See, for example, Joshua Margolis and Andrew Molinksy, "Navigating the Bind of Necessary Evils: Psychologicial Engagement and the Production of Interpersonally Sensitive Behavior," *Academy of Management Journal* 51, no. 5 (2008), 847–872.

4. Daniel Goleman, *Emotional Intelligence* (New York: Bantam Books, 1995); and Daniel Goleman, Richard E. Boyatzis, and Annie McKee, *Primal Leadership: Realizing the Power of Emotional Intelligence* (Boston: Harvard Business School Press, 2002).

5. Alan Alda, *Never Have Your Dog Stuffed: And Other Things I've Learned* (New York: Random House Trade Paperbacks, 2006), 161–162.

6. See, for example, Salvatore R. Maddi and Deborah M. Khoshaba, *Resilience at Work: How to Succeed No Matter What Life Throws at You* (New York: AMACOM, 2005); Joshua D. Margolis and Paul G. Stoltz, "How to Bounce Back from Adversity," *Harvard Business Review*, January–February 2010, 86–92; and Karen Reivich and Andrew Shatte, *The Resilience Factor: 7 Keys to Finding Your Inner Strength and Overcoming Life's Hurdles* (New York: Broadway Books, 2002).

Chapter 5

1. For an example of the limitations of holding such a perspective on managerial effectiveness, see Herminia Ibarra and Otilia Obodaru, "Women and the Vision Thing," *Harvard Business Review*, January 2009, 62–70.

2. Henry Mintzberg, *The Nature of Managerial Work* (New York: Harper & Row, 1973).

3. See, for example, Linda A Hill, "Moral Leadership: A Development Agenda for Future Managers," in *Moral Leadership: The Theory and Practice of Power, Judgment, and Policy*, ed. Deborah Rhode (San Francisco: Jossey-Bass, 2006); and Rosabeth M. Kanter, "Power Failure in Management Circuits," *Harvard Business Review*, July 1979, 65–75.

4. Harold J. Leavitt, *Top Down: Why Hierarchies Are Here to Stay and How to Manage Them More Effectively* (Boston: Harvard Business School Press, 2005), 163.

5. See, for example, Linda A. Hill et al., "Unlocking the Slices of Genius in Your Organization: Leading for Innovation," in *Handbook of Leadership Theory and Practice: An HBS Centennial Colloquium on Advancing Leadership*, eds. Nitin Nohria and Rakesh Khurana (Boston: Harvard Business Press, 2010).

6. See, for example, Larry Hirschhorn and Thomas Gilmore, "The New Boundaries of the 'Boundaryless' Company," *Harvard Business Review*, May 1992, 104–115.

7. Herminia Ibarra, "Making Partner: A Mentor's Guide to the Psychological Journey," *Harvard Business Review*, March–April 2000, 146–154.

Chapter 6

1. Henry Mintzberg, *Managing* (San Francisco: Berrett-Koehler, 2009), 167–168.

2. See, for example, Linda A. Hill and Nancy A. Kamprath, "Beyond the Myth of the Perfect Mentor: Building a Network of Development Relationships (A)," Case 9-491-096 (Boston: Harvard Business School, 1991); and Kathy E. Kram, *Mentoring at Work: Developmental Relationships in Organizational Life* (Glenview, IL: Scott Foresman, 1985).

3. See, for example, Wayne Baker, *Networking Smart: How to Build Relationships for Personal and Organizational Success* (New York: McGraw-Hill, 1994); Robert L. Cross and Andrew Parker, *The Hidden Power of Social Networks: Understanding How Work Really Gets Done in Organizations* (Boston: Harvard Business School Press, 2004); Jeffrey R. Hanson and David Krackhardt, "Informal Networks: The Company Behind the Charts," *Harvard Business Review*, July 1993, 104–111; and Jeffrey Pfeffer, *Managing with Power: Politics and Influence in Organizations* (Boston: Harvard Business School Press, 1992).

4. See, for example, Robert J. House et al., eds., *Culture, Leadership, and Organizations: The Globe Study of 62 Societies* (Thousand Oaks, CA: Sage Publications, 2004); Geert H. Hofstede, *Culture's Consequences: International Differences in Work-Related Values* (Beverly Hills, CA: Sage Publications, 1980); Charlene M. Solomon and Michael S. Schell, *Managing Across Cultures: The Seven Keys to Doing Business with a Global Mindset* (New York: McGraw-Hill, 2009); and Alfons Trompenaars and Charles Hampden-Turner, *Riding the Waves of Culture: Understanding Cultural Diversity in Global Business*, 2nd ed. (New York: McGraw Hill, 1998).

5. John P. Kotter, *The General Managers* (New York: Free Press, 1982), 86; and Mintzberg, *Managing*, 87.

6. See, for example, Ronald S. Burt, *Structural Holes: The Social Structure of Competition* (Cambridge, MA: Harvard University Press, 1992).

7. Tiziana Casciaro and Miguel Sousa Lobo, "Competent Jerks, Lovable Fools, and the Formation of Social Networks," *Harvard Business Review*, June 2005, 92–99.

Chapter 7

1. See, for example, Nancy Adler, *International Dimensions of Organizational Behavior*, 3rd ed. (Belmont, CA: PWS-Kent Publishing Company, 1996); Robert J. House et al., eds., *Culture, Leadership, and Organizations: The Globe Study of 62 Societies* (Thousand Oaks, CA: Sage Publications, 2004); and Charlene M. Solomon and Michael S. Schell, *Managing Across Cultures: The Seven Keys to Doing Business with a Global Mindset* (New York: McGraw-Hill, 2009).

2. See, for example, Gene Boccialetti, *It Takes Two: Managing Yourself When Working with Bosses and Other Authority Figures* (San Francisco, CA: Jossey-Bass, 1995); and Harvey A. Hornstein, *Brutal Bosses and Their Prey* (New York: Riverhead Books, 1996).

3. Michael Maccoby, "Narcissistic Leaders," *Harvard Business Review*, January 2004, 92–101.

Part III

1. See, for example, Linda A. Hill et al., "Unlocking the Slices of Genius in Your Organization: Leading for Innovation," in *Handbook of Leadership Theory and Practice: An HBS Centennial Colloquium on Advancing Leadership*, eds. Nitin Nohria and Rakesh Khurana (Boston: Harvard Business Press, 2010).

2. See, for example, Morgan W. McCall Jr. and Michael M. Lombardo, *Off the Track: Why and How Successful Executives Get Derailed, Technical Report No. 21* (Greensboro, NC: Center for Creative Leadership, 1983).

Chapter 8

1. Michael Kanazawa and Robert H. Miles, *Big Ideas to Big Results: Remake and Recharge Your Company, Fast* (Upper Saddle River, NJ: Financial Times Press, 2008); and Rosemary Stewart, *Choices for the Manager* (Englewood Cliffs, NJ: Prentice-Hall, 1982), 75.

2. Rodd Wagner and James K. Harter, *12: The Elements of Great Managing* (New York: Gallup Press, 2006), 114–117.

3. For a summary of relevant research, see Maria Farkas and Linda A. Hill, "A Note on Team Process (A)," Case 9-402-032 (Boston: Harvard Business School, 2001).

4. Dwight D. Eisenhower, BrainyQuote.com, April 24, 2010, http://www.brainyquote.com/quotes/quotes/d/dwightdei149111.html.

5. See, for example, Deborah L. Duarte and Nancy Tennant Snyder, *Mastering Virtual Teams: Strategies, Tools, and Techniques That Succeed*, 3rd ed. (San Francisco: Jossey-Bass, 2006); Bradley L. Kirkman et al., "Five Challenges to Virtual Team Success: Lessons from Sabre, Inc.," *Academy of Management Executive* 16, no. 3 (2002): 67–79; and Jessica Lipnack and Jeffrey Stamps, *Virtual Teams: People Working Across Boundaries with Technology*, 2nd ed. (New York: John Wiley & Sons, 2000).

6. See, for example, Thomas J. DeLong, John J. Gabarro, and Robert J. Lees, *When Professionals Have to Lead: A New Model for High Performance* (Boston: Harvard Business School Press, 2007); and Jay W. Lorsch and Peter F. Mathias, "When Professionals Have to Manage," *Harvard Business Review*, July–August 1987, 78–83.

7. Morten T. Hansen, *Collaboration: How Leaders Avoid the Traps, Create Unity, and Reap Big Results* (Boston: Harvard Business Press, 2009); Herminia Ibarra and Mark Hunter, "How Leaders Create and Use Networks," *Harvard Business Review*, January 2007, 124–131; and Herminia Ibarra and Otilia Obodaru, "Women and the Vision Thing," *Harvard Business Review*, January 2009, 62–70.

8. Andrew S. Grove, *Only the Paranoid Survive: How to Exploit the Crisis Points That Challenge Every Company and Career* (New York: Currency Doubleday, 1996).

9. See, for example, Michael L. Tushman and Charles A. O'Reilly III, *Winning Through Innovation: A Practical Guide to Leading Organizational Change and Renewal* (Boston: Harvard Business School Press, 2002), on the distinction between performance and opportunity gaps. It turns out that one of the criteria for becoming a high

potential is in fact the pursuit of opportunity gaps and not simply performance gaps. See, for example, Douglas A. Ready, Jay A. Conger, and Linda A. Hill, "Are You a High Potential?" *Harvard Business Review*, June 2010, 78–85.

10. See, for example, Michael Beer, *High Commitment, High Performance: How to Build a Resilient Organization for Sustained Advantage* (San Francisco: Jossey-Bass, 2009); Michael Beer, "Leading Change (A)," Case 9-488-03 (Boston: Harvard Business School, 1988, rev. 2007); and John P. Kotter, *A Sense of Urgency* (Boston: Harvard Business Press, 2008).

11. See, for example, Kathleen M. Eisenhardt, Jean Kahwajy, and L. J. Bourgeois, "How Management Teams Can Have a Good Fight," *Harvard Business Review*, July 1997, 77–85.

12. See, for example, Jeffrey R. Hanson and David Krackhardt, "Informal Networks: The Company Behind the Charts," *Harvard Business Review*, July 1993, 104–111; Rosabeth M. Kanter, "The Middle Manager as Innovator," *Harvard Business Review*, July–August 1982, 95–105; and Jeffrey Pfeffer, *Managing with Power: Politics and Influence in Organizations* (Boston: Harvard Business School Press, 1992).

Chapter 9

1. See, for example, Jennifer A. Chatman and Sandra A. Cha, "Leading by Leveraging Culture," *California Management Review* 45 (Summer 2003): 20–34; Edgar Schein, *Organizational Culture and Leadership: A Dynamic View* (San Francisco: Jossey-Bass, 1985); and Robert Simons, *Levers of Control: How Managers Use Innovative Control Systems to Drive Strategic Renewal* (Boston: Harvard Business School Press, 1995).

2. Robert N. Ford, "Job Enrichment Lessons from AT&T," *Harvard Business Review*, January–February 1973, 96–106; J. Richard Hackman et al., "A New Strategy for Redesigning Work," *California Management Review* 4, no. 17 (Summer 1975): 57–71; and Robert L. Simons, "Designing High-Performance Jobs," *Harvard Business Review*, July 2005, 2–10.

3. See, for example, Maria Farkas and Linda A. Hill, "A Note on Team Process (A)," Case 9-402-032 (Boston: Harvard Business School, 2001); David A. Garvin and Michael A. Roberto, "What You Don't Know About Making Decisions," *Harvard Business Review*, September 2001, 108–116; Linda A. Hill, "A Note on Building and Leading Your Senior Team," Case 9-402-037 (Boston: Harvard Business School, 2002); and Victor H. Vroom and Philip W. Yetton, *Leadership and Decision-Making* (Pittsburgh, PA: University of Pittsburgh Press, 1973).

4. See, for example, Linda A. Hill and Michel J. Anteby, "Analyzing Work Groups (A)," Case 9-496-026 (Boston: Harvard Business School, 2006), for an illustration of how to analyze your team culture.

5. See, for example, Kathleen M. Eisenhardt, Jean Kahwajy, and L. J. Bourgeois, "How Management Teams Can Have a Good Fight," *Harvard Business Review*, July 1997, 77–85; Garvin and Roberto, "What You Don't Know About Making Decisions," 108–116; and Peter M. Senge, *The Fifth Discipline: The Art and Practice of the Learning Organization* (New York: Doubleday/Currency, 1990).

6. See, for example, Robert S. Kaplan and David P. Norton, *The Balanced Scorecard: Translating Strategy into Action* (Boston: Harvard Business School Press, 1996); and Robert Simons, *Levers of Organization Design: How Managers Use Accountability Systems for Greater Performance and Commitment* (Boston: Harvard Business School Press, 2005).

7. See, for example, Deborah L. Duarte and Nancy T. Snyder, *Mastering Virtual Teams: Strategies, Tools, and Techniques That Succeed*, 3rd ed. (San Francisco: Jossey-Bass, 2006); Bradley L. Kirkman et al., "Five Challenges to Virtual Team Success: Lessons from Sabre, Inc.," *Academy of Management Executive* 16, no. 3 (2002): 67–79; and Jessica Lipnack and Jeffrey Stamps, *Virtual Teams: People Working Across Boundaries with Technology*, 2nd ed. (New York: John Wiley & Sons, 2000).

8. Kirkman et al., "Five Challenges to Virtual Team Success," 71–72.

9. Irving L. Janis, *Victims of Groupthink: A Psychological Study of Foreign-Policy Decisions and Fiascoes* (Boston: Houghton, 1972).

Chapter 10

1. For insights into how to build effective relationships with your people, see, for example, Linda A. Hill, "Building Effective One-on-One Work Relationships (A)," Case 9-497-028 (Boston: Harvard Business School, 1996).

2. Thomas DeLong and Vineeta Vijayaraghavan, "Let's Hear It for B Players," *Harvard Business Review*, June 2003, 96–102.

3. See, for example, Sumantra Ghoshal and Christopher A. Bartlett, *The Individualized Corporation: A Fundamentally New Approach to Management: Great Companies Are Defined by Purpose, Process, and People* (New York: HarperCollins Publishing, 1997), chap. 8 and 9.

4. See for example, Jane E. Dutton and Robert E. Quinn, *Positive Organizational Scholarship: Foundations of a New Discipline* (San Francisco: Berrett-Koehler, 2003); and James L. Heskett, Earl W. Sasser, and Joe Wheeler, *The Ownership Quotient: Putting the Service Profit Chain to Work for Unbeatable Competitive Advantage* (Boston: Harvard Business Press, 2008).

5. See, for example, Marshall Goldsmith, Laurence Lyons, and Alyssa Freas, eds., *Coaching for Leadership: How the World's Greatest Coaches Help Leaders Learn* (San Francisco: Jossey Bass/Pfeiffer, 2000); and Noel M. Tichy. *The Cycle of Leadership: How Great Leaders Teach Their Companies to Win* (New York: HarperCollins Publishers, Inc., 2002).

6. William Oncken Jr. and Donald L. Wass, "Management Time: Who's Got the Monkey?" *Harvard Business Review*, November–December 1974, 27–36.

7. See, for example, Carol R. Rogers and Fritz J. Roethlisberger, "Barriers and Gateways to Communication," *Harvard Business Review*, November–December 1991, 46–52; and Douglas Stone, Bruce Patton, and Sheila Heen, *Difficult Conversations: How to Discuss What Matters Most* (New York: Penguin Books, 2000).

8. Jean-François Manzoni and Jean-Louis Barsoux, "The Set-Up-to-Fail-Syndrome," *Harvard Business Review*, March–April 1998, 101–113.

9. See, for example, Claudio Fernandez-Araoz, *Great People Decisions: Why They Matter So Much, Why They Are So Hard, and How You Can Master Them* (Hoboken, NJ: John Wiley & Sons, 2007).

Chapter 11

1. John P. Kotter, *The General Managers* (New York: Free Press, 1982), 91–92, 127; Henry Mintzberg, *Managing* (San Francisco: Berrett-Koehler, 2009), 26–33; and Henry Mintzberg, *The Nature of Managerial Work* (Englewood Cliffs, NJ: Prentice-Hall, 1973), 50–51, 180–181.

2. Linda A. Hill and Kristin D. Doughty, "Taran Swan at Nickelodeon Latin America (A)," Case 9-400-036 (Boston: Harvard Business School, 1999, rev. 2008).

3. Eliyahu M. Goldratt and Jeff Cox, *The Goal: A Process of Ongoing Improvement* (Croton-on-Hudson, NY: North River Press, 1986).

Chapter 12

1. See, for example, Linda A. Hill and Nancy A. Kamprath, "Beyond the Myth of the Perfect Mentor: Building a Network of Development Relationships (A)," Case 9-481-096 (Boston: Harvard Business School, 1991); Monica C. Higgins and David A. Thomas, "Constellations and Careers: Toward Understanding the Effects of Multiple Developmental Relationships," *Journal of Organizational Behavior* 22, no. 3 (2001): 223–227; Kathy E. Kram, *Mentoring at Work: Developmental Relationships in Organizational Life* (Glenview, IL: Scott Foresman, 1985); and David A. Thomas, "Truth About Mentoring Minorities," *Harvard Business Review*, April 2001, 99–107.

2. Patrick Barwise and Sean Meehan, "So You Think You're a Good Listener," *Harvard Business Review*, April 2008, 22; and Rodd Wagner and James K. Harter, *12: The Elements of Great Managing* (New York: Gallup Press, 2006), 157–158.

3. See, for example, Jean-Francois Manzoni and Jean-Louis Barsoux, "The Set-Up-to-Fail Syndrome," *Harvard Business Review*, March–April 1998, 101–113.

4. Herminia Ibarra, "Making Partner: A Mentor's Guide to the Psychological Journey," *Harvard Business Review*, March–April 2000, 146–154.

5. Chris Argyris, "Teaching Smart People to Learn," *Harvard Business Review*, May–June 1991, 99–109.

SELECTED REFERENCES

For a complete list of references, please visit http://www.hbr.org/beingtheboss.

Used Throughout the Book

Hill, Linda A. *Becoming a Manager.* 2nd ed. Boston: Harvard Business School Press, 2003.

———. "Where Will We Find Tomorrow's Leaders?" *Harvard Business Review,* January 2008, 123–129.

———. "Becoming the Boss." *Harvard Business Review,* January 2007, 48–57.

Introduction: Where Are You on Your Journey?

Argyris, Chris. "Teaching Smart People to Learn." *Harvard Business Review,* May–June 1991, 99–109.

George, Bill, and Peter Sims. *True North: Discover Your Authentic Leadership.* San Francisco: Jossey-Bass, 2007.

Sayles, Leonard. *Leadership: Managing in Real Organizations.* New York: McGraw-Hill, 1989.

Schön, Donald A. *The Reflective Practitioner: How Professionals Think in Action.* New York: Basic Books, 1983.

Skinner, Wickman, and Earl W. Sasser. "Managers with Impact: Versatile and Inconsistent." *Harvard Business Review,* November–December 1977, 140–148.

Spreier, Scott. "Leadership Run Amok." *Harvard Business Review,* June 2006, 72–82.

Chapter 1: Your 3 Imperatives as a Manager

Alder, Nancy. *International Dimensions of Organizational Behavior.* 3rd ed. Belmont, CA: PWS-Kent Publishing Company, 1996.

Ciampa, Dan, and Michael Watkins. *Right from the Start: Taking Charge in a New Leadership Position.* Boston: Harvard Business School Press, 1999.

Dychtwald, Ken, Tamara J. Erickson, and Robert Morison. *Workforce Crisis: How to Beat the Coming Shortage of Skills and Talent.* Boston: Harvard Business School Press, 2006.

Gabarro, John J. *The Dynamics of Taking Charge.* Boston: Harvard Business School Press, 1987.

Goleman, Daniel. *Emotional Intelligence*. New York: Bantam Books, 1995.

Goleman, Daniel, Richard E. Boyatzis, and Annie McKee. *Primal Leadership: Realizing the Power of Emotional Intelligence*. Boston: Harvard Business School Press, 2002.

Hamel, Gary, and Bill Breen. *The Future of Management*. Boston, MA: Harvard Business Publishing, 2007.

Hofstede, Geert H. *Culture's Consequences, International Differences in Work-Related Values*. Beverly Hills, CA: Sage Publications, 1980.

House, Robert J., Paul J. Hanges, Mansour Javidan, Peter W. Dorfman, and Vipin Gupta, eds. *Culture, Leadership, and Organizations: The Globe Study of 62 Societies*. Thousand Oaks, CA: Sage Publications, 2004.

Kotter, John P. *The General Managers*. New York: Free Press, 1982.

Luthans, Fred, Richard M. Hodgetts, and Stuart A. Rosenkrantz. *Real Managers*. Cambridge, MA: Ballinger, 1988.

Mintzberg, Henry. *Managing*. San Francisco: Berrett-Koehler, 2009.

——. *The Nature of Managerial Work*. New York: Harper & Row, 1973.

Nicholson, Nigel, and Michael West. *Managerial Job Change: Men and Women in Transition*. Cambridge, UK: Cambridge University Press, 1988.

Sayles, Leonard. *Leadership: Managing in Real Organizations*. New York: McGraw-Hill, 1989.

Solomon, Charlene M., and Michael S. Schell. *Managing Across Cultures: The Seven Keys to Doing Business with a Global Mindset*. New York: McGraw-Hill, 2009.

Stewart, Rosemary. "Studies of Managerial Jobs and Behavior: The Ways Forward." *Journal of Management Studies* 26, no. 1 (1989): 1–10.

Watkins, Michael. *The First 90 Days: Critical Success Strategies for New Leaders at All Levels*. Boston: Harvard Business School Press, 2003.

Chapter 2: I'm the Boss!

Heifetz, Ronald A. *Leadership Without Easy Answers*. Cambridge, MA: Belknap Press of Harvard University Press, 1994.

Leavitt, Harold J. *Top Down: Why Hierarchies Are Here to Stay and How to Manage Them More Effectively*. Boston: Harvard Business School Press, 2005.

Magretta, Joan. *What Management Is: How It Works and Why It's Everyone's Business*. New York: Free Press, 2002.

Mintzberg, Henry. *Managing*. San Francisco: Berrett-Koehler, 2009.

Ready, Douglas A., Jay A. Conger, and Linda A. Hill. "Are You a High Potential?" *Harvard Business Review*, June 2010, 78–85.

Wagner, Rodd, and James K. Harter. *12: The Elements of Great Managing*. New York: Gallup Press, 2006.

Chapter 3: I'm Your Friend!

Leavitt, Harold J. *Top Down: Why Hierarchies Are Here to Stay and How to Manage Them More Effectively*. Boston: Harvard Business School Press, 2005.

Chapter 4: Can People Trust You?

Heifetz, Ronald A. *Leadership Without Easy Answers*. Cambridge, MA: Belknap Press of Harvard University Press, 1994.

Hill, Linda A. "Moral Leadership: A Development Agenda for Future Managers." In *Moral Leadership: The Theory and Practice of Power, Judgment, and Policy*, edited by Deborah Rhode, 267–290. San Francisco: Jossey-Bass, 2006.

Chapter 5: Understand the Reality of Your Organization

Cohen, Allan R., and David L. Bradford. *Influence Without Authority.* New York: John Wiley & Sons, 1991.

Hill, Linda A. "Moral Leadership: A Development Agenda for Future Managers." In *Moral Leadership: The Theory and Practice of Power, Judgment, and Policy,* edited by Deborah Rhode, 267–290. San Francisco: Jossey-Bass, 2006.

Kotter, John P. *The General Managers.* New York: Free Press, 1982.

———. *Power and Influence.* New York: Free Press, 1985.

Leavitt, Harold J. *Top Down: Why Hierarchies Are Here to Stay and How to Manage Them More Effectively.* Boston: Harvard Business School Press, 2005.

Mintzberg, Henry. *The Nature of Managerial Work.* New York: Harper & Row, 1973.

Pfeffer, Jeffrey. *Managing with Power: Politics and Influence in Organizations.* Boston: Harvard Business School Press, 1992.

Chapter 6: Weave Your Own Web of Influence

Cohen, Allan R., and David L. Bradford. *Influence Without Authority.* New York: John Wiley & Sons, 1991.

Hansen, Morten T. *Collaboration: How Leaders Avoid the Traps, Create Unity, and Reap Big Results.* Boston: Harvard Business Press, 2009.

Heifetz, Ronald A., and Martin Linsky. *Leadership on the Line: Staying Alive Through the Dangers of Leading.* Boston: Harvard Business School Press, 2002.

Hill, Linda A. "Building Effective One-on-One Work Relationships (A)." Case 9-497-028. Boston: Harvard Business School, 1996.

Ibarra, Herminia, and Mark Hunter. "How Leaders Create and Use Networks." *Harvard Business Review,* January 2007, 124–131.

Katzenbach, Jon R., and Zia Khan. *Leading Outside the Lines: How to Mobilize the (In) Formal Organization, Energize Your Team, and Get Better Results.* San Francisco: Jossey-Bass, 2010.

Kotter, John P. *Power and Influence.* New York: Free Press, 1985.

Pfeffer, Jeffrey. *Managing with Power: Politics and Influence in Organizations.* Boston: Harvard Business School Press, 1992.

Uzzi, Brian, and Shannon Dunlap. "How to Build Your Network." *Harvard Business Review,* December 2005, 53–60.

Chapter 7: Don't Forget Your Boss

Gabarro, John J., and John P. Kotter. "Managing Your Boss." *Harvard Business Review,* January 2005, 92–99.

Watkins, Michael. *The First 90 Days: Critical Success Strategies for New Leaders at All Levels.* Boston: Harvard Business School Press, 2003.

Chapter 8: Define the Future

Avolio, Bruce J., and Fred Luthans. *The High Impact Leader.* New York: McGraw Hill, 2006.

Beer, Michael. "Leading Change (A)." Case 9-488-037. Boston: Harvard Business School, 1988, rev. 2007.

Beer, Michael, and Nitin Nohria. "Cracking the Code of Change." *Harvard Business Review,* May 2000, 133–141.

Bennis, Warren G. *On Becoming a Leader.* Reading, MA: Addison-Wesley, 1989.

Drucker, Peter F. *The Effective Executive*. New York: Harper & Row, 1967.

———. *Peter Drucker on the Profession of Management*. Boston: Harvard Business School Press, 1998.

Hansen, Morten T. *Collaboration: How Leaders Avoid the Traps, Create Unity, and Reap Big Results*. Boston: Harvard Business Press, 2009.

Heifetz, Ronald A. *Leadership Without Easy Answers*. Cambridge, MA: Belknap Press of Harvard University Press, 1994.

Heifetz, Ronald A., and Martin Linsky. *Leadership on the Line: Staying Alive Through the Dangers of Leading*. Boston: Harvard Business School Press, 2002.

Hill, Linda A. "A Note on Building and Leading Your Senior Team (A)." Case 9-402-037. Boston: Harvard Business School, 2002.

Kotter, John P. "Leading Change: Why Transformation Efforts Fail." *Harvard Business Review*, March 1995, 1–10.

———. *A Force for Change: How Leadership Differs from Management*. New York: Free Press, 1990.

———. *The General Managers*. New York: Free Press, 1982.

———. "What Leaders Really Do." *Harvard Business Review*, March 1990, 103–111.

Schein, Edgar. *Organizational Culture and Leadership: A Dynamic View*. San Francisco: Jossey-Bass, 1985.

Watkins, Michael. *Your Next Move: The Leader's Guide to Navigating Major Career Transitions*. Boston: Harvard Business Press, 2009.

Chapter 9: Be Clear About How Your Team Works

Ancona, Deborah G., and Henrik Bresman. *X-Teams: How to Build Teams that Lead, Innovate, and Succeed*. Boston, MA: Harvard Business School Press, 2007.

Coutu, Diane. "Why Teams Don't Work (an Interview with Richard Hackman)." *Harvard Business Review*, May 2009, 99-103.

Farkas, Maria, and Linda A. Hill. "A Note on Team Process (A)." Case 9-402-032. Boston: Harvard Business School, 2001.

Hackman, J. R. "Why Teams Don't Work." In *Theory and Research on Small Groups*, edited by R. Scott Tindale, Linda Heath, John Edwards, Emil J. Posavac, Fred B. Bryant, Yolanda Suarez-Balcazar, Eaaron Henderson-King, and Judith Myers. New York: Plenum Press, 1988.

Hackman, J. Richard. *Groups That Work (and Those That Don't): Creating Conditions for Effective Teamwork*. San Francisco: Jossey-Bass, 1990.

———. *Leading Teams: Setting the Stage for Great Performances*. Boston: Harvard Business School Press, 2002.

Hill, Linda A., and Michel J. Anteby. "Analyzing Work Groups (A)." Case 9-496-026. Boston: Harvard Business School, 2006.

Katzenbach, Jon R., and Douglas K. Smith. "The Discipline of Teams." *Harvard Business Review*, July–August 2005, 162–171.

———. *The Wisdom of Teams: Creating the High-Performance Organization*. Boston: Harvard Business School Press, 1993.

Sayles, Leonard. *Leadership: Managing in Real Organizations*. New York: McGraw-Hill, 1989.

Simons, Robert. *Levers of Control: How Managers Use Innovative Control Systems to Drive Strategic Renewal*. Boston: Harvard Business School Press, 1995.

———. *Levers of Organization Design: How Managers Use Accountability Systems for Greater Performance and Commitment*. Boston: Harvard Business School Press, 2005.

Chapter 10: Your Team Members Are Individuals Too

Avolio, Bruce J., and Fred Luthans. *The High Impact Leader.* New York: McGraw Hill, 2006.

Dutton, Jane E., and Robert E. Quinn. *Positive Organizational Scholarship: Foundations of a New Discipline.* San Francisco: Berrett-Koehler, 2003.

Dychtwald, Ken, Tamara J. Erickson, and Robert Morison. *Workforce Crisis: How to Beat the Coming Shortage of Skills and Talent.* Boston: Harvard Business School Press, 2006.

Fernandez-Araoz, Claudio. *Great People Decisions: Why They Matter So Much, Why They Are So Hard, and How You Can Master Them.* Hoboken, NJ: John Wiley & Sons, 2007.

Margolis, Joshua, and Andrew Molinksy. "Navigating the Bind of Necessary Evils: Psychological Engagement and the Production of Interpersonally Sensitive Behavior." *Academy of Management Journal* 51, no. 5 (2008): 847–872.

Sayles, Leonard. *Leadership: Managing in Real Organizations.* New York: McGraw-Hill, 1989.

Schein, Edgar H. *Helping: How to Offer, Give and Receive Help.* San Francisco: Berrett-Koehler, 2009.

Stone, Douglas, Bruce Patton, and Sheila Heen. *Difficult Conversations: How to Discuss What Matters Most.* New York: Penguin Books, 2000.

Chapter 11: Manage Through Your Daily Work

Kotter, John P., *The General Managers.* New York: The Free Press, 1982.

Chapter 12: Completing Your Journey

Higgins, Monica C., and David A. Thomas. "Constellations and Careers: Toward Understanding the Effects of Multiple Developmental Relationships." *Journal of Organization Behavior* 22, no. 3 (2001): 223–247.

Hill, Linda A. "Beyond the Myth of the Perfect Mentor: Building a Network of Developmental Relationships." Harvard Business School Note 491-096. Boston: Harvard Business School, 1998.

Kram, Kathy E. *Mentoring at Work: Developmental Relationships in Organizational Life.* Glenview, IL: Scott Foresman, 1985.

McCall, Morgan W., Jr. *High Flyers: Developing the Next Generation of Leaders.* Boston: Harvard Business School Press, 1998.

Roberts, Laura Morgan, Gretchen Spreitzer, Jane Dutton, Robert Quinn, Emily Heaphy, and Brianna Baker. "How to Play to Your Strengths." *Harvard Business Review*, January 2005, 75–80.

INDEX

ABOUT THE AUTHORS

LINDA A. HILL is the Wallace Brett Donham Professor of Business Administration at Harvard Business School, and faculty chair of the Leadership Initiative. She has chaired numerous HBS Executive Education programs, including the High Potentials Leadership Program, and was a key developer of the School's required Leadership and Organizational Behavior course.

Hill's consulting and executive education activities are in the areas of managing change, managing cross-organizational relationships, implementing global strategy, innovation, talent management, and leadership development. She has worked with organizations worldwide, including General Electric, Reed Elsevier, Accenture, Pfizer, IBM, MasterCard, Mitsubishi, Morgan Stanley, the National Bank of Kuwait, Areva, and *The Economist*.

She is the author of *Becoming a Manager* (2nd edition) and numerous *Harvard Business Review* articles. She is also the author of course modules, award-winning multimedia management development programs, and the e-learning programs *Stepping Up to Management* and *Harvard ManageMentor*.

Hill is a member of the boards of State Street Corporation, Cooper Industries, and Harvard Business Publishing. She is a trustee of the Nelson Mandela Children's Fund USA, The Bridgespan Group, Bryn Mawr College, and The Children's Museum, Boston. She is also on the Advisory Board of the Aspen Institute Business and Society Program. She serves on the Editorial Board of the *Leadership Quarterly*.

Dr. Hill holds a PhD in behavioral sciences and an MA in educational psychology, both from the University of Chicago. She received a BA summa cum laude in psychology from Bryn Mawr College.

KENT LINEBACK was, for nearly thirty years, a manager and executive in a variety of organizations.

He served as Assistant to the President at the consulting company Sterling Institute, where he ran management development projects for *Fortune* 500 companies. He managed business administration for two public broadcasting organizations in Washington, D.C.—the Public Broadcasting Service (PBS) and the Corporation for Public Broadcasting (CPB). He ran marketing for the professional, Boston-based publisher Warren Gorham & Lamont. He built a successful, $40 million, internal computer-products start-up for New England Business Service, a national business-products direct marketer in Groton, Massachusetts. He then led the company's main $200 million division through strategic reorganization and change. Finally, he co-led the production of film and video management-development programs for Harvard Business School Publishing.

In the late 1990s, he began coauthoring and collaborating with authors of business books. His first book, coauthored with Randy Komisar, was *The Monk and the Riddle,* a *BusinessWeek* bestseller that was later selected as one of "The 100 Best Business Books of All Time." Other authors or coauthors he's worked with include several Harvard faculty members, the CEO of a nationally known company, the governor of a major state, and prominent consultants.

He holds a BA from Harvard College and an MBA from Boston College.